P9-DFL-876

NEW & REVISED EDITION

Marden's Guide to
Manhattan
Booksellers

Doug Van Valkenburgh 10298

NEW & REVISED EDITION

Marden's Guide to Manhattan Booksellers

WITH A PREFACE BY ARTHUR MILLER

WILLIAM MARDEN

CITY & COMPANY • NEW YORK

Front and Back Cover photographs:
Interior of Rizzoli Bookstore, 31 West 57th Street.

Copyright © 1997 by William Marden
Photography copyright ©1997 by Russell Dian
Preface copyright © 1997 by Arthur Miller

All rights reserved. No portion of this book may be reproduced
without written permission from the publisher.

City & Company
22 West 23rd Street
New York, N.Y. 10010

Printed in the United States of America

Design by Leah Lococo

Library of Congress Cataloging-in-Publication Data is available upon request.

ISBN 1-885492-45-6
Second Edition 1997
First Edition 1994

NOTE TO READERS: Neither City & Company nor the author has any interest, financial or personal, in the locations listed in this book. No fees were
paid or services rendered in exchange for inclusion in these pages.

While every effort was made to ensure that information regarding
addresses, phone numbers, and hours was accurate at the time of publica-
tion, it is always best to call ahead.

To Joan and Abigail

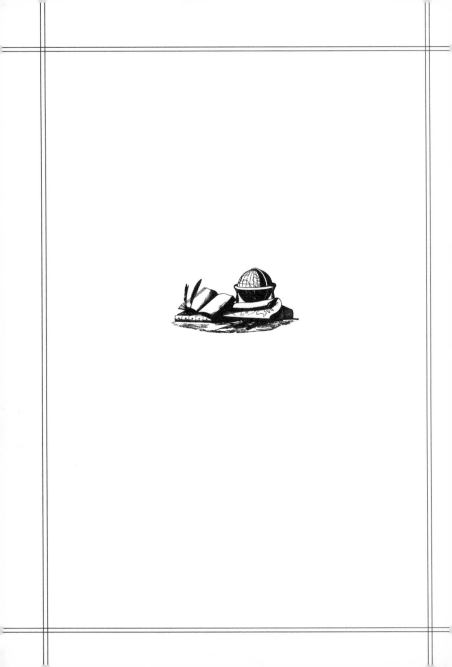

Contents

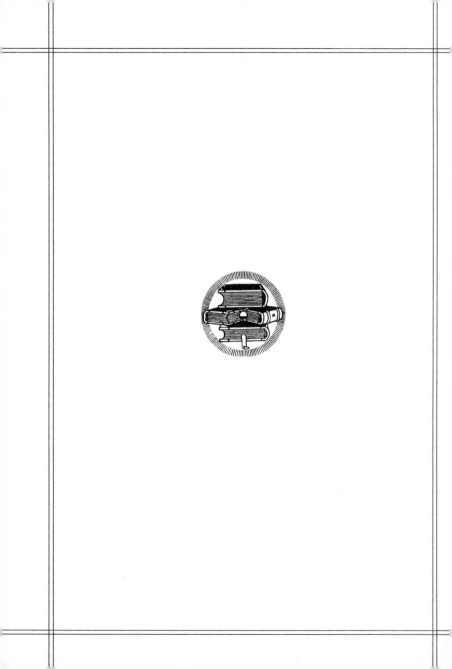

Preface by Arthur Miller

It can be laid flat or stood on end; it can be shaken or
dropped without damage; it does not need to be plugged
in, yet has no batteries; information can be retrieved
from it without pressing a button, merely by slipping any
piece of paper, a napkin, a thin stick or an apple stem at
the desired place one wishes to return to. It can be plain
or highly decorated for display purposes and many examples of it will fit into a coat pocket or a woman's purse. It
makes no clicks or buzzes, does not flash indecipherable
lights or without warning cast away all its contents as
though into a hurricane in a spasm of despair, fury or
misplaced sense of humor. It can be used in all kinds of

circumstances—on a windy beach with sand blowing harmlessly over its contents, on the surface of a swimming pool while floating on an air mattress without fear of contamination by a few errant drops of water, in a hammock while facing upward or straight down, on a subway without fear of it attracting assault and robbery. It can be stood on in order to reach a high shelf or sat on to stay off a cold floor. Held prominently on one hand it can be used to indicate intellectuality, a high spiritual tone or fashionable angst. It can be all things to all men or nothing at all to anybody. It can tell ghastly lies or painfully constructive truths and is thus the invention of the human race which most accurately represents it in all its variety and range of mood and attitude from self-disgust to visionary elation . . . It is called a book.

And if the present volume is indicative, a surprisingly large number of people seem eager to own examples of it.

Introduction

As the publishing capital of the world, New York City is a natural habitat for book dealers of all types. While many of them operate from the traditional street-level storefront, hundreds sell books from office suites, apartments, or by mail order. Add to this the bookstores in the city's museums, schools, and other cultural institutions, and the number of places where books are available is tremendous.

This comprehensive guide brings together all the essential information you need on 580 booksellers who operate in Manhattan, including dealers in new, used, out-of-print, and rare books. You'll find shops and dealers ranging from mega-stores to specialty shops to auction houses, offering everything from rare, multi-million-dollar volumes to discount tables of used and remaindered books.

All entries in this guide appear in alphabetical order. Hours are listed only for days on which a business is open. Assume that a business is closed on any days not listed. "By Appointment Only" means just that. (Many dealers operate their businesses out of their homes. Dropping in on them unexpectedly can create an awkward situation and there is always the possibility that the bookseller may not be home.) Businesses take credit cards and/or checks only if such payment methods are noted. Be mindful that this is always subject to change.

The category "Type of Store" delineates the predominant type of book sold by a dealer. "New" means new, unused copies of in-print or recently out-of-print books. "Used" means books that have been sold then resold, as well as review copies of newly-published titles. "Out of print" books are those which are no longer available through the publisher or its normal channels of distribution. "Mail order" refers to businesses that deal with clients exclusively through the mail and by phone. A "remainder" book is one that has been declared "out of print" by the publisher, but still remains in the publisher's warehouse in sizable quantities. These unsold books are liquidated by making them available to booksellers at a reduced price.

I would appreciate any reader's comments about this book's content and, particularly, the names of any booksellers I may have missed. The mailing address is: William Marden, P.O. Box 6794, FDR Station, New York, N.Y. 10150. Or you may send e-mail to me at: 72124.2360@compuserve.com

Antiquarian and Rare Books

British librarian A.W. Pollard once wrote that rare book collecting was "the bringing together of books which in their contents, their form or the history of the individual copy possess some element of permanent interest, and either actually or prospectively are rare, in the sense of being difficult to procure." A somewhat stuffy description, perhaps, but one that hints at the delights of this vast and complex corner of the book world.

For those completely new to the subject of antiquarian books, some very readable surveys include Alan Thomas's <u>Great Books and Book Collectors</u> (NY: Putnam, 1975) and the recent, well-written <u>A Gentle Madness: Bibliophiles, Bibliomanes, and the Eternal Passion for Books</u>, by Nicholas Basbanes (NY: Henry Holt, 1995). Among the more practical how-to guides for neophytes, I can recommend <u>Understanding Book Collecting</u>, by Grant Uden (Wappingers Falls, NY: Antique Collectors' Club, 1982) and <u>Miller's Collecting Books</u> (Antique Collectors' Club, 1996) by Catherine Porter, a Sotheby's book expert.

For the beginner who wants to dive in head first, there is the essential <u>ABC for Book Collectors</u> by John Carter, now in its 7th edition (New Castle, Del.: Oak Knoll Books, 1995). An excellent introduction to how books are (and were) physically put together is Philip Gaskell's <u>A New Introduction to Bibliography</u> (Oak Knoll Books, 1996).

The most widely-read periodical relating to the antiquarian book trade in the United States is <u>AB Bookman's Weekly</u> (P.O. Box AB, Clifton, NJ 07015; phone: 201-772-0020). The Internet provides an enormous pool of World Wide Web sites, newsgroups, FTP files, and e-mail addresses all related to rare books and book collecting. They are expanding and changing so rapidly that even a cursory list would do the reader a disservice. Despite (or perhaps, partly because of) its constant flux, the Internet has become an important resource for the rare book community.

America's professional organization of antiquarian book dealers is based in Manhattan. The Antiquarian Booksellers' Association of America (50 Rockefeller Plaza, New York, NY 10020; phone: 212-757-9395), sponsors the annual New York Antiquarian Book Fair in April and also issues a free annual directory of its members.

Also to be noted are the many public exhibitions and displays of rare books regularly presented at the New York Public Library (the branch at 42nd Street and Fifth Avenue) and the Pierpont Morgan Library.

For those who truly want to immerse themselves in this field, I can highly recommend the Rare Book School, open every summer at the University of Virginia. A previous offering included dozens of one-week courses in subjects as diverse as typography, the history of bookbinding, and book illustration. For more information contact: Terry Belanger. Rare Book School. 114 Alderman Library. Univ. of Virginia. Charlottesville, VA 22903. Phone: 804-924-8851.

On the subject of manuscripts and documents, two good primers are Charles Hamilton's <u>Collecting Autographs and Manuscripts</u> (Santa Monica, Calif: Modoc Press, 1993) and Kenneth Rendell's <u>History Comes to Life: Collecting Historical Letters and Documents</u> (Norman, Okla.: University of Oklahoma Press, 1995). You also might want to join The Manuscript Society, whose membership includes dealers, collectors, scholars, and archivists with a common interest in the autograph field. For information write to: The Manuscript Society, David Smith, 350 N. Niagara St., Burbank, CA 91505.

Acknowledgments

Thanks are due to many people for their advice, support, and help. My great appreciation and thanks are owed to Arthur Miller, who very kindly responded to my request to write the preface for this edition. His words are an eloquent testament to why the printed book still bears importance in the electronic age.

Thanks to Russell Dian for the cover photos; to my publisher Helene Silver, and Rosalind Colman at City & Company for all their help; and to Manhattan's multitude of booksellers for their cooperation. I would also like to thank Kevin Goering and Bob Lemstrom-Sheedy for their assistance.

Finally, love and gratitude to my wife, Joan, who has proven to be my better half throughout this whole endeavor.

Booksellers A-Z

Abraham's Magazine Service

56 E. 13th St. (bet. University Pl. & Broadway)
New York, NY 10003 • (212) 777-4700
Hours: By appointment only
Type of store: Mail order, antiquarian
Subject Specialties: Magazines/Journals/Newspapers
• Facsimile Editions
Year Established: 1889
Sidelines and Services: Appraise library collections, back issues of periodicals, search service

Academy Book Store

10 W. 18th St. (bet. Fifth & Sixth Aves.) New York, NY 10011
(212) 242-4848 Fax: (212) 675-9595
Hours: Mon.-Sat. 11 A.M. to 9 P.M.; Sun. 11 A.M. to 7 P.M.
Form of payment: Visa, MC, Discover, Checks
Type of store: Used, antiquarian
Subject Specialties: Art – General • Decorative Arts • History
• Literature – General • Philosophy • Photography • Psychology/
Psychiatry • Social Science/Cultural History
Manager: Macklin Trimnell
Year Established: 1977
No. of Volumes: 100,000
Sidelines and Services: Appraise library collections, autographs
Comments: Store also operates Academy Records and CDs
(used and rare classical/jazz/rock LPs and CDs) next door at
12 W. 18th Street.

Acanthus Books

54 W. 21st St., Rm. 908 (bet. Fifth & Sixth Aves.)
New York, NY 10010 • (212) 463-0750 Fax: (212) 463-0752
E-mail address: acanthus@pipeline.com
Hours: By appointment only
Form of payment: Visa, MC, Checks
Type of store: New, antiquarian
Subject Specialties: Architecture • Antiques/Collectibles
• Decorative Arts • Landscape Architecture • Design
Owner: Barry Cenower
Year Established: 1982
No. of Volumes: 3,000
Sidelines and Services: Appraise library collections
Catalogs: Annual catalog

Action Comics

1551 Second Ave. (bet. 80th & 81st Sts.) New York, NY 10028
(212) 639-1976
Hours: Mon.-Sat. 11 A.M. to 8 P.M.; Sun. 11 A.M. to 6 P.M.
Form of payment: Visa, MC, AMEX, Checks
Type of store: New, used, mail order
Subject Specialties: Comic Books
Owner: Stephen Passarelli
Year Established: 1981
Sidelines and Services: Restoration, evaluation
Comments: You can also buy sports and non-sports
trading cards here.

Adventist Book Center

12 W. 40th St. (bet. Fifth & Sixth Aves.) New York, NY 10018

(212) 944-2788 Fax: (212) 819-1973

Hours: Mon.-Thu. 9 A.M. to 6 P.M.; Fri. 9 A.M. to 1 P.M.;
Sun. 10 A.M. to 3 P.M. Closed Sat.

Form of payment: Visa, MC, AMEX, Discover, Checks

Subject Specialties: Religion - Christianity

Manager: Nelly Harris

Year Established: 1905

No. of Volumes: 75,000

Sidelines and Services: Religious goods

Comments: This store is owned by the Greater New York Conference of Seventh-Day Adventists.

Agueybana Bookstore

192 Avenue B (at E. 12th St.) New York, NY 10009

(212) 539-1662

Hours: Tue.-Sat. Noon to 7 P.M.

Form of payment: Checks

Type of Store: New

Subject Specialties: Literature - Latin American/Caribbean
• Literature - Puerto Rican

Manager: Sery Colon

Year Established: 1993

Sidelines and Services: CDs, artwork, author readings

Catalogs: Catalog available

Comments: This shop specializes in Puerto Rican and Latin literature in both Spanish and English.

Aids Thrift Shop/Out of the Closet

**220 E. 81st St. (bet. Second & Third Aves.) New York, NY 10028
(212) 472-3573**
Hours: Tue.-Sat. 10 A.M. to 5 P.M. Closed August and Tues. after
Mon. holidays.
Form of payment: Visa, MC, AMEX; No checks
Type of store: Used
Subject Specialties: Art - General • Biography/Autobiography
• Cooking • Erotica/Curiosa • Gay/Lesbian Studies • History
• Literature - General • Travel • Children's/Juvenile • Cinema/Films
• Reference • Performing Arts
Manager: Edward Maloney
Year Established: 1991
No. of Volumes: 10,000
Comments: Occasionally sells new books and publishers'
proofs donated by publishing houses.

William Alatriste

**10 Downing St. (on Sixth Ave. bet. Houston & Bleecker Sts.)
New York, NY 10014 • (212) 366-0604**
Hours: By appointment only
Form of payment: Visa, MC, AMEX, Checks
Type of store: Antiquarian
Subject Specialties: Literature - European to 1900 • Literature -
American • Colorplate Books
Owner: William Alatriste

Alba House Cornerstone Book and Gift Shop

16 Barclay St. (bet. Broadway & Church St., near City Hall)
New York, NY 10007 • (212) 732-4140 Fax: (212) 349-3063
Hours: Mon.-Fri.: 10 A.M. to 5:30 P.M.; Sat. 12:30 P.M. to 5 P.M.
Form of payment: Visa, MC, AMEX, Discover, Checks
Type of store: New
Subject Specialties: Religion - Christianity • Bibles • History
• Theology • Spirituality • Catholicism • Scripture Study
Owner: Society of St. Paul
Year Established: 1976
No. of Volumes: 3,000
Sidelines and Services: Tapes, videos, gifts, music, cards
Catalogs: Semiannual catalog
Comments: Branch of Alba House Centers, Society of St. Paul

Amen Ra and Isis

260 W. 125th St. (bet. Frederick Douglass Blvd.
& Adam Clayton Powell Jr. Blvd.) New York, NY 10027
(212) 316-3680 Fax: (212) 866-4747,
Hours: Mon.-Tue. 10 A.M. to 6:30 P.M.; Wed.-Sat. 10 A.M.
to 7:30 P.M.; Sun. Noon to 5 P.M.
Form of payment: Visa, MC, AMEX, Discover; No checks
Type of store: New
Subject Specialties: African-American Studies • Children's/Juvenile
• Black Comics
Owner: Lana Drakes
Sidelines and Services: Gifts, greeting cards, ethnic wrapping paper

America East Book Co.

46 Bowery (near Canal St.) New York, NY 10013 • (212) 233-4926
Hours: Mon.-Sun.: 10 A.M. to 8 P.M.
Type of store: New
Subject Specialties: China (including Chinese Language and Literature)

America's Hobby Center

146 W. 22nd St. (bet. Sixth & Seventh Aves.)
New York, NY 10011 • (212) 675-8922 Fax: (212) 633-2754
Hours: Mon.-Fri. 9 A.M. to 5:30 P.M.; Sat. 9 A.M. to 3:30 P.M.
Form of payment: Visa, MC, Discover
Type of store: New, mail order
Subject Specialties: Hobbies • Transportation
Year Established: 1931
No. of Volumes: 200,000
Sidelines and Services: Mail order
Catalogs: Annual catalog

Comments: Also sells instructional books for building models.

American Bible Society Bookstore

1865 Broadway (at 61st St.) New York, NY 10023
(212) 408-1201 (800) 322-4253 Fax: (212) 408-1512
Hours: Mon-Fri: 9 A.M. to 5 P.M.
Form of payment: Visa, MC, Checks
Type of store: New
Subject Specialties: Religion - Christianity • Bibles - English

and foreign language

Manager: Miriam Rivera

Year Established: 1966

No. of Volumes: 2,500

Sidelines and Services: Religious goods

Catalogs: 4/year

Comments: Also sells scholarly scripture resources and publications of the American Bible Society.

American Companion Inc.

121 Madison Ave. New York, NY 10016 • (212) 545-8554

Fax: (212) 889-2044

Type of store: Mail order

Comments: This store advertises its stock as "American books for international readers."

American Craft Museum

40 W. 53rd St. (bet. Fifth & Sixth Aves.) New York, NY 10019

(212) 956-3535

Hours: Tues: 10 A.M. to 8 P.M. / Wed-Sun: 10 A.M. to 5 P.M.

Form of payment: Visa, MC, AMEX, Checks

Type of store: New

Subject Specialties: Crafts

American Folk Art Books

145 W. 55th St. (bet. Sixth & Seventh Aves.)

New York, NY 10019 • (212) 245-5042

Hours: By mail or appointment only

Form of payment: Checks

Type of store: Used

Subject Specialties: Americana • Art - General • Art History • Art - American • Folk Art

Owners: Priscilla Brandt, Dorothy Kaufman

Year Established: 1982

No. of Volumes: 1,500

Catalogs: Annual catalog

Comments: Specializes in American folk art.

American Management Association Bookstore

135 W. 50th St., 7th fl. (bet. Sixth & Seventh Aves.)

New York, NY 10020 • (212) 903-8286 Fax: (212) 903-8309

Hours: Mon.-Fri. 8:30 A.M. to 5 P.M.

Form of payment: Visa, MC, AMEX, Discover, Diners Club, Checks

Type of store: New, mail order

Subject Specialties: Accounting • Advertising • Business/ Management • Computers • Reference • Self-Help

Manager: Evan Miller

Year Established: 1965   **No. of Volumes:** 5,500

Sidelines and Services: Special orders, college supplies, audio-tapes, CD-ROMs, study aids, corporate accounts

Catalogs: Semiannual catalog

American Museum of Natural History Museum Shop

79th St. & Central Park West New York, NY 10024

(212) 769-5150 Fax: (212) 769-5044

Hours: Sun.-Thu. 10 A.M. to 5:45 P.M.;

Fri.-Sat. 10 A.M. to 8:45 P.M.

Form of payment: Visa, MC, AMEX, Checks

Type of store: New

Subject Specialties: Natural History • Children's/Juvenile

No. of Volumes: 3,200

Sidelines and Services: Videotapes, audio cassettes, CDs, CD-ROMs

Ampersand Books

P.O. Box 674, Cooper Station New York, NY 10276

(212) 674-6795

Hours: Mail order only

Form of payment: Checks

Type of store: Antiquarian, new, mail order

Subject Specialties: Limited Editions • Literature - Modern First Editions

Owner: George Bixby

Year Established: 1968

No. of Volumes: 10,000

Sidelines and Services: Appraise library collections, mail order

Catalogs: 3-4/year

Angelica's Herbs

147 First Ave. (corner of E. 9th St.) New York, NY 10003
(212) 529-4335
Hours: Mon.-Sat. 10 A.M. to 7:45 P.M.; Sun. 11 A.M. to 6:45 P.M.
Type of store: New
Subject Specialties: Health/Nutrition
Manager: Paul Broaddus
Year Established: 1976
No. of Volumes: 2,000
Sidelines and Services: You can also purchase a variety
of herbal products here.

Animation Art Guild Ltd.

330 W. 45th St., Suite 9D New York, NY 10036
(212) 765-3030 Fax: (212) 765-2727
Hours: Mail order only
Form of payment: Checks
Type of store: Mail order
Subject Specialties: Animation Art • Cinema/Films • Signed
Editions • Walt Disney
President: Michael Scoville
Year Established: 1991
Sidelines and Services: Search service
Catalogs: 4/year

Ann St. Adult Entertainment Center

21 Ann St. (bet. Broadway & Nassau St.) New York, NY 10038

(212) 267-9760
Hours: Mon-Fri: 7 A.M. to 11 P.M.; Sat: 10 A.M. to 11 P.M.;
Sun: 10 A.M. to 7 P.M.
Form of payment: Visa, MC
Subject Specialties: Adult

Aperture Book Center

20 E. 23rd St. (bet. Broadway & Park Ave.) New York, NY 10010
(212) 505-5555 Fax: (212) 979-7759
Hours: Mon.-Fri. 9 A.M. to 5 P.M.
Form of payment: Visa, MC, AMEX
Type of store: New
Subject Specialties: Photography • Social Science/Cultural History
• Environment/Conservation/Ecology • Judaica
Manager: Katherine Miller
Year Established: 1992
Sidelines and Services: Cards, postcards, posters
Catalogs: Semiannual catalog

Appelfeld Gallery

1372 York Ave. (bet. 73rd & 74th Sts.) New York, NY 10021
(212) 988-7835 Fax: (212) 876-8915
Hours: Mon.-Fri. 10 A.M. to 5 P.M.; Sat. 11 A.M. to 4 P.M.
Form of payment: Visa, MC, Checks
Type of store: Antiquarian
Subject Specialties: Children's/Juvenile • History - America
19th c. • Literature - American • Travel • Americana • History -

Britain • Literature - British • Autographs/Manuscripts

Owner: Michael Colon

Year Established: 1960

No. of Volumes: 25,000

Sidelines and Services: Book appraisals

Catalogs: 4/year

Applause Theater Books Inc.

**211 W. 71st St. (bet. Broadway & West End Ave.,
below street level) New York, NY 10023 • (212) 496-7511
Fax: (212) 721-2856**

Hours: Mon.-Sat. 10 A.M. to 8 P.M.; Sun. Noon to 6 P.M.

Form of payment: Visa, MC, AMEX, Discover, Checks

Type of store: New, mail order

Subject Specialties: Performing Arts • Theater/Drama • Cinema/
Films • Video Production • Popular Culture • Radio/Television
• Acting • Directing • Theater Criticism

Owners: Glenn Young, David Cleave

Year Established: 1979

No. of Volumes: 50,000

Sidelines and Services: Videotapes, audiotapes

Catalogs: Annual catalog

W. Graham Arader III

**29 E. 72nd St. (at Madison Ave.) New York, NY 10021
(212) 628-3668 Fax: (212) 879-8714**

Hours: Mon.-Sat. 10 A.M. to 6 P.M.; Sun. 11 A.M. to 5 P.M.

Form of payment: Visa, MC, AMEX, Checks
Type of store: Antiquarian, illustrated books
Subject Specialties: Americana • Books About Books/Bibliography • Reference • Travel • Maps/Atlases/Cartography • Prints/Drawings • Facsimile Editions
Owner: W. Graham Arader III
Manager: Bevin Bravacos
Sidelines and Services: Appraise library collections, paper restoration

Arcade Books

P.O. Box 5176, FDR Station New York, NY 10150
(212) 724-5371
Hours: By appointment only
Type of store: Used
Subject Specialties: Architecture • Engineering • Decorative Arts • Design • New York City • Environment/Conservation/Ecology • Art - Modern • Urban Planning • New York State • Printmaking
Owner: Michael T. Sillerman
No. of Volumes: 5,000
Catalogs: Periodically

Archivia: The Art Book Shop

944 Madison Ave. (bet. 74th & 75th Sts.) New York, NY 10021
(212) 439-9194 Fax: (212) 744-1626
Hours: Mon.-Fri. 10 A.M. to 6 P.M.; Sat. 11 A.M. to 5 P.M.; Sun. (Oct.-June only) Noon to 5 P.M. Closed for 1 week during August.

Form of payment: Visa, MC, AMEX, Checks

Type of store: New, used, antiquarian, mail order, out-of-print, imports

Subject Specialties: Architecture • Gardening • Decorative Arts • Painted Finishes

Owners: Joan Gers, Cynthia Conigliaro

Year Established: 1987

No. of Volumes: 4,000

Sidelines and Services: Book searches for in-print, out-of-print, and foreign books; collection development

Catalogs: Semiannual catalog (Christmas & Gardening); plus 6-8 free flyers announcing new titles

Argosy Book Store

116 E. 59th St. (bet. Lexington and Park Aves.) New York, NY 10022 • (212) 753-4455 Fax: (212) 593-4784 • E-mail address: argosybk@interloc.com

Hours: Mon.-Fri.: 9 A.M. to 6 P.M.; Sat. 10 A.M. to 5 P.M. Open Sat. October through May.

Form of payment: Visa, MC, AMEX

Type of store: Used, antiquarian, fine bindings, first editions

Subject Specialties: Autographs/Manuscripts • Americana • Art - General • Medicine • Maps/Atlases/Cartography • Prints/Drawings

Owners: Naomi Hample, Judith Lowry, Adina Cohen

Year Established: 1924

No. of Volumes: 500,000

Sidelines and Services: Appraise library collections

Catalogs: 10/year

Arka Gift Shop

26 First Ave. (bet. 1st & 2nd Sts.) New York, NY 10009
(212) 473-3550
Hours: Mon.-Sat. 10 A.M. to 6 P.M.; Sun. 11 A.M. to 3 P.M.
Form of payment: Checks accepted
Type of store: New
Subject Specialties: Ukraine (including Ukrainian Language and Literature) • Russia (including Russian Language and Literature)
Manager: J. Pastushenko
No. of Volumes: 2,500
Sidelines and Services: Gifts, greeting cards, stationery, embroidery

Richard B. Arkway

59 E. 54th St., Suite 62 (bet. Park & Madison Aves.)
New York, NY 10022 • (212) 751-8135 or (800) 453-0045
Fax: (212) 832-5389 • E-mail address: 74563.2265@
compuserve.com
Hours: Mon.-Fri. 9:30 A.M. to 5 P.M., plus evenings and Sats. by appointment
Form of payment: Visa, MC, AMEX, Checks
Type of store: Antiquarian
Subject Specialties: Exploration/Voyages • Maps/Atlases/ Cartography • Illustrated Books • Travel • Science • Medicine
President: Richard Arkway

Art Market

75 Grand St. (bet. Wooster & Greene Sts.) New York, NY 10013
(212) 226-4370 Fax: (212) 226-4350
Hours: Mon.-Sun.: Noon to 7 P.M.
Form of payment: Visa, MC, AMEX, Checks
Type of store: New
Subject Specialties: Photography
Manager: Douglas Lee
Sidelines and Services: Posters, T-shirts, CDs, greeting cards

Asahiya Bookstores New York, Inc.

52 Vanderbilt Ave. (bet. 44th & 45th Sts., west of Grand Central
Station) New York, NY 10017 • (212) 883-0011 Fax: (212) 883-1011
Hours: Mon.-Sun. 10 A.M. to 8 P.M.
Form of payment: Visa, MC, AMEX, Checks (with I.D.)
Type of store: New
Subject Specialties: Japan (including Japanese Language
and Literature)
Year Established: 1993
No. of Volumes: 110,000
Sidelines and Services: Mail service (on premises and by phone)
Comments: The majority of the books, about 95 percent, are
in Japanese; 5 percent are English-language books about Japan
and the Japanese language.

The Asia Society Bookstore

725 Park Ave. (bet. 70th & 71st Sts.) New York, NY 10021

(212) 288-6400 Fax: (212) 517-8315
Hours: Tue.-Wed., Fri.-Sat. 11 A.M. to 6 P.M.; Thu. 11 A.M. to 8 P.M.; Sun. Noon to 5 P.M.
Form of payment: Visa, MC, AMEX, Checks
Type of store: New
Subject Specialties: Asian Studies • Children's/Juvenile
Year Established: 1981
No. of Volumes: 35,000
Sidelines and Services: Stationery, sound recordings, periodicals, audiotapes, videotapes
Catalogs: 3/year

Asian Rare Books

175 W. 93rd St., Suite 16-D (bet. Columbus & Amsterdam Aves.)
New York, NY 10025 • (212) 316-5334 Fax: (212) 316-3408
E-mail address: ARB@maestro.com
Hours: By appointment only Mon.-Sat. 9 A.M. to 5 P.M.
Type of store: Antiquarian, mail order
Subject Specialties: Asian Studies • Middle Eastern Languages and Literature • China (including Chinese Language and Literature) • Japan (including Japanese Language and Literature) • Orient • Art - Asian • Exploration/Voyages
Assoc. Director: Stephen Feldman
Year Established: 1974
No. of Volumes: 3,000
Catalogs: Regularly issued

Asian American Bookshop

37 St. Marks Pl. (at Second Ave., in basement of Gap store)
New York, NY 10003 • (212) 228-6718 Fax: (212) 228-7718
E-mail address: aaww@panix.com
Hours: Tue.-Fri. 11 A.M. to 8 P.M.; Sat. 11 A.M. to 7 P.M.;
Sun. Noon to 6 P.M.
Type of store: New
Subject Specialties: Asian Studies • Literature - Asian • Children's/
Juvenile • Poetry • Theater/Drama
Manager: Calvin Chin
Year Established: 1995
Sidelines and Services: Journals, newspapers, catalogs,
newsletters

Association of Independent Video and Film Makers

304 Hudson St., 6th fl. North (bet. Spring & Vandam Sts.)
New York, NY 10013 • (212) 807-1400 Fax: (212) 463-8519
E-mail address: aivffivf@aol.com
Hours: Mon.-Fri. 11 A.M. to 6 P.M.
Form of payment: Visa, MC
Type of store: New, mail order
Subject Specialties: Cinema/Films • Video Production
Manager: Ruby Lerner
Year Established: 1974
Sidelines and Services: Information services, magazines, seminars

Bart Auerbach

411 West End Ave. New York, NY 10024 • (212) 724-4054
Hours: By appointment only
Type of store: Antiquarian
Subject Specialties: Autographs/Manuscripts
Owner: Bart Auerbach

Aurora Fine Books

548 W. 28th St. (bet. Tenth & Eleventh Aves.)
New York, NY 10001 • (212) 947-0422 Fax: (212) 947-0422
Hours: By appointment only Mon.-Fri. 9 A.M. to 4 P.M.
Type of store: Used
Subject Specialties: Art - Modern • Art - Middle Eastern • Judaica
• Classical Studies • Germany (including German Language
and Literature)
Owner: Yaakov Mashiah
Year Established: 1989

The Baha'i Bookstore

53 E. 11th St. (bet. University Pl. & Broadway)
New York, NY 10003 • (212) 674-8998 Fax: (212) 677-7300
Hours: Fri. 7:30 P.M. to 9 P.M.; Sun. Noon to 4 P.M.
Other hours by appointment.
Form of payment: Visa, MC, AMEX, Checks
Type of store: New
Subject Specialties: General
Manager: Riaz Jurney

Year Established: 1992
Sidelines and Services: Greeting cards, religious goods

Bank Street College Bookstore

610 W. 112th St. (at corner of Broadway) New York, NY 10025
(212) 678-1654 or (800) 724-1486 Fax: (212) 316-7026
Hours: Mon.-Thu. 10 A.M. to 8 P.M.; Fri.-Sat. 10 A.M. to 6 P.M.;
Sun. Noon to 5 P.M.
Form of payment: Visa, MC, AMEX, Checks
Type of store: New
Subject Specialties: Children's/Juvenile • Education • Juvenile
Development
Manager: Beth Puffer
Year Established: 1970
No. of Volumes: 200,000
Sidelines and Services: Games, special order, video cassettes,
mail order, audio cassettes, CDs, story hours, author appearances
Catalogs: Annual catalog

C. Virginia Barnes

2 Fifth Ave., Rm. 16M New York, NY 10011 • (212) 227-4714
Fax: (212) 732-9453
Hours: Mail order only
Form of payment: Checks
Type of store: Antiquarian
Subject Specialties: Genealogy • Magic
• Mnemonics/Memory • Metiodism

Owner: C. Virginia Barnes
Year Established: 1954
Catalogs: Subject list on request

Barnes & Noble Bookstore (Store No. 1003)

600 Fifth Ave. (at 48th St.) New York, NY 10020
(212) 765-0590 Fax: (212) 489-2355
Hours: Mon.-Fri. 8:30 A.M. to 6:45 P.M.; Sat. 9:45 A.M. to 6 P.M.;
Sun. Noon to 6 P.M.
Form of payment: Visa, MC, AMEX, Discover, Checks
Type of store: New
Subject Specialties: General • Travel
Year Established: 1977
Sidelines and Services: Gift wrapping, mailing

Barnes & Noble Bookstore (Store No. 1006)

1 Penn Plaza (33rd St. & Seventh Ave.) New York, NY 10019
(212) 695-1677 Fax: (212) 695-3396
Hours: Mon.-Fri.: 8 A.M. to 8 P.M.; Sat. 10 A.M. to 7 P.M.;
Sun. 10 A.M. to 7 P.M.
Form of payment: Visa, MC, AMEX, Discover, Checks
Type of store: New
Subject Specialties: General
Year Established: 1986

Barnes & Noble Bookstore (Store No. 1020)

750 Third Ave. (at 47th St.) New York, NY 10017

(212) 697-2251 Fax: (212) 697-9273

Hours: Mon.-Fri.: 8 A.M. to 8 P.M.; Sat. 10 A.M. to 6 P.M.;

Sun. Noon to 5 P.M.

Form of payment: Visa, MC, AMEX, Discover, Checks

Type of store: New

Subject Specialties: General

Year Established: 1979

Barnes & Noble Bookstore (Store No. 1050)

385 Fifth Ave. (at 36th St.) New York, NY 10016

(212) 779-7677 Fax: 696-9525

Hours: Mon.-Fri. 8 A.M. to 7 P.M.; Sat.-Sun. 10 A.M. to 6 P.M.

Form of payment: Visa, MC, AMEX, Discover, Checks

Type of store: New

Subject Specialties: General

Year Established: 1987

Barnes & Noble Bookstore (Store No. 1051)

109 E. 42nd St. (bet. Lexington & Vanderbilt Aves., inside Grand Central Station) New York, NY 10017 • (212) 818-0973

Hours: Mon.-Fri. 8 A.M. to 8 P.M.; Sat. 10 A.M. to 6 P.M.;

Sun. Noon to 5 P.M.

Form of payment: Visa, MC, AMEX, Discover, Checks

Type of store: New

Subject Specialties: General   **Year Established:** 1988

Barnes & Noble Bookstore (Store No. 1071)

901 Sixth Ave. (at 33rd St., inside the Manhattan Mall, 6th fl.)
New York, NY 10001 • (212) 268-2505
Hours: Mon.-Sat. 10 A.M. to 8 P.M.; Sun. 11 A.M. to 6 P.M.
Form of payment: Visa, MC, AMEX, Discover, Checks
Type of store: New
Subject Specialties: General
Year Established: 1989

Barnes & Noble Junior Bookstore

(Store No. 1941)
120 E. 86th St. (bet. Lexington & Park Aves.)
New York, NY 10029 • (212) 427-0686 Fax: (212) 360-1957
Hours: Mon.-Sat. 9 A.M. to 9 P.M.; Sun. 11 A.M. to 7 P.M.
Form of payment: Visa, MC, AMEX, Discover, Checks
Type of store: New
Subject Specialties: Children's/Juvenile
Year Established: 1992
Sidelines and Services: Gift wrapping, mailing

Barnes & Noble Bookstore (Store No. 1979)

2289 Broadway (at 82nd St.) New York, NY 10024
(212) 362-8835 Fax: (212) 362-6908
Hours: Sun.-Thu. 9 A.M. to 11 P.M.; Fri.-Sat. 9 A.M. to Midnight
Form of payment: Visa, MC, AMEX, Discover, Checks
Type of store: New, periodicals
Subject Specialties: General

Year Established: 1993
Sidelines and Services: Café, gift wrapping, mailing, CDs, gifts

Barnes & Noble Bookstore (Store No. 2525)
1280 Lexington Ave. (bet. 86th & 87th Sts.) New York, NY 10028
(212) 423-9900 Fax: (212) 369-7859
Hours: Mon.-Sat. 9 A.M. to 11 P.M.; Sun. 10 A.M. to 9 P.M.
Form of payment: Visa, MC, AMEX, Discover, Checks
Type of store: New
Subject Specialties: General
Year Established: 1992
Sidelines and Services: Gift wrapping, mailing

Barnes & Noble Bookstore (Store No. 2538)
675 Sixth Ave. (bet. 21st & 22nd Sts.) New York, NY 10010
(212) 727-1227 Fax: (212) 727-1672
Hours: Mon.-Sun.: 9 A.M. to 11 P.M.
Form of payment: Visa, MC, AMEX, Discover, Checks
Type of store: New
Subject Specialties: General
Year Established: 1994
No. of Volumes: 150,000

Sidelines and Services: Café, gift wrapping
and mailing, CDs, gifts, magazines

Barnes & Noble Bookstore (Store No. 2618)
160 E. 54th St. (bet. Third & Lexington Aves.,

inside the Citicorp Building) New York, NY 10022
(212) 750-8033 Fax: (212) 750-8038
Hours: Mon.-Fri. 8 A.M. to 9 P.M.; Sat. 9 A.M. to 9 P.M.;
Sun. 11 A.M. to 6 P.M.
Form of payment: Visa, MC, AMEX, Discover, Checks
Type of store: New, periodicals, mail order
Subject Specialties: General • Business/Management
• Computers • Art - General • Cooking • History - General
• Literary Criticism • Travel
Year Established: 1994
Sidelines and Services: Café, music recordings; will special order
books, CDs and cassettes

Barnes & Noble Bookstore **(Store No. 2619)**

4 Astor Pl. (bet. Broadway and Lafayette St.)
New York, NY 10003 • (212) 420-1322 Fax: (212) 420-1652
Hours: Mon.-Sat. 10 A.M. to Midnight; Sun. 10 A.M. to 10 P.M.
Form of payment: Visa, MC, AMEX, Discover, Checks
Type of store: New
Subject Specialties: General
Year Established: 1994
Sidelines and Services: Café, free gift wrap, mailing service

Barnes & Noble Bookstore **(Store No. 2628)**

1960 Broadway (at 66th St., at Lincoln Triangle)
New York, NY 10023 • (212) 595-6859 Fax: (212) 595-8946
Hours: Mon.-Sun. 9 A.M. to Midnight

Form of payment: Visa, MC, AMEX, Discover, Checks
Subject Specialties: General
Year Established: 1995
Sidelines and Services: Café, music recordings, computer software, gift wrapping, mailing

Barnes & Noble Bookstore (Store No. 2675)

33 E. 17th St. (bet. Broadway & Park Ave. South, just north of Union Square Park) New York, NY 10003
(212) 253-0810 Fax: (212) 253-0820
Hours: Mon.-Sun. 10 A.M. to 10 P.M.
Form of payment: Visa, MC, AMEX, Discover, Checks
Type of store: New
Subject Specialties: General
Year Established: 1995
Sidelines and Services: Café, music recordings, computer software

Barnes & Noble Bookstore—Annex

(Store No. 1002)
128 Fifth Ave. (at 18th St., directly across the street from main Barnes & Noble store) New York, NY 10011
(212) 691-3770 Fax: (212) 691-6010
Hours: Mon.-Fri. 9:30 A.M. to 8 P.M.; Sat. 9:30 A.M. to 6:30 P.M.; Sun. 11 A.M. to 6 P.M.
Form of payment: Visa, MC, AMEX, Discover, Checks
Type of store: Used, remainders

Subject Specialties: General
Year Established: 1984
No. of Volumes: 250,000

Barnes & Noble Bookstore—Main Store

105 Fifth Ave. (at 18th St.) New York, NY 10003
(212) 675-5500 Fax: (212) 633-2522
Hours: Mon.-Fri. 9:30 A.M. to 7:45 P.M.; Sat. 9:30 A.M.
to 6:15 P.M.; Sun. 11 A.M. to 5:45 P.M.
Form of payment: Visa, MC, AMEX, Discover, Diners Club,
Corporate checks
Type of store: New, used, mail order
Subject Specialties: Academic • Engineering • Law • Medicine
• Nursing • Reference • Technology
No. of Volumes: 3 million
Catalogs: Catalogs of medical/science/technical books
issued 4 times/year
Comments: Barnes and Noble's main store

J. N. Bartfield

30 W. 57th St., 3rd fl. (bet. Fifth & Sixth Aves.)
New York, NY 10019 • (212) 245-8890 Fax: (212) 541-4860
Hours: Mon.-Fri. 10 A.M. to 5 P.M.; Sat. 10 A.M. to 3 P.M.
During the summer, open on Sat. by appointment only.
Form of payment: AMEX, Checks
Type of store: Antiquarian
Subject Specialties: Fine Bindings • Fore-edge Paintings

• Americana • Illustrated Books • Western Americana • Maps/
Atlases/Cartography • Colorplate Books • Natural History
• Art - General • Canada • Exploration/Voyages • Sports
• Autographs/Manuscripts • Prints/Drawings

Owner: George Bartfield

Year Established: 1937

No. of Volumes: 37,500

Sidelines and Services: Appraise library collections, original art,
wholesale

Catalogs: On occasion; special catalogs of stock made
on request.

Comments: Also carries leatherbound sets and singles.

Baruch College Bookstore

360 Park Ave. South (bet. 25th & 26th Sts.) New York, NY 10010

(212) 889-4327 Fax: (212) 679-2014

Hours: Mon.-Thu. 9 A.M. to 7 P.M.; Fri. 10 A.M. to 3 P.M.
Summer hours: Mon.-Thu. 10 A.M. to 6 P.M.; Fri. 10 A.M. to 3 P.M.
Hours vary; best to phone ahead.

Form of payment: Visa, MC, AMEX, Discover, Checks

Type of store: New, used

Subject Specialties: Business/Management • Accounting
• Computers • Foreign Language Instruction • Marketing

Manager: Michael Cram

Year Established: 1979

Sidelines and Services: College supplies, stationery

Bauman Rare Books

301 Park Ave. (bet. 49th & 50th Sts., inside Waldorf-Astoria Hotel lobby) New York, NY 10022 • (212) 759-8300

Fax: (212) 759-8350 • E-mail address: brb@baumanrarebk.com

Hours: Mon.-Sat. 10 A.M. to 7 P.M.

Form of payment: Visa, MC, AMEX, Checks

Type of store: Antiquarian

Subject Specialties: Literature - General • Autographs/Manuscripts • Signed Editions • Americana • Law • Science • Travel • History - General • Economics • Judaica • Children's/Juvenile

Owners: David L. Bauman, Natalie Bauman

No. of Volumes: 3,000

Catalogs: 3-4/year

Comments: Company headquarters are located in Philadelphia

Ronald Belanske—Rare Books & Manuscripts

245 E. 40th St. (at Second Ave.) New York, NY 10016

(212) 697-3091 or (908) 687-6220 Fax: (908) 687-8195

Hours: By appointment only

Form of payment: Checks

Type of store: Antiquarian, mail order

Subject Specialties: Literature - Modern • Fiction - Crime/Mystery/Suspense • Autographs/Manuscripts

Owner: Ronald Belanske

Year Established: 1982   **No. of Volumes:** 2,000

Sidelines and Services: Appraisals

Catalogs: Semiannual catalog

Benjamin Books

408 World Trade Center, Concourse Level New York, NY 10048

(212) 432-1103 Fax: (212) 432-1104

Hours: Mon.-Fri. 7 A.M. to 6:30 P.M.; Sat. 11 A.M. to 4 P.M.

Form of payment: Visa, MC, AMEX; No checks

Type of store: New

Subject Specialties: General • Business/Management • Computers

Manager: Valerie Catchings

Sidelines and Services: Corporate/volume discounts

Better Book Getter

310 Riverside Dr., Apt. 202 New York, NY 10025

(212) 316-5634 Fax: (212) 316-5634

Hours: Phone/mail order only

Form of payment: Visa, MC, AMEX, Checks

Type of store: Used, antiquarian

Subject Specialties: General

Owner: Richard Chalfin

Sidelines and Services: Search service

Biblio's Cafe and Bookstore

317 Church St. (bet. Lispenard & Walker Sts.)
New York, NY 10013 • (212) 334-6990 Fax: (212) 334-6991
E-mail address: biblio's@gmx1.com

Hours: Sun.-Wed. 7:30 A.M. to 9 P.M.; Thu.-Sat. 7:30 A.M. to 11 P.M.
Summer hours: Mon.-Sun. 7:30 A.M. to 8 P.M.

Form of payment: Visa, MC, AMEX, Checks

Type of store: New, periodicals
Subject Specialties: Literature - American • Literature - Modern
• Poetry • Science • Philosophy • Religion - General • Sexology
• Popular Culture • Politics/Political Science
Owner: Joseph Manuse
Manager: Alford Faulkner
Year Established: 1993
No. of Volumes: 3,000
Sidelines and Services: Literary magazines, newspapers,
special orders
Comments: For those in the know, this store is also referred
to as Java Joe's.

Bilingual Publications Co.

270 Lafayette, Suite 705 (at Prince St.) New York, NY 10012
(212) 431-3500 Fax: (212) 431-3567
Hours: Mon.-Fri. 9 A.M. to 5 P.M., primarily by appointment
Form of payment: Checks
Type of store: New, mail order
Subject Specialties: Spanish Language and Literature • Literature-
Latin American/Caribbean • History - Latin America/Caribbean
• How-To Books
Owner: Linda E. Goodman
Year Established: 1974
Sidelines and Services: Book importing
Catalogs: 3/year (free)

Biography Bookshop

400 Bleecker St. (at W. 11th St.) New York, NY 10014

(212) 807-8655

Hours: Mon.-Thu. Noon to 8 P.M.; Fri. Noon to 10 P.M.;
Sat. 11 A.M. to 11 P.M.; Sun. 11 A.M. to 7 P.M.

Form of payment: Visa, MC, AMEX

Type of store: New, used

Subject Specialties: Biography/Autobiography

Owners: Carolyn Epstein, Charles Mullen

Year Established: 1984

Sidelines and Services: Maps

Black Books Plus

702 Amsterdam Ave. (corner of 94th St.) New York, NY 10025

(212) 749-9632

Hours: Tue.-Wed., Fri. 11 A.M. to 6 P.M.; Thu. 11 A.M. to 7 P.M.; Sat.
11 A.M. to 5 P.M. Closed Sun. & Mon.

Form of payment: AMEX

Type of store: New, used

Subject Specialties: African-American Studies • History - Africa
• Children's/Juvenile • Literature - African

Owner: Glenderlyn Johnson

Year Established: 1989

No. of Volumes: 3,000 titles

Sidelines and Services: Mail order, special order, book signings,
greeting cards, posters, calendars, Black memorabilia

Comments: This store specializes in books relating to African-
American history, art, literature, and politics.

Black Orchid Bookshop

303 E. 81st St. (bet. First & Second Aves.) New York, NY 10028
(212) 734-5980 • E-mail address: borchid@aol.com
Hours: Mon.-Fri. Noon to 8 P.M.; Sat. 11 A.M. to 7 P.M.;
Sun. Noon to 5 P.M.
Form of payment: Visa, MC, AMEX, Traveler's checks
Type of store: New, used
Subject Specialties: Fiction - Crime/Mystery/Suspense
Owners: Bonnie Claeson, Joseph Guglielmelli
Year Established: 1994   **No. of Volumes:** 10,000
Sidelines and Services: Search service
Catalogs: Newsletter of upcoming signings

Black Sun Books

157 E. 57th St. (bet. Lexington & Third Aves.)
New York, NY 10022 • (212) 688-6622 Fax: (212) 751-6529
E-mail address: blksnbks@panix.com
Hours: Mon.-Fri. 9 A.M. to 5 P.M. by appointment only
Form of payment: AMEX, Visa, MC, Checks
Type of store: Antiquarian
Subject Specialties: Illustrated Books • Fine Printing
• Autographs/Manuscripts • Livres d'Artiste • Prints/Drawings
• Literature - British • Literature - American
Owners: Harvey Tucker, Linda Tucker
Year Established: 1969
Sidelines and Services: Appraise library collections; original art
for books
Catalogs: 4/year

Blackout Books

50 Avenue B (bet. 3rd & 4th Sts.) New York, NY 10009
(212) 777-1967 Fax: (212) 777-4091 • E-mail address:
blackout@panix.com
Hours: Mon.-Sun. 11 A.M. to 10 P.M.
Form of payment: Checks
Type of store: New
Subject Specialties: Radical Issues • Comic Books • Left-Wing
Issues • Anarchism • Anti-Authoritarianism
Year Established: 1994

Bleecker Street Books

350 Bleecker St. (bet. W. 10th & Charles Sts.)
New York, NY 10014 • (212) 675-2084
Hours: Mon.-Sun. 10:30 A.M. to 11 P.M.
Form of payment: Visa, MC, AMEX, Checks
Type of store: New, used
Subject Specialties: General • Mathematics • Physics
• Science
Owner: Paul Valluzzi
Manager: Gary Nargi
Year Established: 1995
No. of Volumes: 40,000
Sidelines and Services: Buys textbooks and
other books on weekends only.
Comments: New books are generally discounted 50%.

The Bohemian Bookworm

110 W. 25th St., 9th fl. (bet. Sixth & Seventh Aves.)
New York, NY 10001 • (212) 620-5627 Fax: (212) 620-5688
E-mail address: antiqarc@panix.com
Hours: Mon.-Tue., Thu.-Sun. 10 A.M. to 6 P.M.;
Wed. 10 A.M. to 8 P.M.
Form of payment: Visa, MC, AMEX, Discover, Checks
Type of store: Used, antiquarian
Subject Specialties: Decorative Arts • Fashion/Costume/Clothing
Travel • Illustrated Books • Literature - General • Books About
Books/Bibliography • Architecture
Owners: Ronald Morris, Myrna Adolph
Year Established: 1991
No. of Volumes: 6,000
Sidelines and Services: Free search service

Book Ark

173 W. 81st St. (bet. Columbus & Amsterdam Aves.)
New York, NY 10024 • (212) 787-3916 Fax: 787-3914
Hours: Sun.-Thu. 11 A.M. to 9 P.M.; Fri.-Sat. 11 A.M. to 11 P.M.
Form of payment: Visa, MC, Checks
Type of store: Used, antiquarian
Subject Specialties: Academic • Philosophy • Literature - General
• Art - General • Performing Arts • France (including French
Language and Literature) • Germany (including German
Language and Literature) • Spanish Language and Literature
• Children's/Juvenile • Theater/Drama • Cinema/Films • Music
• Illustrated Books • Architecture • Photography

Owners: Daniel Wechsler, Jorge Souto Silva
Manager: Thomas Dukleth
Year Established: 1995

The Book Chest

322 W. 57th St., Rm. 34-S (bet. Eighth & Ninth Aves.)
New York, NY 10019 • (212) 246-8955 Fax: (212) 757-8817
E-mail address: bkchest@pipeline.com
Hours: By appointment only
Form of payment: Checks
Type of store: Used, antiquarian
Subject Specialties: Colorplate Books • Humor • Literature -
General • Humor • Etiquette
Owners: Estelle Chessid, Sigmund Chessid
Year Established: 1972
No. of Volumes: 2,800
Sidelines and Services: Caricatures, appraise library collections
Catalogs: 1 or 2/year

Book Fairs

There are a number of book fairs in Manhattan in the course of
a year. These are events at which dealers of used and antiquarian books, manuscripts, prints, and maps set up booths in an
exhibition hall and sell selected items from their stock.

The typical book fair begins on a Fri. evening and runs
through Sun., with an average of 100 dealers. It's an ideal place
to both see and handle a wide variety of antiquarian books and

to meet the booksellers themselves. Some of the regular book fairs held every year in Manhattan are listed below. For up-to-date information, check <u>AB Bookman's Weekly</u> magazine.

Trinity Antiquarian
Westside Book Fair
Late October
Trinity School
101 West 91st Street, New York

Upper West Side
Antiquarian Book Fair
Early March
Temple Rodeph Sholom
7 West 83rd Street, New York

Greenwich Village Book Fair
Late February
P.S. 3
490 Hudson Street, New York

Metropolitan Antiquarian
Book Fair
Spring and Autumn
Metropolitan Antiques Pavilion
110 West 19th Street, 1st floor,
New York

New York Antiquarian
Book Fair
April
(This is the main book fair
of the year in New York City.)
Seventh Regiment Armory
643 Park Avenue, New York

Book Resource

41 E. 11th St., 3rd fl. New York, NY 10003 • (212) 254-6031
Fax: (212) 777-9224 • E-mail address: service@bookresource.com
Hours: Mon.-Fri.: 9:30 A.M. to 5:30 P.M. Mail order by phone only.
Form of payment: Visa, MC, AMEX, Checks
Type of store: New, used, antiquarian, mail order
Subject Specialties: General

Owner: Cynthia Gillis

Year Established: 1989

Sidelines and Services: Search service

Comments: The Book Resource Center either has or will order any book listed in Books in Print. They also offer a 10 percent discount on orders of $75 or more.

Book Scientific

10 W. 19th St., 3rd fl. (bet. Fifth & Sixth Aves.)

New York, NY 10011 • (212) 206-1310 or (888) BOOK-SCI

Fax: (212) 675-4230

Hours: Mon.-Sat. 10 A.M. to 6 P.M.; Sun. 11 A.M. to 5 P.M.

Form of payment: Visa, MC, AMEX, Checks

Type of store: New, used

Subject Specialties: Science • Chemistry
• Engineering • Mathematics • Physics

Book Smart

27 W. 20th St., #506 (bet. Fifth & Sixth Aves.)

New York, NY 10011 • (212) 675-8677 Fax: (212) 675-8713

Hours: Mon.-Fri. 9 A.M. to 5 P.M., by appointment only

Form of payment: AMEX

Type of store: New

Subject Specialties: Children's/Juvenile • Cooking

Bookberries

983 Lexington Ave. (at 71st St.) New York, NY 10021
(212) 794-9400 Fax: (212) 794-7042
Hours: Mon.-Fri. 10 A.M. to 9 P.M.; Sat. 10 A.M. to 6 P.M.;
Sun. Noon to 6 P.M. Summer hours: Mon.- Sun. 10 A.M. to 7 P.M.
Form of payment: Visa, MC, AMEX, Checks
Type of store: New
Subject Specialties: General • Literature - General • Children's/
Juvenile • Art - General • Cooking • New York City • Philosophy
Owner: Hope Feinberg
Manager: David Graham
Year Established: 1990
No. of Volumes: 35,000
Sidelines and Services: Special orders, free neighborhood
delivery, books on tape, gift wrapping, worldwide shipping,
readings, book signings
Catalogs: Free monthly newsletter

Bookfinders General

P.O. Box G, Madison Square Station New York, NY 10159
(212) 689-0772 Fax: (212) 481-0552 • E-mail address:
bkfindgen@aol.com
Hours: Mail order only
Type of store: Antiquarian, mail order
Subject Specialties: Medicine • Genealogy • History - General
• Literature - General • Religion - General
Year Established: 1963
Sidelines and Services: Back issues of periodicals, search

service, computer software
Catalogs: 3/year

Bookleaves

304 W. 4th St. (off Bank St.) New York, NY 10014
(212) 924-5638
Hours: Tue.-Sun. 11 A.M. to 9 P.M.
Form of payment: Checks
Type of store: Used, antiquarian
Subject Specialties: Art - General • Literature - General
• Cinema/Films • Performing Arts • Photography • History -
20th c. • Biography/Autobiography
Owner: Arthur Farrier
Year Established: 1992
No. of Volumes: 2,500

Books and Binding

33 W. 17th St. (bet. Fifth & Sixth Aves.) New York, NY 10011
(212) 229-0004 Fax: (212) 229-0044
Hours: Mon.-Fri. 9.30 A.M. to 8 P.M.; Sat. 10 A.M. to 7 P.M.;
Sun. 11 A.M. to 5 P.M.
Form of payment: Visa, MC
Type of store: New, used, antiquarian
Subject Specialties: Art - General • Dictionaries/Encyclopedias
• Fine Bindings • Photography • Architecture • Scholarly
Publications
Owner: Joe Landau

Sidelines and Services: This store also does bookbinding.

Catalogs: Upon request

Books & Co.

939 Madison Ave. (bet. 74th & 75th Sts.) New York, NY 10021

(212) 737-1450 Fax: (212) 472-6251

Hours: Mon.-Fri. 10 A.M. to 7 P.M.; Sat. 10 A.M. to 6 P.M.;
Sun. Noon to 6 P.M.

Form of payment: Visa, MC, AMEX, Checks

Type of store: New

Subject Specialties: Art - General • Photography • Philosophy
• Literature - General

Owner: Jeannette Watson

Year Established: 1978

Sidelines and Services: Literary magazines, art shows, readings

Books of Wonder

16 W. 18th St. (bet. Fifth & Sixth Aves.) New York, NY 10011

(212) 989-3270 or (800) 835-4315 Fax: (212) 989-1203

E-mail address: bookswon@ix.netcom.com

Hours: Mon.-Sat. 11 A.M. to 7 P.M.; Sun. Noon to 6 P.M.

Form of payment: Visa, MC, AMEX, Discover, JCB, Checks

Type of store: New, used, rare

Subject Specialties: Children's/Juvenile • Folklore/Mythology
• Baumiana

Owners: Peter Glassman, James Carey

Year Established: 1980

No. of Volumes: 15,000

Sidelines and Services: Greeting cards, toys, original illustrations

Catalogs: Monthly newsletter (free); catalog of collectible children's books ($3/issue; $30 for 12 issues); semiannual "Oz Collector" catalog ($2/issue)

Borders Books and Music

5 World Trade Center (at corner of Church & Vesey Sts.)
New York, NY 10048 • (212) 839-8049 Fax: (212) 839-0806
Hours: Mon.-Fri. 7 A.M. to 8:30 P.M.; Sat. 10 A.M. to 8:30 P.M.;
Sun. 11 A.M. to 8:30 P.M.

Form of payment: Visa, MC, AMEX, Discover, Checks

Type of store: New

Subject Specialties: General

General Manager: Mark Schneyer

Asst. Manager: April Bart-Locque

Year Established: 1996

No. of Volumes: 165,000 titles

Sidelines and Services: Special orders, café, music CDs (70,000; all categories), worldwide shipping, gift certificates, magazines, author appearances, CD-ROMs

Borough of Manhattan
Community College Bookstore

199 Chambers St. (bet. Greenwich & West Sts., 3 blocks west of City Hall) New York, NY 10007 • (212) 608-1023 Fax: 732-4287
Hours: Mon.-Thu. 9 A.M. to 6 P.M.; Fri. 9 A.M. to 5 P.M.

Form of payment: Visa, MC, AMEX, Discover, Checks
Type of store: New
Subject Specialties: General
Comments: Operated by Barnes & Noble.

William G. Boyer

P.O. Box 763, Planetarium Station New York, NY 10024
(212) 724-9402
Hours: Call for appointment
Form of payment: Checks
Type of store: Used, antiquarian, mail order
Subject Specialties: Architecture • Art - General • Children's/
Juvenile • History - General • Illustrated Books • Performing Arts
• Travel • Collectibles
Owner: William G. Boyer
Year Established: 1965
No. of Volumes: 5,000
Comments: This shop is located at the
owner's residence, at W. 81st St. & Broadway.

Bradlees

40 E. 14th St. (at Broadway) New York, NY 10003
(212) 673-5814
Hours: Mon.-Sat. 9 A.M. to 9 P.M.; Sun. 10 A.M. to 7 P.M.
Form of payment: Visa, MC, AMEX, Checks
Type of store: New
Subject Specialties: General

Brazen Head Books

235 E. 84th St. (bet. Second & Third Aves.) New York, NY 10028
(212) 879-9830 or (212) 535-3734
Hours: By appointment only
Form of payment: Checks
Type of store: Used, rare
Subject Specialties: Biography/Autobiography • History - General
• First Editions • Literature - Modern • Theater/Drama • Cinema/
Films • Theater/Drama
Owner: Michael Seidenberg
Year Established: 1980
No. of Volumes: 10,000
Sidelines and Services: Search service

Martin Breslauer

P.O. Box 607 New York, NY 10028
(212) 794-2995 Fax: (212) 794-4913
Hours: By appointment only
Form of payment: Checks
Type of store: Antiquarian
Subject Specialties: Fine Bindings • Illustrated Books • Incunabula
Owner: Bernard H. Breslauer

Bridge World Magazine

39 W. 94th St. (bet. Central Park West & Columbus Ave.)
New York, NY 10025 • (212) 866-5860
Hours: Mon.-Fri. 9 A.M. to 5 P.M. (best to call ahead)

Form of payment: Checks
Type of store: New, used, periodicals, mail order
Subject Specialties: Games/Gambling • Contract Bridge
President: Edgar Kaplan
Vice-President: Jeff Rubens
Year Established: 1929
No. of Volumes: 15,000
Sidelines and Services: Periodicals, special orders, monthly magazine on contract bridge, back issues of "Bridge World" magazine (back to the 1950s)
Catalogs: Free monthly catalog

E. W. Brill Antiquarian Books

505 Eighth Ave., 11th fl. (at E. 35th St.) New York, NY 10018
(212) 864-1269 or (800) 562-9911 Fax: (212) 695-3860
Hours: Mail order only
Form of payment: Visa, MC, AMEX, Checks
Type of store: Out-of-print
Subject Specialties: Judaica • Hebraica
Owner: Elliott Brill

British Travel Bookshop

551 Fifth Ave., 7th fl. (corner of 45th St. & Fifth Ave.)
New York, NY 10176 • (212) 490-6688 Fax: (212) 490-0219
Hours: Mon.-Fri. 9 A.M. to 5 P.M.
Form of payment: Visa, MC, AMEX, Discover, Checks
Type of store: New

Subject Specialties: United Kingdom • Travel • Maps/Atlases/ Cartography
Owner: Gerlinde Woititz
Year Established: 1974
No. of Volumes: 500 titles
Sidelines and Services: Maps, tickets and transport passes, UK travel videos
Catalogs: Annual catalog

Brown's Music Co.

44 W. 62nd St. (corner of Columbus Ave., across from Lincoln Center) New York, NY 10023 • (212) 541-6236
Hours: Mon.-Sat. 10 A.M. to 7 P.M.; Sun. Noon to 5 P.M.
Form of payment: Visa, MC, AMEX, Discover, Checks
Type of store: New
Subject Specialties: Music
Owner: Jack Brown
Year Established: 1861
No. of Volumes: 10,000
Sidelines and Services: Greeting cards, periodicals, sheet music/scores (classical and popular), international shipping

Brunner-Mazel

19 Union Square West, 8th fl. (east of Fifth Ave., corner of 15th St.) New York, NY 10003 • (212) 924-3344 or (800) 825-3089
Fax: (212) 242-6339 • E-mail address: postmaster@bmpub.com
Hours: Mon.-Fri. 9 A.M. to 6 P.M.; Sat. 10:30 A.M. to 3:30 P.M.

Closed Sun.

Form of payment: Visa, MC, AMEX

Type of store: New

Subject Specialties: Psychology • Psychiatry • Psychoanalysis • Psychotherapy • Child Development

Owner: Mark Tracten

Year Established: 1946

No. of Volumes: 8,000

Sidelines and Services: Videotapes, audiotapes

Catalogs: 6/year

Comments: You can visit this shop's home page on the World Wide Web located at: http://www.bmpub.com

Bryn Mawr Bookshop

502 E. 79th St. (bet. York & East End Aves.) New York, NY 10021 (212) 744-7682

Hours: Thu.-Sat. Noon to 7 P.M.; Sun. Noon to 5 P.M. Closed Mon.-Wed.

Form of payment: Checks

Type of store: Used

Subject Specialties: Literature - General

Manager: Jon Boorstein

Chairman: Rolly Phillips

Year Established: 1974

No. of Volumes: 20,000

Sidelines and Services: LP records, audiotapes, CDs, videotapes

Comments: Will buy your used books and records.

Susi Buchanan

325 E. 79th St., #2E (bet. First & Second Aves.)
New York, NY 10021 • (212) 288-4018
Hours: By appointment only
Form of payment: Checks
Type of store: Antiquarian
Subject Specialties: Children's/Juvenile
Owner: Susi Buchanan
Year Established: 1981

Jutta Buck, Antiquarian Book and Print Sellers

4 E. 95th St. (bet. Madison & Fifth Aves.) New York, NY 10128
(212) 289-4577 Fax: (212) 797-1189
Type of store: Antiquarian
Subject Specialties: Natural History • Botany • Natural History
• Illustrated Books

Bus Terminal Books and Periodicals

625 Eighth Ave. (inside New York Port Authority building,
north wing, 2nd floor) New York, NY 10018
(212) 736-4380 Fax: 564-4226
Hours: Mon.-Fri. 7:30 A.M. to 8 P.M.; Sat. 9 A.M. to 6 P.M.
Form of payment: Visa, MC, AMEX, Discover, Diners Club, Checks
Type of store: New
Subject Specialties: General
Owner: Peter Sanjanwals

Manager: Joseph Guyton
Sidelines and Services: Stationery

CFM Gallery

112 Greene St. (bet. Spring & Prince Sts.) New York, NY 10012
(212) 966-3864 Fax: (212) 226-1041
Hours: Mon.-Fri. Noon to 6 P.M.
Form of payment: Visa, MC, AMEX
Type of store: New, used
Subject Specialties: Art - Symbolism • Art - Surrealism • Leonor Fini
Owner: Neil P. Zukerman
Year Established: 1986   **No. of Volumes:** 1,000
Sidelines and Services: Original art, prints
Comments: You can also visit this gallery on the Internet at:
http://www.galleryguide.com/gallerycfm

Calvary Christian Book Store

139 W. 57th St. (bet. Sixth & Seventh Aves.) New York, NY 10019
(212) 315-0230 Fax: (212) 974-1945
Hours: Sun. 12:30 P.M. to 4 P.M.; Mon. 10 A.M. to 6 P.M.;
Wed. 10 A.M. to 7 P.M.
Form of payment: Visa, MC, AMEX, Checks
Type of store: New
Subject Specialties: Religion - Christianity • Bibles
No. of Volumes: 4,000
Sidelines and Services: Gifts, greeting cards, audiotapes,
Sunday school supplies, videotape rentals, Bible study courses

Camel Book Co.

P.O. Box 1936, Cathedral Station New York, NY 10025

(516) 883-5650 Fax: (516) 944-6389

E-mail address: cA.M.elbooks@gnn.com

Hours: Mail order only

Form of payment: Checks

Type of store: Used, antiquarian, mail order

Subject Specialties: Religion - Islam • Middle Eastern Languages and Literature • Judaica • Art - Middle Eastern • History - Middle East • Arabic • Travel • Exploration/Voyages

Owners: Carl Wurtzel, Faith Wurtzel

Year Established: 1985

No. of Volumes: 3,000

Sidelines and Services: Computer software for booksellers and book collectors

Catalogs: 3/year

Benjamin Cardozo School of Law Bookstore

55 Fifth Ave. (bet. 12th & 13th Sts.) New York, NY 10003

(212) 790-0339/0200 Fax: (212) 391-6736

Hours: Mon-Tues: 10:30 A.M. to 3:30 P.M. / Wed: 9:30 A.M. to 11:30 A.M. / Thurs: 10:30 A.M. to 3:30 P.M.

Form of payment: Visa, MC, AMEX, Checks

Type of store: New

Subject Specialties: Law

Manager: Esther Hollander

Sidelines and Services: College supplies

James F. Carr

227 E. 81st St. (bet. Second & Third Aves.) New York, NY 10028
(212) 535-8110
Hours: By appointment only
Form of payment: Checks
Type of store: Used, antiquarian
Subject Specialties: Americana • Fine Bindings • Christmas
• Ephemera • Mari Sandoz • Christmas Keepsake Books
Owner: James F. Carr
Year Established: 1959
No. of Volumes: 50,000
Sidelines and Services: Autographs, original art

Jo Ann and Richard Casten Ltd.

101 W. 81st St., Suite 207 New York, NY 10024
(212) 496-5483 Fax: (516) 689-8909
Hours: By appointment only
Type of store: Antiquarian
Subject Specialties: Maps/Atlases/Cartography
Owners: Jo Ann Casten, Richard Casten
Comments: This store specializes in historical maps of the 15th
through 18th centuries and maps of the Holy Land.

Castle Clinton Monument Bookstore

Battery Park New York, NY 10004 • (212) 344-7220
Hours: Mon.-Sun. 8:30 A.M. to 4:30 P.M.
Form of payment: Visa, MC, AMEX, Discover, Checks

Type of store: New
Subject Specialties: History - America - Colonial/Revolution
• New York City • Statue of Liberty • Ellis Island • National Parks
Manager: Daniel T. Brown
No. of Volumes: 180
Comments: The mailing address for this store is: Eastern
National at Castle Clinton, P.O. Box 1593, New York, NY 10274.

Cathedral Shop of Saint John the Divine

**1047 Amsterdam Ave. (at 112th St., inside north transept
of the Cathedral) New York, NY 10025 • (212) 222-7200**
Hours: Mon.-Sun. 9 A.M. to 5 P.M.
Form of payment: Visa, MC, AMEX, Discover, Checks
Type of store: New
Subject Specialties: Theology • Bibles • Religion - Christianity
• Spirituality • Ethnic Studies
No. of Volumes: 800 titles
Sidelines and Services: Gifts, greeting cards, mail order, stone
reproductions, jewelry, religious art

Center for Book Arts

626 Broadway, 5th fl. (bet. Houston & Bleecker Sts.)
New York, NY 10012 • (212) 460-9768 Fax: (212) 673-4635
E-mail address: bookarts@pipeline.com
Hours: Mon.-Fri. 10 A.M. to 6 P.M.; Sat. 10 A.M. to 4 P.M.
Form of payment: Visa, MC, AMEX, Checks

Type of store: New
Subject Specialties: Book Arts • Fine Bindings • Fine Printing
Executive Director: Brian Hannon
Year Established: 1974
Sidelines and Services: Reference library, slide registry, bookmaking classes, exhibitions, workspace rental, membership program, lectures, newsletter
Catalogs: Free semiannual catalog
Comments: This is a non-profit organization dedicated to the art of the book.

Central Yiddish Culture Organization

25 E. 21st St., 3rd fl. (bet. Broadway & Park Ave.)
New York, NY 10010 • (212) 505-8305 Fax: (212) 505-8044
Hours: Tue. & Thu. 10 A.M. to 3 P.M.
Form of payment: Checks
Type of store: New, used, periodicals
Subject Specialties: Judaica • Yiddish Literature
Manager: David Kirshenweig
Year Established: 1942
No. of Volumes: 9,000

Chartwell Booksellers

55 E. 52nd St. (bet. Park & Madison Aves.,
inside Park Avenue Plaza bldg.) New York, NY 10055
(212) 308-0643 Fax: (212) 838-7423
Hours: Mon-Fri: 9:30 A.M. to 6:30 P.M.

Form of payment: Visa, MC, AMEX, Discover, Checks

Type of store: New, antiquarian

Subject Specialties: Literature - American • Literature - British • Photography • Automobiles • Business/Management • Cooking • Gardening • First Editions • Winston Churchill • Fishing

Owner: Barry Singer

Year Established: 1983

No. of Volumes: 50,000

Sidelines and Services: Search service

Catalogs: Christmas catalog

Chelsea Books and Records

111 W. 17th St. (bet. Sixth & Seventh Aves.) New York, NY 10011 (212) 645-4340

Hours: Mon.-Fri. 10 A.M. to 7 P.M.; Sat.-Sun. 11 A.M. to 6 P.M.

Form of payment: Checks

Type of store: Used

Subject Specialties: Literature - General • History - General • Music • Mathematics • Art - General • Theater/Drama • Philosophy • Social Science/Cultural History • Psychology/Psychiatry • Architecture • Photography • Travel • Children's/Juvenile • Occult/Mysticism

Owner: Isaac Kosman

Year Established: 1993

No. of Volumes: 25,000

Chess Forum

219 Thompson St. (bet. Bleecker & 3rd Sts.) New York, NY 10012 • (212) 475-2369 Fax: (212) 475-2369
Hours: Mon.-Sun. Noon to Midnight
Type of store: New
Subject Specialties: Chess • Games/Gambling

Chess Shop

230 Thompson St. (bet. Bleecker & 3rd Sts.)
New York, NY 10012 • (212) 475-9580/8130 Fax: (212) 982-7471
Hours: Mon.-Sun. Noon to Midnight
Form of payment: Visa, MC, AMEX, Discover, Checks
Type of store: New, periodicals, mail order
Subject Specialties: Chess • Board Games
Owner: George S. Frohlinde
Year Established: 1972

Children of Paradise

154 Bleecker St. (bet. Thompson St. & LaGuardia Pl.)
New York, NY 10012 • (212) 473-7148
Hours: Mon.-Sat. 11 A.M. to 7 P.M.; Sun. Noon to 7 P.M.
Form of payment: Visa, MC, AMEX
Type of store: New
Subject Specialties: Children's/Juvenile
Owner: Laurie Maoz
Year Established: 1980   **No. of Volumes:** 400
Sidelines and Services: Toys, collectible dolls

Children's Museum of Manhattan

212 W. 83rd St. (bet. Broadway & Amsterdam Ave.)
New York, NY 10024 • (212) 721-1234 Fax: (212) 721-1127
Hours: Mon., Wed.-Thu.: 1:30 P.M. to 5:30 P.M.;
Fri.-Sun. 10 A.M. to 5 P.M.
Form of payment: Visa, MC, AMEX
Type of store: New
Subject Specialties: Science • Children's/Juvenile • Photography
Manager: Linda Obser
Year Established: 1980
Sidelines and Services: Toys, educational toys, games

Chip's Bookshop

P.O. Box 123, Planetarium Station New York, NY 10024
(212) 362-9336
Hours: By appointment only
Form of payment: All major credit cards, Checks
Type of store: Used, antiquarian, mail order
Subject Specialties: Literary Criticism • Literature - General
• Literature - Modern • First Editions • Performing Arts • Belles
Lettres • Joseph Conrad
Owner: Chip Greenberg
Year Established: 1957
No. of Volumes: 7,000
Sidelines and Services: Appraise library collections,
search service
Catalogs: Free semiannual catalog

Choices — The Recovery Bookshop

220 E. 78th St. (bet. Second & Third Aves.) New York, NY 10021
(212) 794-3858

Hours: Tue.-Fri. 11 A.M. to 7 P.M.; Sat. 11 A.M. to 6 P.M.;
Sun. Noon to 4 P.M. Closed Mon. from July 1 through Labor Day.

Form of payment: Visa, MC, AMEX, Checks

Type of store: New

Subject Specialties: Substance Abuse • Women's Studies
• Self-Help • Spirituality • Eating Disorders • Family Dynamics
• Counseling • Grief & Loss • Abuse • Gambling Addiction

Owner: Miriam Pollack

Year Established: 1989

No. of Volumes: 6,000

Sidelines and Services: Gifts, greeting cards

Christian Publications Book and Supply Center

315 W. 43rd St. (bet. Eighth & Ninth Aves.) New York, NY 10036
(212) 582-4311 Fax: (212) 262-1825

Hours: Mon.-Wed. 9:30 A.M. to 6:45 P.M.; Thu.-Fri. 9:30 A.M.
to 7:45 P.M.; Sat. 9:30 A.M. to 5:45 P.M.

Form of payment: Visa, AMEX, Discover, Checks

Type of store: New

Subject Specialties: Religion - Christianity • Bibles

Manager: Gary Gin

Year Established: 1885

No. of Volumes: 30,000

Sidelines and Services: Videos, records, tapes, sheet music,

Sunday school supplies, gifts, greeting cards, religious goods, games, Christmas cards, audio-visual materials

Christian Science Reading Room (1st Church)

1 W. 96th St. (at Central Park West) New York, NY 10025
(212) 749-3088
Hours: Mon.-Tue., Thu.-Sat. Noon to 7 P.M.; Wed. Noon to 7:15 P.M. (and 1/2 hour after services)
Form of payment: Checks
Type of store: New
Subject Specialties: Religion - Christianity • Bibles

Christian Science Reading Room (2nd Church)

10 W. 68th St. (at Central Park West) New York, NY 10023
(212) 877-6169
Hours: Mon.-Fri. 3 P.M. to 8 P.M.; Wed. 3 P.M. to 7:15 P.M.; Sat. & Sun. Noon to 5 P.M. Holidays: 2 P.M. to 5 P.M.
Form of payment: Checks
Type of store: New
Subject Specialties: Religion - Christianity • Bibles

Christian Science Reading Room (3rd Church)

147 E. 62nd St. (bet. Third & Lexington Aves.)
New York, NY 10021 • (212) 838-2855
Hours: Mon.-Fri. Noon to 7:30 P.M. Wed. Noon to 7 P.M.; Sat. 10 A.M. to 4 P.M.; Sun. 1 P.M. to 4 P.M.

Form of payment: Checks
Type of store: New, used, periodicals
Subject Specialties: Religion - Christianity • Bibles • Christian Science • Mary Baker Eddy
Managers: Betty Bayfield, James Logan
No. of Volumes: 600
Sidelines and Services: Special orders
Comments: Also sells works by Mary Baker Eddy in many foreign languages.

Christian Science Reading Room (5th Church)

342 Madison Ave., Rm. 1526 (bet. 43rd & 44th Sts.)
New York, NY 10173 • (212) 682-0165
Hours: Mon.-Fri. 8 A.M. to 6 P.M.
Form of payment: Checks
Type of store: New, periodicals
Subject Specialties: Religion - Christianity • Bibles • Christian Science
Sidelines and Services: Lending library, study/reference room

Christian Science Reading Room (7th Church)

516 W. 112th St. (bet. Amsterdam Ave. & Broadway)
New York, NY 10025 • (212) 662-5129
Hours: Mon.-Fri. 1 P.M. to 4 P.M.; Sat. Noon to 3 P.M.
Closed Wed. & Sun.
Form of payment: Checks
Type of store: New
Subject Specialties: Religion - Christianity • Bibles • Christian Science

Christian Science Reading Room (8th Church)

925 Madison Ave. (bet. 73rd & 74th Sts.) New York, NY 10021
(212) 737-8040
Hours: Mon., Tue., Thu.-Sat.: 10 A.M. to 8 P.M. Wed. 10 A.M.
to 7:15 P.M. Sun. & Holidays: 1:30 P.M. to 4:30 P.M.
Form of payment: Checks
Type of store: New
Subject Specialties: Religion - Christianity • Bibles • Christian Science

Christian Science Reading Room (9th Church)

223 E. 25th St. (bet. Second & Third Aves.) New York, NY 10010
(212) 679-8193
Hours: Tue., Wed., Fri.: Noon to 3 P.M.; Sat. 10 A.M. to 1 P.M.
Form of payment: Checks
Type of store: New
Subject Specialties: Religion - Christianity • Bibles • Christian Science

Christian Science Reading Room (10th Church)

171 Macdougal St. (bet. W. 8th St. & Washington Square North)
New York, NY 10011 • (212) 777-0323 or (212) 777-1717
Hours: Mon., Tue., Thu.-Fri. 8 A.M. to 9 P.M.; Wed. 8 A.M.
to 7:30 P.M.; Sat. Noon to 6 P.M.; Sun. 1 P.M. to 7 P.M.
Holidays: 2 P.M. to 5 P.M.
Form of payment: Checks
Type of store: New, used
Subject Specialties: Religion - Christianity • Bibles • Christian Science
Sidelines and Services: Periodicals, audiotapes, book lending

Christian Science Reading Room (12th Church)

2315 Adam Clayton Powell Jr. Blvd. (at 136th St.)
New York, NY 10030 • (212) 281-6595
Hours: Mon. & Sat. Noon to 3 P.M.; Wed. 3 P.M. to 6:45 P.M.
Form of payment: Checks
Type of store: New
Subject Specialties: Religion - Christianity • Bibles • Christian Science

Christian Science Reading Room (14th Church)

555 W. 141st St. (bet. Broadway & Hamilton Pl.)
New York, NY 10031 • (212) 283-5158
Hours: Wed. 3 P.M. to 6:45 P.M.; Sun. Noon to 1 P.M.
Form of payment: Checks
Type of store: New
Subject Specialties: Religion - Christianity • Bibles • Christian Science

Christian Science Reading Room

(Tri-State Reading Room)
5 World Trade Center (Plaza Level, Rm. 2341)
New York, NY 10048 • (212) 432-9272
Hours: Mon.-Fri. 7:30 A.M. to 5:30 P.M.
Form of payment: Checks
Type of store: New
Subject Specialties: Religion - Christianity • Bibles • Christian Science

Christie's Book and Manuscript Department

502 Park Ave. (at 59th St.) New York, NY 10022

(212) 546-1195 Fax: (212) 980-2043

Hours: Mon.-Fri.: 9:30 A.M. to 5:30 P.M.

Form of payment: Checks

Type of store: Auction house

Subject Specialties: Auction House

Senior Director: Stephen C. Massey

Vice-President: Chris Coover

Year Established: 1766

Catalogs: 4-6/year ($150/year)

Church of St. Paul the Apostle Book and Gift Shop

415 W. 59th St. (at Columbus Ave., inside the Church of St. Paul the Apostle) New York, NY 10019

(212) 315-0918 Fax: (212) 262-9239

Hours: Mon.-Fri. 10 A.M. to 6 P.M.; Sat. 4 P.M. to 6:15 P.M.; Sun. 8:30 A.M. to 1:30 P.M.; 4:30 P.M. to 6:30 P.M.

Form of payment: Visa, MC, AMEX, Checks

Type of store: New, periodicals, mail order

Subject Specialties: Religion - Christianity • Self-Help • Psychology/Psychiatry • Fiction - Religious

Manager: Robert Fucci

Year Established: 1978   **No. of Volumes:** 4,500

Sidelines and Services: Gifts, religious goods, greeting cards, music tapes

City Books Stores

1 Centre St., Rm. 2223 (at Chambers St., inside NYC Municipal Building, 22nd floor) New York, NY 10007 • (212) 669-8245
Hours: Mon.-Fri. 9 A.M. to 5 P.M. (except legal holidays)
Form of payment: Checks
Type of store: New
Subject Specialties: Government publications

City College of New York Bookstore

W. 138th St. and Convent Ave. New York, NY 10031
(212) 368-4000 Fax: (212) 491-5771
E-mail address: moacc.cunyvm.cuny.edu
Hours: Mon.-Thu. 9 A.M. to 7:30 P.M.; Fri. 9 A.M. to 3 P.M.
Form of payment: Visa, MC, AMEX, Checks
Type of store: New, used
Subject Specialties: General
Manager: Cosmo Oleviri
No. of Volumes: 20,000
Sidelines and Services: Art and college supplies, gifts, greeting cards, maps
Comments: Operated by Barnes & Noble.

Civil Service Book Shop

89 Worth St. (bet. Broadway & Church Sts.) New York, NY 10013
(212) 226-9506
Hours: Mon.-Fri.: 8:30 A.M. to 5 P.M.
Type of store: New, mail order

Subject Specialties: Reference • Self-Help • Travel • Crafts
• Maps/Atlases/Cartography • Dictionaries/Encyclopedias
• Children's/Juvenile • Civil Service Study
Owner: Roslyn Bergenfeld
Manager: Amy Bergenfeld
Year Established: 1943
No. of Volumes: 500,000 (800 titles)
Sidelines and Services: Maps, globes, mail order

The Civilized Traveler

**2 World Financial Center, 225 Liberty St. (inside Winter Garden
shopping complex) New York, NY 10281**
(212) 786-3301 Fax: (212) 786-3302
Hours: Mon.-Fri. 10 A.M. to 7:30 P.M.; Sat. 10 A.M. to 6:30 P.M.;
Sun. 10 A.M. to 5:30 P.M.
Form of payment: Visa, MC, AMEX, Checks
Type of store: New
Subject Specialties: Travel • Maps/Atlases/Cartography
Year Established: 1992
Sidelines and Services: Videos, tapes, travel accessories
and clothes, globes

Coliseum Books

1771 Broadway (at 57th St.) New York, NY 10019
(212) 757-8381 or (800) 833-1543 Fax: (212) 586-5607
E-mail address: nycolbooks@aol.com
Hours: Mon. 8 A.M. to 10 P.M.; Tue.-Thu. 8 A.M. to 11 P.M.; Fri. 8 A.M.

to 11:30 P.M.; Sat. 10 A.M. to 11:30 P.M.; Sun. Noon to 8 P.M.
Form of payment: Visa, MC, AMEX, Discover, Checks
Type of store: New
Subject Specialties: General • Literature - General
President: Irwin Hersch
Vice-President: George S. Leibson
Year Established: 1974
No. of Volumes: 70,000 titles
Sidelines and Services: Literary periodicals, mail order, greeting
cards, maps, posters

College of Insurance Bookstore

101 Murray St. (at West St.) New York, NY 10007
(212) 962-4111 Fax: (212) 964-3381
Hours: Mon.-Thu. Noon to 5:30 P.M.
Form of payment: Visa, MC, AMEX, Discover, Checks
Type of store: New
Subject Specialties: Business/Management • History - General
• Computers • Insurance • Actuarial Science
Manager: Karen Thomas
Sidelines and Services: School supplies, clothing

Colony Inc.

1619 Broadway (at 49th St.) New York, NY 10019
(212) 265-2050 Fax: (212) 956-6009
Hours: Mon.-Sat. 9:30 A.M. to 1 A.M.; Sun. 10 A.M. to Midnight
Form of payment: Visa, MC, AMEX

Type of store: New
Subject Specialties: Music

Columbia-Presbyterian Medical Center Bookstore

3954 Broadway (at 166th St.) New York, NY 10032
(212) 923-2149 Fax: (212) 923-7539
Hours: Mon.-Thu. 9 A.M. to 6 P.M.; Fri. 9 A.M. to 5 P.M.
Form of payment: Visa, MC, AMEX, Discover, Checks
Type of store: New
Subject Specialties: Medicine
Manager: Sandra Martinez
Comments: Formerly known as the Columbia University Medical Center Bookstore

Columbia University Bookstore

1187 Amsterdam Ave. (bet. 118th & 119th Sts.)
New York, NY 10027 • (212) 854-4131 Fax: (212) 866-8713
Hours: Mon.-Thu. 9 A.M. to 6 P.M.; Fri. 9 A.M. to 5 P.M.;
Sat. Noon to 4 P.M. Closed Sun.
Form of payment: Visa, MC, AMEX, Checks
Type of store: New
Subject Specialties: Law • Business/Management • Engineering
• International Affairs
Manager: Kevin Renshaw
No. of Volumes: 5,000
Comments: This is one of two temporary locations during con-

struction of new main store, which is scheduled to open in 1999 at Broadway & 114th Street. This location sells books for the Schools of Law, Business, Graduate Engineering and SIPA (School of International Public Affairs). See also next entry, below.

Columbia University Bookstore At Lion's Court

1187 Amsterdam Ave. New York, NY 10027 (mailing address only)
(212) 854-4131 Fax: (212) 866-8713
Hours: Mon.-Thu. 9 A.M. to 7 P.M.; Fri. 9 A.M. to 5 P.M.;
Sat. 11 A.M. to 5 P.M.; Sun. Noon to 5 P.M.
Form of payment: Visa, MC, AMEX, Checks
Subject Specialties: General
Manager: Kevin Renshaw
No. of Volumes: 5,000
Comments: This store is located in a temporary structure next to John Jay Hall during construction of the new main store, scheduled to open in 1999 at Broadway & 114th Street.

Gary Combs Autographs

3 Sheridan Square, Rm. 7-H (W. 4th St. & Seventh Ave.)
New York, NY 10014 • (212) 242-7209 Fax: (212) 924-9006
Hours: By appointment only
Form of payment: Visa, MC, AMEX, Checks
Type of store: Antiquarian, mail order
Subject Specialties: Autographs/Manuscripts • Music • Opera
• Signed Editions

Owner: Gary Combs
Year Established: 1985
Comments: You can also purchase signed music scores here.

Come Again

353 E. 53rd St. (bet. First & Second Aves.) New York, NY 10022
(212) 308-9394
Hours: Mon.-Fri. 11 A.M. to 7:30 P.M.; Sat. 11 A.M. to 6 P.M.
Form of payment: Visa, MC, AMEX
Type of store: New, mail order, periodicals
Subject Specialties: Erotica/Curiosa • Gay/Lesbian Studies
• Sexology • Massage
Year Established: 1980
No. of Volumes: 2,000
Sidelines and Services: Mail order, videos
Catalogs: Catalog available

Comic Art Gallery

940 Third Ave. (bet. 56th & 57th Sts.) New York, NY 10022
(212) 759-6255
Hours: Mon. & Tue. Noon to 6 P.M.; Wed. 11 A.M. to 7 P.M.;
Thu. & Fri. 11:30 A.M. to 7:30 P.M.
Form of payment: Visa, MC, Discover, JVC, Checks
Type of store: New, used, periodicals, mail order
Subject Specialties: Comic Books • Graphic Arts • Humor
• Prints/Drawings • Magazines/Journals/Newspapers • Signed
Editions • Toys

Owner: Joseph Lihach
Year Established: 1978
Sidelines and Services: Comic Art, collectibles, T-shirts, Japanimation

The Compleat Strategist

**11 E. 33rd St. (bet. Fifth & Madison Aves.) New York, NY 10016
(212) 685-3880 Fax: (212) 685-2123**
Hours: Mon.-Wed., Fri., Sat. 10:30 A.M. to 6 P.M.;
Thu. 10:30 A.M. to 9 P.M.
Form of payment: Visa, MC, AMEX, Discover, Checks
Type of store: New
Subject Specialties: Military/War • Wargames • Fiction - Science Fiction • Fiction - Fantasy/Horror • Chess
Owners: Danny Kilbert, Mike Kilbert
Year Established: 1976
No. of Volumes: 3,000
Sidelines and Services: Games, maps, posters, computer software, wholesale
Catalogs: Annual catalog

The Compleat Strategist

**342 W. 57th St. (bet. Eighth & Ninth Aves.) New York, NY 10019
(212) 582-1272**
Hours: Mon.-Sat. 11 A.M. to 8 P.M.; Sun. Noon to 5 P.M.
Form of payment: Visa, MC, AMEX, Discover, Checks
Type of store: New

Subject Specialties: Military/War • Wargames • Fiction - Science
Fiction • Fiction - Fantasy/Horror • Chess
Manager: Vincent Amella
Sidelines and Services: Games, maps, posters, computer
software, wholesale
Comments: This is a branch of the 33rd Street main store.

The Compleat Strategist

**630 Fifth Ave. (bet. 50th & 51st Sts., inside International Bldg.
at Rockefeller Center) New York, NY 10111 • (212) 265-7449**
Hours: Mon.-Fri.: 10:30 A.M. to 5:30 P.M.
Form of payment: Visa, MC, AMEX, Discover
Type of store: New
Subject Specialties: Military/War • Wargames • Fiction - Science
Fiction • Fiction - Fantasy/Horror • Chess
Manager: Enid Kilbert
Sidelines and Services: Games, maps, posters, computer
software, wholesale

Complete Traveller Bookstore

**199 Madison Ave. (at 35th St.) New York, NY 10016
(212) 685-9007 Fax: (212) 481-3253**
Hours: Mon.-Fri.: 9 A.M. to 7 P.M. (9 A.M. to 6:30 P.M., October
through March); Sat. 10 A.M. to 6 P.M. Sun. 11 A.M. to 5 P.M.
Form of payment: AMEX, Visa, MC, Diners, Discover, Checks
(w/photo ID)
Type of store: New, antiquarian, mail order

Subject Specialties: Travel • Maps/Atlases/Cartography • Travelogs

Owners: Arnold Greenberg, Harriet Greenberg

Year Established: 1978

No. of Volumes: 10,000

Sidelines and Services: Maps, manuscripts, audiotapes (foreign language instruction), travel accessories, money belts, converters, and magnifying glasses

Catalogs: One catalog every two years (newsletters in off years). $2 for first catalog only.

Comments: Also sells antiquarian travel books.

The Compulsive Collector

1082 Madison Ave. (bet. 81st & 82nd Sts.) New York, NY 10028

(212) 879-7443

Hours: Tue.-Sat. 1 P.M. to 6 P.M.

Form of payment: Visa, MC, AMEX, Checks

Type of store: Used

Subject Specialties: Fine Bindings • Limited Editions

Owner: Ami Megiddo

Year Established: 1981

No. of Volumes: 5,000

Comments: Mailing address: P.O. Box 544, Forest Hills, NY 11375

Computer Book Works

25 Warren St. (bet. Broadway & Church St., 1 block south of Chambers St.) New York, NY 10007 • (212) 385-1616

Fax: (212) 385-8193 • E-mail address: bookman@cnct.com

Hours: Mon.-Fri. 10 A.M. to 6:30 P.M.; Sat. 10 A.M. to 6 P.M.; Sun. 11 A.M. to 5 P.M.

Form of payment: Visa, MC, AMEX, Checks

Type of store: New, used, mail order

Subject Specialties: Computers • Business/Management • Engineering • Mathematics • Chemistry • Physics

Manager: Jack Rosenblatt

Year Established: 1992

Sidelines and Services: Mail and phone orders

Catalogs: 4/year

Continental Book Search

P.O. Box 1163 New York, NY 10009 • (212) 254-8719

Fax: (212) 533-2046 • E-mail address: alkatz@spacelab.net

Hours: Mon-Fri: 9 A.M. to 6 P.M. (mail and phone order only)

Form of payment: Checks only

Type of store: Used, antiquarian, mail order

Subject Specialties: Philosophy • Anthropology • Literature - General • Travel • Business/Management • Social Science/Cultural History • Education • Psychology/Psychiatry

Owner: Alvin M. Katz

Year Established: 1977

No. of Volumes: 10,000 titles

Sidelines and Services: Search service

Catalogs: As available

Cooper-Hewitt Museum Shop— Book Department

2 E. 91st St. (corner of Fifth Ave.) New York, NY 10128

(212) 860-6939 Fax: (212) 860-6909

Hours: Tue. 10 A.M. to 9 P.M.; Wed.-Sat. 10 A.M. to 5 P.M.;
Sun. Noon to 4:45 P.M.

Form of payment: Visa, MC, AMEX

Type of store: New, used, mail order

Subject Specialties: Textiles • History - General • Design
• Architecture • Decorative Arts • Jewelry • Children's/Juvenile
• Furniture

Manager: Matt Hahn

Year Established: 1979

No. of Volumes: 2,300 titles

Sidelines and Services: Gifts, greeting cards,
posters, reproductions, stationery, toys, Christmas cards

Catalogs: Free annual catalog

Cornell University Medical College Bookstore

424 E. 70th St. (bet. First & York Aves.) New York, NY 10021

(212) 988-0400 Fax: (212) 717-4169

Hours: Mon.-Thu. 9 A.M. to 6 P.M.; Fri. 9 A.M. to 5 P.M.;
Sat. 11 A.M. to 4 P.M.

Form of payment: Visa, MC, AMEX, Checks

Type of store: New

Subject Specialties: Medicine

Manager: Michelle Rothmen-Mendel

Sidelines and Services: Gifts, stationery
Comments: Operated by Barnes & Noble. Visit their World Wide Web site at: http://www.lb.com

Corner Bookstore

1313 Madison Ave. (at 93rd St.) New York, NY 10128
(212) 831-3554 Fax: (212) 831-2930
Hours: Mon.-Fri. 10 A.M. to 8 P.M.; Sat. 11 A.M. to 6 P.M.;
Sun. Noon to 6 P.M.
Form of payment: Visa, MC, Checks
Type of store: New
Subject Specialties: Architecture • Art - General • Cooking • Poetry • Children's/Juvenile • Literature - General • History - General • Belles Lettres • Parenting
Owners: Raymond Sherman, Helene Golay
No. of Volumes: 40,000
Sidelines and Services: Special order, search service

Corporate Book Express

173 W. 81st St., Lower Level (bet. Columbus & Amsterdam Aves.) New York, NY 10024 • (212) 501-8181
Fax: (212) 501-8926 • E-mail address: aes26@cornel.edu
Hours: Mon.-Fri. 9 A.M. to 6 P.M.
Form of payment: AMEX, Visa, MC, Discover, Business checks
Type of store: New, mail order
Subject Specialties: Dictionaries/Encyclopedias • Business/Management • Computers • Medicine • Nursing • Science

• Reference • Academic • Banking • Engineering • Accounting
Owner: Elliot Saltman
Manager: Gary Larson
Year Established: 1989
Catalogs: Catalogs on oil/petroleum, business, and finance books
Comments: Does special orders of book for any book or monograph in print, especially for schools, as well as for technical and corporate training programs.

Crawford Doyle Booksellers

1082 Madison Ave. (bet. 81st & 82nd Sts.) New York, NY 10028
(212) 288-6300 Fax: (212) 517-8002
Hours: Mon.-Sat. 10 A.M. to 6 P.M. Sun. Noon to 5 P.M.
Form of payment: Visa, MC, AMEX
Type of store: New
Subject Specialties: History - General • Art - General • Photography
Owners: Judy Crawford, John Doyle
Sidelines and Services: Literary magazines, search service

Creative Living Bookstore

(First Church of Religious Science)
14 E. 48th St. (bet. Madison & Fifth Aves.) New York, NY 10017
(212) 688-0600 Fax: (212) 688-0603
Hours: Mon.-Thu. 10 A.M. to 6 P.M.; Fri. 10 A.M. to 5 P.M.
Closes at 1:30 P.M. on Fri. during July and August.
Form of payment: Visa, MC
Type of store: New

Subject Specialties: Metaphysics • Self-Help • Psychology/Psychiatry
Manager: C. C. Banks
Sidelines and Services: Videotapes, audiotapes

Creative Visions Bookstore

548 Hudson St. (bet. Charles & Perry Sts.) New York, NY 10014
(212) 645-7573
Hours: Mon.-Thu. 1 P.M. to 8 P.M.; Fri. 1 P.M. to 9 P.M.;
Sat. & Sun. Noon to 9 P.M.
Form of payment: Visa, MC, AMEX, Checks
Type of store: New
Subject Specialties: Gay/Lesbian Studies
Manager: Mark Wisniewski
Year Established: 1994

Cultured Oyster Books

P.O. Box 404, Planetarium Station New York, NY 10024
(212) 362-0269 • E-mail address: Ci+OysBks@aol.com.
Hours: By appointment only
Form of payment: Checks
Type of store: Antiquarian
Subject Specialties: Literature - Modern • Poetry • Theater/Drama
• Literary Criticism
Owners: George Koppelman, Becky Koppelman

James Cummins Bookseller

699 Madison Ave., 7th fl. (bet. 62nd & 63rd Sts.)
New York, NY 10021 • (212) 688-6441 Fax: (212) 688-6192
E-mail address: hercher@pilot.njin.net
Hours: Mon.-Sat. 10 A.M. to 6 P.M.
Form of payment: AMEX, Visa, MC, Checks
Type of store: Antiquarian
Subject Specialties: Literature - British • Literature - American
• Illustrated Books • Private Press • Travel • Sports • Fishing
• Fine Bindings • First Editions • Graphic Arts • History - Britain
• History - America
Owner: James B. Cummins Jr.
Year Established: 1978
No. of Volumes: 50,000
Sidelines and Services: Appraise library collections, books purchased
Catalogs: 4/year
Comments: Also sells book sets.

G. Curwen Books

1 W. 67th St., Suite 710 New York, NY 10023 • (212) 595-5904
E-mail address: basho@gramercy.ios.com
Hours: Mail order only
Form of payment: Checks
Type of store: New
Subject Specialties: First Editions • Fiction - Crime/Mystery/
Suspense • Performing Arts • Popular Culture • Cooking • Magic
Owners: Jack Nessel, Ginger Curwen
Year Established: 1977

No. of Volumes: 4,000+
Catalogs: Occasional free catalogs

D.A.P. Bookstore at Exit Art

548 Broadway (bet. Prince & Spring Sts.) New York, NY 10012
(212) 966-7745 Fax: (212) 925-2928
Hours: Tue.-Sat. 11 A.M. to 6 P.M.
Form of payment: Visa, MC, AMEX, Checks
Subject Specialties: Art - General
Comments: D.A.P. is an abbreviation for "Distributed Art Publications."

DG Antiquarian Books

1150 Fifth Ave. (at 96th St.) New York, NY 10128 • (212) 996-4629
E-mail address: antiquarianbooks@msn.com
Hours: By appointment only
Form of payment: Checks
Type of store: Antiquarian
Subject Specialties: Architecture • Fine Arts • Decorative Arts
• Fine Printing • Horace Walpole
Owner: Dey Gosse
Year Established: 1988
No. of Volumes: 500
Catalogs: Lists issued

Comments: Carries general antiquarian books, 17th-19th centuries; including books about Horace Walpole and his contemporaries.

Da Dochi Bookstore

3441 Broadway (bet. 140th & 141st Sts.) New York, NY 10031
(212) 862-5500
Hours: Mon.-Sun. 8 P.M. to 6 P.M.
Type of store: New
Subject Specialties: Spanish Language and Literature
Owner: V. Chinea

Dahesh Heritage Fine Books

304 W. 58th St. (Eighth Ave. at Columbus Circle)
New York, NY 10019 • (212) 265-0600 Fax: (212) 265-0601
Hours: Mon.-Fri. 9 A.M. to 6 P.M.; Sat. 10 A.M. to 5 P.M.
Form of payment: Checks
Type of store: New
Subject Specialties: Dictionaries/Encyclopedias • Arabic
• Publishing • Art - European, 1600-1900 • Philosophy • Poetry
• Religion • Fiction - Science Fiction
Manager: Mike Masri
Sidelines and Services: Foreign newspapers and magazines
Catalogs: Free catalog
Comments: Also carries literary works of Dr. Dahesh in Arabic,
English, German, French, and Spanish.

Howard C. Daitz Photographica

355 W. 19th St. (bet. Eighth & Ninth Aves.)
New York, NY 10011 • (212) 929-8987
Hours: By appointment only

Form of payment: Cash only
Type of store: Used, antiquarian, periodicals
Subject Specialties: Photography
Owner: Howard C. Daitz
Year Established: 1972
No. of Volumes: 3,000
Sidelines and Services: Autographs, back issues of periodicals, original art, sheet music, wholesale (all as related to photography), appraise library collections
Comments: Specializes in 19th-century books on photography. Mailing address is: P.O. Box 530, Old Chelsea Station, New York, NY 10011

B. Dalton Bookseller (Store No. 1167)

396 Avenue of the Americas (at W. 8th St.) New York, NY 10011
(212) 674-8780 or (212) 674-8725 Fax: (212) 475-9082
Hours: Mon.-Sat. 9:30 A.M. to 11 P.M.; Sun. Noon to 8 P.M.
Form of payment: All major credit cards, Checks
Type of store: New, periodicals, mail order
Subject Specialties: General
Manager: Edward Shreve
Comments: B. Dalton is a division of Barnes & Noble Inc.

B. Dalton Bookseller (Store No. 300)

666 Fifth Ave. (at 52nd St.) New York, NY 10103
(212) 247-1740 Fax: (212) 262-9833
Hours: Mon.-Fri. 8:30 A.M. to 7 P.M.; Sat. 9:30 A.M. to 6:30 P.M.; Sun. Noon to 5 P.M.

Form of payment: All major credit cards, Checks

Subject Specialties: General

Manager: Dorothy McNally

Comments: B. Dalton is a division of Barnes & Noble Inc.

Daughters of St. Paul Bookstore

SEE: Pauline Books & Media

Nicholas Davies & Co.

23 Commerce St. (bet. Seventh Ave. and Bedford St.)

New York, NY 10014 • (212) 243-6840 Fax: (212) 243-6842

E-mail address: dimber@aol.com

Hours: Tue.-Sat. 11 A.M. to 6 P.M. Closed Sun. & Mon.

Form of payment: Visa, MC, AMEX, JCB

Type of store: Used, antiquarian

Subject Specialties: Biography/Autobiography • Etiquette
• Fashion/Costume/Clothing • Prints/Drawings • Sexology
• Social Science/Cultural History

Owner: Nicholas Davies

No. of Volumes: 1,000

Sidelines and Services: Art gallery (contemporary fine art)

Comments: This space functions primarily as an art gallery, with a selection of out-of-print books.

Dean and Deluca

560 Broadway (corner of Prince St.) New York, NY 10012

(212) 431-1691 or (800) 221-7714 Fax: (212) 334-6183

Hours: Mon.-Sat. 8 A.M. to 8 P.M.; Sun. 8 A.M. to 7 P.M.

Form of payment: Visa, MC, AMEX, Checks

Type of store: New, periodicals, mail order

Subject Specialties: Cooking • Wine • Children's/Juvenile • Recipes

Year Established: 1978

No. of Volumes: 2,000 (500 titles)

Sidelines and Services: Periodicals

Comments: Also carries essays and histories regarding food.
You can stop by their Web site at: http://www.dean-delucca.com

Demes Books

229 W. 105th St., #46 New York, NY 10025 • (212) 865-1273

Hours: By appointment only

Type of store: Antiquarian, used

Subject Specialties: Natural History • Travel • First Editions
• Illustrated Books • Children's/Juvenile • Zoology • Exploration/
Voyages • Art - African

Owner: James M. Demes

Year Established: 1993

No. of Volumes: 15,000

Sidelines and Services: Search service

Dianetics Center

227 W. 46th St. (bet. Broadway & Eighth Ave.)
New York, NY 10036 • (212) 921-1210

Hours: Mon.-Sun. 9 A.M. to 11 P.M.

Form of payment: Visa, MC, AMEX, Checks
Type of store: New
Subject Specialties: Scientology

The Dictionary Store
SEE: French and European Publications

Dieu Donne Papermill—The Mill Store
433 Broome St. (bet. Broadway & Crosby St.)
New York, NY 10013 • (212) 226-0573 Fax: (212) 226-6088
E-mail address: ddpaper@cybernex.net
Hours: Tue.-Sat. 10 A.M. to 6 P.M.
Form of payment: Visa, MC, Checks
Type of store: New
Subject Specialties: Book Arts • Books About Books/Bibliography
• Limited Editions • Papermaking • Paper Conservation
Director: Mina Takahashi
Year Established: 1994
No. of Volumes: 30 titles
Sidelines and Services: Handmade papers, papermaking
supplies, periodicals
Catalogs: Free annual catalog
Comments: This is a non-profit organization dedicated to all
aspects of papermaking.

A Different Light Bookstore

151 W. 19th St. (bet. Sixth & Seventh Aves.) New York, NY 10011
(212) 989-4850 or (800) 343-4002 Fax: (212) 989-2158
E-mail address: adl@adlbooks.com
Hours: Mon.-Sun.: 10 A.M. to Midnight
Form of payment: Visa, MC, AMEX
Type of store: New, periodicals, mail order
Subject Specialties: Gay/Lesbian Studies • Erotica/Curiosa • Travel
• Poetry • Theater/Drama • Fiction - Gay/Lesbian
Owner: Norman Laurila
Manager: Dan Seitler
Year Established: 1984
No. of Volumes: 15,000 titles
Sidelines and Services: Greeting cards, literary magazines, maps,
book search service, video rentals, records, audiotapes, posters,
buttons, mail order
Catalogs: 3/year
Comments: This store has a site on the World Wide Web at:
http://www.adlbooks.com/~adl

Dinosaur Hill Books

306 E. 9th St. (bet. First & Second Aves.) New York, NY 10003
(212) 473-5850
Hours: Mon.-Sun. 11 A.M. to 7 P.M.
Form of payment: Visa, MC, AMEX, Checks
Subject Specialties: Children's/Juvenile
Owner: Pamela Pier

Dog Lovers Bookshop

9 W. 31st St. (bet. Fifth Ave. & Broadway) New York, NY 10001
(212) 594-3601 Fax: (212) 576-4343 • E-mail address:
info@dogbooks.com
Hours: Mon.-Sat. Noon to 6 P.M.
Form of payment: Visa, MC, AMEX
Type of store: New, used, antiquarian, mail order
Subject Specialties: Pets • Animals • Dogs • Wolves • Foxes
Owners: Bernard Marcowitz, Margot Rosenberg
Year Established: 1994
No. of Volumes: 8,400
Sidelines and Services: Gifts
Catalogs: Free "Dogalog," issued semiannually
Comments: Visit Dog Lovers' Web site at:
http://www.dogbooks.com

Dokya Bookstore

106 Park St. (bet. Mott and Mulberry Sts.) New York, NY 10013
(212) 349-1979 Fax: (212) 349-1979
Hours: Mon.-Sun. 10 A.M. to 8:30 P.M.
Form of payment: Visa, MC
Type of store: New
Subject Specialties: Orient • Thailand
Owner: Watana Wongsriskulchai
No. of Volumes: 150,000

Doubleday Book Shops (Store No. 1601)

724 Fifth Ave. (bet. 56th & 57th Sts.) New York, NY 10019

(212) 397-0550 or (800) 635-0045 Fax: (212) 307-7681

Hours: Mon.-Sat. 9 A.M. to 11 P.M.; Sun. Noon to 7 P.M.
Extended hours Nov. 27-Dec. 23: Mon.-Sat. 9 A.M. to 11 P.M.

Form of payment: AMEX, Visa, MC, Discover, Checks

Type of store: New, periodicals, mail order

Subject Specialties: General • Travel • Business/Management
• Photography • Children's/Juvenile

Manager: Don Rieck

Year Established: 1961

No. of Volumes: 150,000

Sidelines and Services: Books on tape, worldwide delivery,
gift wrapping, corporate accounts, mail & telephone orders,
gift certificates, audio CDs

Catalogs: No

Comments: Doubleday is a division of Barnes & Noble Inc.

Dover Publications Bookstore

180 Varick St., 9th fl. (bet. Charlton & King Sts.)
New York, NY 10014 • (212) 255-6399

Hours: Mon.-Fri. 9 A.M. to 4:30 P.M.

Form of payment: Checks

Type of store: new

Subject specialties: art and design, science, math, music,
natural history; reprints of 18th and 19th century works

Comments: Main headquarters are located at 31 E. Second St.,
Mineola, NY 11501.

Down East Enterprises

50 Spring St. (bet. Lafayette & Mulberry Sts.)
New York, NY 10012 • (212) 925-2632
Hours: Mon.-Fri. 11 A.M. to 6 P.M.
Form of payment: Visa, MC, AMEX, Checks
Type of store: New, mail order
Subject Specialties: Travel • Skiing • Hiking • Mountaineering
• Camping • Canoeing
Owner: Leon R. Greenman
Year Established: 1976
No. of Volumes: 5,000
Sidelines and Services: Maps, repairing and modifying outdoor
equipment, National Park maps of U.S. Geological Survey
Comments: Also sells guidebooks to the mountainous
areas of the U.S.

William Doyle Galleries

175 E. 87th St. (bet. Third & Lexington Aves.)
New York, NY 10128 • (212) 427-2730 Fax: 369-0892
Hours: Mon.-Fri. 8 A.M. to 5 P.M.
Form of payment: checks
Type of store: Auction house
Subject Specialties: Auction House
Book Specialist: Brendan Cahill

250 W 40th

Drama Book Shop

723 Seventh Ave., 2nd fl. (bet. 48th & 49th Sts.)

New York, NY 10019 • (212) 944-0595 or (800) 322-0595
Fax: (212) 921-2013
Hours: Mon., Tue., Thu., Fri. 9:30 A.M. to 7 P.M.; Wed. 9:30 A.M.
to 8 P.M.; Sat. 10:30 A.M. to 5:30 P.M.; Sun. Noon to 5 P.M.
Form of payment: Visa, MC, AMEX, Checks
Type of store: New
Subject Specialties: Theater/Drama • Dance • Cinema/Films
• Radio/Television • Music • Opera • Design • Reference
Owner: Arthur Seelen
Year Established: 1923
No. of Volumes: 50,000
Sidelines and Services: Periodicals, greeting cards, musical
scores, vocal selections
Catalogs: 1-2/year

Drougas Books

34 Carmine St.(bet. Bleecker & Bedford Sts.)
New York, NY 10014 • (212) 229-0079 Fax: (212) 243-6261
Hours: Mon.-Sun. Noon to 9 P.M. Closed holidays;
summer hours vary.
Form of payment: Visa, MC, AMEX, Discover
Type of store: New (remainders only)
Subject Specialties: Cinema/Films • Art - General • New Age
• Native Americans • Photography • Women's Studies • Literature -
General • Popular Culture
Owners: James Drougas, Indiana Bervis
Year Established: 1991
No. of Volumes: 5,000

Sidelines and Services: Wholesale also
Comments: All of the books here are discounted.

E & D Books

136 W. 42nd St. (bet. Sixth Ave. & Broadway)
New York, NY 10017 • (212) 391-0005
Hours: Mon.-Sun. open 24 hours
Form of payment: Visa, MC, AMEX
Type of store: New
Subject Specialties: Adult

The East Africa Safari Co.

1500 Broadway, Suite 2201 New York, NY 10036
(212) 840-7800 Fax: (212) 840-9411
Hours: Mail and phone order only
Form of payment: Visa, MC, AMEX, Checks
Type of store: New
Subject Specialties: Travel • Geography
Manager: Mackey Arnstein

East Village Books and Records

101 St. Marks Place (bet. Avenue A & First Ave.)
New York, NY 10009 • (212) 477-8647
Hours: Mon.-Thu. 3 P.M. to 11:30 P.M.; Fri. 2:30 P.M. to Midnight;
Sat. Noon to Midnight; Sun. 1 P.M. to 9 P.M. During winter, opens
and closes earlier.

Form of payment: Visa, MC, AMEX, Discover, Checks
Type of store: New, used
Subject Specialties: Art - General • Children's/Juvenile • Cinema/
Films • Literature - General • Music • Occult/Mysticism
• Philosophy • Poetry • Private Press
Owners: Edith Harari, Donald Davis
Year Established: 1994
No. of Volumes: 12,000
Sidelines and Services: CDs, audio cassettes
Comments: Fifty percent of profits from donated books go
to support local causes. Also specializes in books published
by the Loompanics Press, and stocks many other underground
press books.

East-West Books

78 Fifth Ave. (bet. 13th & 14th Sts.) New York, NY 10011
(212) 243-5994 or (212) 243-5995 Fax: (212) 243-7591
Hours: Mon.-Sun. 10 A.M. to 7:30 P.M.
Form of payment: Visa, MC, AMEX, Checks
Type of store: New
Subject Specialties: Self-Help • Religion - Oriental • Psychology/
Psychiatry • Spirituality • Yoga • Alternative Medicine • Cooking
• Holistics • Natural Healing • Zen Buddhism • Spiritual Teaching
• Women's Studies
Manager: Serge Ledan
Year Established: 1978
No. of Volumes: 15,000
Catalogs: Annual catalog

East-West Books

568 Columbus Ave. (bet. 87th & 88th Sts.) New York, NY 10024
(212) 787-7552 Fax: (212) 787-7613
Hours: Mon.-Sat. 10 A.M. to 7 P.M.; Sun. 11 A.M. to 7 P.M.
Form of payment: Visa, MC, AMEX, Discover, Checks
Type of store: New
Subject Specialties: Self-Help • Religion - Oriental • Psychology/
Psychiatry • Spirituality • Yoga • Alternative Medicine • Cooking
• Holistics • Natural Healing • Zen Buddhism • Spiritual Teaching
• Women's Studies
Manager: Subash Dhamiji
Year Established: 1978
Sidelines and Services: Worldwide shipping

Eastern Mountain Sports (Store No. 34)

20 W. 61st St. (bet. Broadway & Columbus Ave.)
New York, NY 10023 • (212) 397-4860
Hours: Mon.-Fri. 10 A.M. to 9 P.M.; Sat. 10 A.M. to 6 P.M.;
Sun. Noon to 6 P.M.
Form of payment: Visa, MC, AMEX, Discover, Checks
Type of store: New
Subject Specialties: Sports • Hiking • Mountaineering • Travel
Manager: David Russell
Year Established: 1983
No. of Volumes: 800 titles
Sidelines and Services: Maps, posters

Eastern Mountain Sports (Store No. 35)

611 Broadway (at Houston St.) New York, NY 10012

(212) 505-9860

Hours: Mon.-Fri. 10 A.M. to 9 P.M.; Sat. 10 A.M. to 6 P.M.;
Sun. Noon to 6 P.M.

Form of payment: Visa, MC, AMEX, Discover, Checks

Type of store: New

Subject Specialties: Sports • Hiking • Mountaineering • Travel

Manager: Eric Fullagar   **Year Established:** 1984

Eastside Books and Paper

P.O. Box 1581, Gracie Station New York, NY 10028

(212) 759-6299

Hours: By appointment only

Form of payment: Checks

Type of store: Antiquarian

Subject Specialties: Autographs/Manuscripts • Typography
• Ephemera • African-American Studies • History - America - Civil
War • Trains/Railways • Trade Catalogs

Owner: Howard Caine

El Cascajero—the old Spanish book mine

506 La Guardia Pl. (bet. Bleecker & Houston Sts.)

New York, NY 10012 • (212) 254-0905 Fax: (212) 254-0905

Hours: Mon.-Fri.: 9 A.M. to 9 P.M. (best to phone ahead
for an appointment)

Form of payment: Checks

Type of store: Used, antiquarian, mail order
Subject Specialties: Hispanic Studies • Semantics • Spanish
Language and Literature • Latin America • History - Latin America/
Caribbean • Earth Sciences • Social Science/Cultural History
• History - General • Hispanic Arts & Crafts • Portuguese Exploration
Owner: Anthony Gran
Year Established: 1956
No. of Volumes: 7,000
Sidelines and Services: Appraise library collections, maps,
free search service, special orders
Catalogs: Free catalog issued periodically

Elite Hong Kong

5 Bowery (at Canal St.) New York, NY 10002
(212) 925-4968 Fax: (212) 226-1227
Hours: Mon.-Sun. 10 A.M. to 7 P.M.
Form of payment: AMEX, Checks
Type of store: New
Subject Specialties: Religion - Christianity • China (including
Chinese Language and Literature)
Owner: Silas Tam
Year Established: 1982
Sidelines and Services: Church supplies, gifts, greeting cards,
religious goods, Sun. school supplies

Episcopal Book Resource Center

815 Second Ave. (bet. 43rd & 44th Sts.) New York, NY 10017

(212) 661-4863 or (800) 334-7626 Fax: (212) 661-1706
Hours: Mon-Fri: 10 A.M. to 5:30 P.M.
Form of payment: Visa, MC, AMEX, Checks
Type of store: New
Subject Specialties: Religion - Christianity • Bibles • Theology
• Children's/Juvenile • Women's Studies • Spirituality
• Environment/Conservation/Ecology • Self-Help • Episcopal
Church • Pastoral Care
Managers: Constancio DeJesus, Ana Hernandez
Year Established: 1952
No. of Volumes: 20,000
Sidelines and Services: Christmas cards, greeting cards, jewelry,
special order, CDs, music tapes, mail order
Comments: Out-of-state callers can call toll-free: (800) 334-7626

Ginesta Eudaldo

264 W. 40th St., 8th fl. (bet. Seventh & Eighth Aves.)
New York, NY 10018 • (212) 302-0303
Hours: Mon.-Fri. 8 A.M. to 3:30 P.M. Call first for an appointment.
Form of payment: Checks
Type of store: Used, rare
Subject Specialties: Spanish Language and Literature • History -
Latin America/Caribbean • Latin America
Owner: Ginesta Eudaldo
Comments: Specializes in Latin American
history of the 17th through 19th centuries.

Eve's Garden International

119 W. 57th St., Suite 420 (bet. Sixth & Seventh Aves.)
New York, NY 10019 • (212) 757-8651 Fax: (212) 977-4306
Hours: Mon.-Sat. Noon to 7 P.M.
Form of payment: Visa, MC, AMEX, Checks
Type of store: New, mail order
Subject Specialties: Women's Studies • Sexology • Spirituality
• Erotica/Curiosa • Gay/Lesbian Studies
President: Dell Williams
Manager: Lorraine Melendez
Year Established: 1975
No. of Volumes: 500
Sidelines and Services: Sexual accessories, massage oils, candles
Catalogs: Semiannual catalog

Everything Angels

9 W. 31st St., 2nd fl. (bet. Fifth & Sixth Aves.)
New York, NY 10001 • (212) 564-6950 or (800) 99-ANGEL
Fax: (212) 564-6944
Hours: Mon.-Sat. Noon to 6 P.M. Other hours by appointment.
Form of payment: Visa, MC. Checks accepted for mail order.
Type of store: New, mail order
Subject Specialties: Religion - General • Spirituality • Theology
• New Age • Occult/Mysticism • Popular Culture • Angels
Owner: Carole Lozoff
Manager: Luella Purse
Year Established: 1992
Catalogs: Annual catalog ($2)

Ex Libris

160-A E. 70th St. (bet. Third & Lexington Aves.)
New York, NY 10021 • (212) 249-2618 Fax: (212) 249-1465
Hours: By appointment only
Form of payment: Checks
Type of store: Antiquarian
Subject Specialties: Design • Posters • Art - Futurism • Art -
Bauhaus School • Art - Modern • Art - Russian Avant-Garde
• Art - Surrealism • Art - Dadaism • Autographs/Manuscripts
Owner: Elaine Lustig Cohen
Manager: W. Michael Sheehe
Year Established: 1974
No. of Volumes: 5,000
Sidelines and Services: Appraise library collections, original art,
ephemera, rare art periodicals

Richard C. Faber Jr.

230 E. 15th St. (bet. Second & Third Aves.)
New York, NY 10003 • (212) 228-7353 Fax: (212) 477-9392
Hours: By appointment only
Form of payment: AMEX, Checks
Type of store: Used, antiquarian, mail order
Subject Specialties: Nautical/Maritime • Oceanliners
Owner: Richard Faber
Sidelines and Services: Maritime ephemera
Comments: Specializes in books about
oceanliners from 1840 to 1939.

Fashion Books and Magazines

1369 Broadway, 5th fl. (entrance on 37th St.)
New York, NY 10018 • (212) 946-5300 Fax: (212) 695-0180
Form of payment: Visa, MC, AMEX
Type of store: New, periodicals
Subject Specialties: Fashion/Costume/Clothing • Graphic Arts
• Design
Sidelines and Services: Subscriptions

Fashion Design Books

234 W. 27th St. (bet. Seventh & Eighth Aves.)
New York, NY 10001 • (212) 633-9646 Fax: (212) 633-0807
Hours: Mon.-Thu. 8:30 A.M. to 8 P.M.; Fri. 8:30 A.M. to 5 P.M.;
Sat. 10 A.M. to 4 P.M. Hours may change outside of school
season; best to call first.
Form of payment: Visa, MC, AMEX, Discover, Checks
Type of store: New, periodicals
Subject Specialties: Fashion/Costume/Clothing
Manager: Martin Ow
Sidelines and Services: Art supplies, sewing supplies, magazines

Fashion Institute of Technology Bookstore

227 W. 27th St. (bet. Seventh & Eighth Aves.)
New York, NY 10001 • (212) 564-4275
Hours: Mon.-Thu. 8:30 A.M. to 7 P.M.; Fri. 8:30 A.M. to 5 P.M.;
Sat. 10 A.M. to 2 P.M.
Form of payment: Visa, MC, AMEX, Discover, Checks

Type of store: New
Subject Specialties: Fashion/Costume/Clothing
Managers: Linda Stewart, Diane Sustad
Comments: Operated by Barnes & Noble.

Fil Caravan Inc.

301 E. 57th St. (entrance on Second Ave.) New York, NY 10022
(212) 421-5972 Fax: (212) 421-5976
Hours: Mon-Sat: 11 A.M. to 6 P.M.
Form of payment: Visa, MC, Discover, Diners Club
Type of store: New, used, antiquarian, mail order
Subject Specialties: Art - Middle Eastern • Russia (including
Russian Language and Literature) • Middle Eastern Languages
and Literature • History - Middle East • Arabic • Art - Russian/
Soviet • Religion - Islam • Calligraphy • Russian Samovars
• Turkish Language • Armenian Language • Koran • Torah
• Autographs/Manuscripts
President: M. Nabi Israfil
Year Established: 1976
No. of Volumes: 200 titles
Sidelines and Services: Antiques, original art, paintings, restora-
tion, framing, Middle Eastern imports, prayer books, Islamic art,
oriental rugs
Catalogs: Annual catalog

Fine Art in Print

SEE: Untitled / Fine Art in Print

First Things First

955 West End Ave. (at 107th St.) New York, NY 10025

(212) 222-2628

Hours: Tue.-Sat. 11 A.M. to 7 P.M.; Sun. Noon to 5 P.M.

Form of payment: Visa, MC, Checks

Type of store: New

Subject Specialties: Substance Abuse • Spiritual Healing
• Conflict Resolution

Owner: Jean Lynch

Year Established: 1996

Sidelines and Services: Special orders, café, evening workshops
offered Tue. through Thu.

Firsts and Company

1100 Madison Ave. (bet. 82nd & 83rd Sts.) New York, NY 10028

(212) 249-4122

Hours: By appointment only

Form of payment: Checks

Type of store: Antiquarian

Subject Specialties: Literature - Modern

Owner: Arnold A. Rogow

Carl Fischer Music Store

56-62 Cooper Square New York, NY 10003 • (212) 777-0900

Hours: Mon.-Wed., Fri.-Sat. 10 A.M. to 5:45 P.M.;

Thu. 10 A.M. to 6:45 P.M.

Form of payment: Visa, MC

Type of store: New
Subject Specialties: Music

Forbidden Planet

840 Broadway (at 13th St.) New York, NY 10003
Store: (212) 473-1576; Office: (212) 475-6161
Fax: (212) 475-6180
Hours: Mon.-Sun.: 10 A.M. to 8:30 P.M. Closed Thanksgiving
& Christmas Day.
Form of payment: Visa, MC, AMEX, Discover, Checks
Type of store: New, periodicals, mail order
Subject Specialties: Fiction - Science Fiction • Fiction -
Fantasy/Horror • Cinema/Films • Comic Books • Magazines/
Journals/Newspapers • Art - General • Radio/Television • Popular
Culture • Star Trek • Star Wars
President: Michael Luckman
Manager: Carol Hanulcik
Year Established: 1981
Sidelines and Services: Mail order service, shipping, toys,
posters, videotapes, games

Fordham University Bookstore

113 W. 60th St. (at Columbus Ave.) New York, NY 10023
(212) 636-6079 or (212) 636-6080
Hours: Mon.-Thu. 10:30 A.M. to 6:30 P.M.; Fri. 10:30 A.M. to 4 P.M.
Form of payment: Visa, MC, AMEX, Discover, Checks
Type of store: New

Subject Specialties: General • Academic
Manager: Art Whatley
Comments: Operated by Barnes & Noble.

Leonard Fox Ltd.

790 Madison Ave., Suite 606 (bet. 66th & 67th Sts.)
New York, NY 10021 • (212) 879-7077 Fax: (212) 772-9692
Hours: Mon.-Fri. 9:30 A.M. to 5 P.M., or by appointment
Form of payment: AMEX, Checks
Type of store: Antiquarian
Subject Specialties: Art - Art Deco/Art Nouveau • Art - Modern
• Prints/Drawings • Livres d'Artiste • Watercolors
Owner: Leonard Fox
Year Established: 1976
No. of Volumes: 500
Sidelines and Services: Appraise library collections,
original art, prints
Catalogs: Semiannual catalog

Frank Music Co.

250 W. 54th St., 3rd fl. (bet. Broadway & Eighth Aves.)
New York, NY 10019 • (212) 582-1999
Hours: Mon.-Fri. 10 A.M. to 6 P.M.
Form of payment: Visa, MC
Type of store: New
Subject Specialties: Music

Fraunces Tavern Museum Store

54 Pearl St. (corner of Broad St.) New York, NY 10004

(212) 425-1778 Fax: (212) 509-3467

Hours: Mon.-Fri. 10 A.M. to 4:45 P.M.; Sat. Noon to 4 P.M.

Form of payment: Visa, MC, AMEX, Checks

Type of store: New, mail order

Subject Specialties: History - America - Colonial/Revolution

• New York City • Art - American • Decorative Arts

Manager: Maureen Sarro

No. of Volumes: 200

Sidelines and Services: Gifts, mail order, souvenirs

Samuel French Bookshop

45 W. 25th St., 2nd fl. (bet. Sixth Ave. & Broadway)

New York, NY 10010 • (212) 206-8990 Fax: (212) 206-1429

Hours: Mon.-Fri. 9 A.M. to 5 P.M. Store closes at 4 P.M.

on Fri. during summer.

Form of payment: Visa, MC, AMEX, Checks

Type of store: New, mail order

Subject Specialties: Theater/Drama • Music

Catalogs: Annual main catalog ($3.00)

French and European Publications

(Librarie de France/Libreria Hispanica/The Dictionary Store)

610 Fifth Ave. (bet. 49th & 50th Sts., on south side of Channel

Gardens promenade) New York, NY 10020

(212) 581-8810 Fax: (212) 265-1094

Hours: Mon.-Sat. 10 A.M. to 6:15 P.M. Open Sun. 11 A.M.
to 6 P.M. during Christmas season.
Form of payment: Visa, MC, AMEX, Corporate checks
Type of store: New
Subject Specialties: Foreign Language Instruction • Dictionaries/
Encyclopedias • France (including French Language and Litera-
ture) • Spanish Language and Literature Magazines/Journals/
Newspapers • Reference
Owner: Emanuel Molho
Year Established: 1928
No. of Volumes: 1,000,000
Sidelines and Services: French magazines & newspapers, posters,
French popular music, foreign books on audiotape and CD,
French & Spanish videotapes, greeting cards, French games,
postcards of France
Catalogs: Occasional

Frick Collection

1 E. 70th St. (bet. Madison & Fifth Aves.) New York, NY 10021
(212) 288-0700
Hours: Tue.-Sat. 10 A.M. to 6 P.M. Sun. 1 P.M. to 6 P.M. Closed Mon.
Form of payment: Visa, MC, Checks
Type of store: New
Subject Specialties: Art - General • Art - European, 1600-1900

A. I. Friedman

44 W. 18th St. (bet. Fifth & Sixth Aves.) New York, NY 10011

(212) 243-9000 Fax: (212) 242-1238
Hours: Mon.-Fri. 9 A.M. to 7 P.M. Sat. 10 A.M. to 5 P.M.
Form of payment: Visa, MC, AMEX, Checks
Type of store: New
Subject Specialties: Art - General • Graphic Arts
Owner: Jim White
Year Established: 1929
No. of Volumes: 500 titles
Sidelines and Services: Art supplies, prints, posters

Funny Business Comics

660-B Amsterdam Ave. (bet. 92nd & 93rd Sts.)
New York, NY 10025 • (212) 799-9477 Fax: (212) 501-8294
Hours: Mon-Sun: Noon to 5 P.M.
Form of payment: Visa, MC, AMEX, Checks
Type of store: New, used
Subject Specialties: Comic Books
Owner: Dr. Roger Smyth
Year Established: 1979
No. of Volumes: 600,000
Sidelines and Services: Collectibles,
back issues of comic books, opera CDs

Galerie St. Etienne

24 W. 57th St. (bet. Fifth & Sixth Aves.) New York, NY 10019
(212) 245-6734 Fax: (212) 765-8493
Hours: Tue.-Sat. 11 A.M. to 5 P.M.

Form of payment: Checks

Type of store: New

Subject Specialties: Art - Modern • Art - Austrian • Art - German

Directors: Hildegard Bachert, Jane Kallir

Year Established: 1939

No. of Volumes: 150

Sidelines and Services: Reproductions

Comments: Specializes in books about Austrian and German art of the 20th century.

Gallagher Paper Collectibles

126 E. 12th St. (bet. Third & Fourth Aves., in basement)
New York, NY 10003 • (212) 473-2404
Hours: Mon.-Fri. 8:30 A.M. to 6 P.M.; Sat. 11 A.M. to 5 P.M.
Closed one Sat. of every month.

Form of payment: Checks

Type of store: Used, periodicals

Subject Specialties: Magazines/Journals/Newspapers • Ephemera

Owner: Mike Gallagher

Year Established: 1993

Sidelines and Services: Libraries bought and sold

Comments: Has a large selection of back isseus of magazines from 1900 to the present.

Gallery 292

120 Wooster St. (bet. Prince & Spring Sts.) New York, NY 10012
(212) 431-0292 Fax: (212) 941-7479

Hours: By appointment only (Tueday-Sat. 11 A.M. to 6 P.M.)
Form of payment: Visa, MC, Checks
Type of store: Antiquarian, gallery
Subject Specialties: Photography • European Studies
Owner: Howard Greenberg
Director: Sarah Morthland
Year Established: 1992
No. of Volumes: 600+
Sidelines and Services: Appraise library
collections, photographs, search service
Catalogs: List available by request only

Ralph D. Gardner

135 Central Park West (bet. 73rd & 74th Sts.)
New York, NY 10023 • (212) 877-6820
Type of store: Mail order, antiquarian, new
Subject Specialties: Antiques/Collectibles • Art - General
• Autographs/Manuscripts • Children's/Juvenile • Cinema/Films
• Cooking • First Editions • Signed Editions
Owner: Ralph D. Gardner
Sidelines and Services: Appraise library collections, auto-
graphs/manuscripts, original art

Gay Pleasures

546 Hudson St. (bet. Charles & Perry Sts.) New York, NY 10014
(212) 255-5756 or (212) 645-7573
Hours: Mon.-Sun. Noon to Midnight

Form of payment: Visa, MC, AMEX, ATM cards
Type of store: New, used, rare
Subject Specialties: Gay/Lesbian Studies • Erotica/Curiosa
Manager: Mark Wisniewski
Year Established: 1985
No. of Volumes: 25,000 (6,000 titles)
Sidelines and Services: Magazines, art reproductions, magazine back issues, video rentals, original art

Gem Antiques

1088 Madison Ave. (at 82nd St.) New York, NY 10028
(212) 535-7399 or (800) 582-2115
Hours: Mon.-Sat. 10:30 A.M. to 5:30 P.M.
Form of payment: Visa, MC, AMEX, Diners Club, Checks
Type of store: Antiquarian
Subject Specialties: Antiques/Collectibles • Ceramics • Paperweights
Owner: Jack Feingold
Year Established: 1967
No. of Volumes: 500

Gemological Institute of America Bookstore

580 Fifth Avenue (bet. 47th & 48th Sts.) New York, NY 10036
Hours: Mon.-Fri. 8 A.M. to 5 P.M.
Form of payment: Visa, MC, AMEX, Discover
Type of Store: New
Subject Specialties: Jewelry • Geology

Year Established: 1974
No. of Volumes: 200
Sidelines and Services: Gemological supplies, kits, study aids, gifts, videotapes, mail order

Bill George International

1370 Broadway (at 37th St.) New York, NY 10018
(212) 688-2693 or (212) 356-1448 Fax: (212) 365-0955
Hours: By appointment only
Form of payment: Checks
Type of store: Antiquarian, rare European
Subject Specialties: Prints/Drawings
Year Established: 1981

V. F. Germack Professional Photography Collectors

1199 Park Ave. (bet. 94th & 95th Sts.) New York, NY 10128
(212) 289-8411
Hours: By appointment only
Form of payment: Checks
Type of store: Antiquarian
Subject Specialties: Photography
Owner: Victor Germack
Year Established: 1978

German Book Center N.A., Inc.

1841 Broadway, Rm. 907 (entrance on 60th St.)
New York, NY 10023 • (212) 307-7733 Fax: (212) 307-7733
Hours: Tue.-Fri. 10 A.M. to 6 P.M.; Sat. 9 A.M. to 4 P.M.
Form of payment: Discover, Checks
Type of store: New, used, antiquarian, mail order
Subject Specialties: Linguistics • Philosophy • Education • Germany
(including German Language and Literature) • History - Europe
• Music • Psychoanalysis/Psychotherapy • Literary Criticism
President: Dr. Thomas Tyrrell
Year Established: 1940
No. of Volumes: 100,000
Sidelines and Services: Audio-visual materials, games, records,
magazine subscription agency, wholesale
Catalogs: Annual catalog of recent German publications
Comments: The center was formerly Mary S. Rosenberg Inc.

E & B Goldbergs' Discount Marine

12 W. 37th St. (bet. Fifth & Sixth Aves.) New York, NY 10018
(212) 594-6065
Hours: Mon.-Sat. 9 A.M. to 6 P.M.; Sun. 9 A.M. to 4 P.M.
Form of payment: Visa, MC, AMEX
Subject Specialties: Boating • Nautical/Maritime

Golden Books Showcase

630 Fifth Ave. (at 50th St.) New York, NY 10111
(212) 582-4323

Hours: Mon.-Sat. 9 A.M. to 7 P.M.; Sun. 10 A.M. to 6 P.M.

Form of payment: Visa, MC, AMEX

Subject Specialties: Children's/Juvenile

Comments: Carries "Golden Books" children's book series

Good Earth Foods

1330 First Ave. (bet. 71st & 72nd Sts.) New York, NY 10021

(212) 472-9055 Fax: (212) 472-8801

Hours: Mon.-Fri. 9 A.M. to 7:30 P.M.; Sat. 9 A.M. to 6 P.M.;
Sun. Noon to 6 P.M.

Form of payment: Visa, MC, AMEX, Discover, Checks

Type of store: New

Subject Specialties: Cooking • Environment/Conservation/Ecology
• Nature

Owner: Gabe Desimone

Year Established: 1952

No. of Volumes: 500

Sidelines and Services: Magazines, special orders

Good Earth Foods

167 Amsterdam Ave. (bet. 67th & 68th Sts.)

New York, NY 10023 • (212) 496-1616

Hours: Mon.-Fri. 9:30 A.M. to 7:30 P.M.; Sat. 9:30 A.M.
to 6:30 P.M.; Sun. Noon to 6 P.M.

Form of payment: Visa, MC, AMEX, Discover, Diners Club, Checks

Type of store: New

Subject Specialties: Cooking • Environment/Conservation/

Ecology • Nature
Manager: Michael Horton
Sidelines and Services: Magazines, special order

Good Field Trading Co.

74-B Mott St. (bet. Canal & Bayard Sts.) New York, NY 10013
(212) 431-4263 Fax: (212) 966-3338
Hours: Mon-Sun: 9:30 A.M. to 7:30 P.M.
Type of store: New
Subject Specialties: China (including Chinese Language and
Literature)

Elliot Gordon Books

150 E. 69th St., #8H (bet. Third & Lexington Aves.)
New York, NY 10021 • (212) 861-2892 • E-mail address:
eqot@nyc.pipeline.com
Type of store: Used, antiquarian
Subject Specialties: Art History • Art - Reference • Books About
Books/Bibliography
Owner: Elliot Gordon
No. of Volumes: 1,500 titles

Dey Gosse

SEE: DG Antiquarian Books

Gotham Book Mart and Gallery

41 W. 47th St. (bet. Fifth & Sixth Aves.) New York, NY 10036
(212) 719-4448
Hours: Mon-Fri: 9:30 A.M. to 6:30 P.M.; Sat: 9:30 A.M. to 6 P.M.
Form of payment: Visa, MC, AMEX, Checks
Type of store: New, used
Subject Specialties: Literature - Modern • Philosophy • Poetry
• Classical Studies • Cinema/Films • Theater/Drama • First Editions
Owner: Andreas L. Brown
Manager: Gina Guy
Year Established: 1920
No. of Volumes: 400,000
Sidelines and Services: Literary magazines, manuscripts, original
art, search service, appraisals

Gotta Have It! Collectibles

153 E. 57th St. (bet. Lexington & Third Aves.)
New York, NY 10022 • (212) 750-7900 Fax: (212) 750-8080
Hours: Mon.-Fri. 10 A.M. to 7 P.M.; Sat. & Sun. 11 A.M. to 6 P.M.
Closed Sat. & Sun. during summer.
Form of payment: Visa, MC, AMEX, Discover, Checks
Subject Specialties: Autographs/Manuscripts

Gozlan's Sefer Israel Inc.

28 W. 27th St., 4th fl. (bet. Sixth Ave. & Broadway)
New York, NY 10001 • (212) 725-5890 Fax: (212) 689-6534
Hours: Mon.-Thu. 9 A.M. to 5 P.M.; Fri. 9 A.M. to 3 P.M.

Form of payment: Checks
Type of store: New, out-of-print
Subject Specialties: Judaica • Children's/Juvenile • Hebrew
• Concordances
Owner: Marc Gozlan
Sidelines and Services: Hebrew books from Israel, computer software, maps
Catalogs: Two different lists available
Comments: Formerly known as Israel Sefer, this shop deals mostly in wholesale.

Granary Books

568 Broadway, Suite 403 (at Prince St.) New York, NY 10012
(212) 226-5462 Fax: (212) 226-6143
Hours: By appointment only
Form of payment: Visa, MC, Checks
Type of store: New
Subject Specialties: Signed Editions
Owner: Steven Clay
Year Established: 1982
No. of Volumes: 2,000
Catalogs: Occasional catalogs

General Ulysses Grant National Memorial Bookstore

Riverside Dr. and W. 122nd St. (inside Riverside Park)
New York, NY 10027 • (212) 666-1640 Fax: (212) 264-3186

Hours: Mon.-Sun. 9 A.M. to 5 P.M.
Form of payment: Checks
Type of store: New
Subject Specialties: History - America - Civil War • Ulysses Grant
Superintendent: Joe Avery
No. of Volumes: 30

Great Judaica Books

136 W. 22nd St., 4th fl. (bet. Sixth & Seventh Aves.)
New York, NY 10011 • (212) 633-2022 Fax: (212) 633-2123
Hours: Mon.-Fri. 10 A.M. to 5:30 P.M.
Form of payment: Visa, MC, Checks
Type of store: New
Subject Specialties: Judaica • Philosophy • Travel • Holocaust
• Current Events • Diaspora • Jewish Mysticism • Jewish Women
Owner: Ian Shapolsky
Manager: Ann Cassonto
Year Established: 1985
No. of Volumes: 30,000 (1,000 titles)
Comments: Warehouse outlet with wholesale prices.

Virginia L. Green Rare Books

424 Broome St. New York, NY 10013
(212) 226-3460 or (212) 226-4265 Fax: (212) 226-8789
Hours: By appointment only
Form of payment: Checks
Type of store: Used

Subject Specialties: Illustrated Books • Art - European 20th c.
• Architecture • Decorative Arts • Marcel Duchamp • Man Ray
Owner: Virginia L. Green
Year Established: 1971
Sidelines and Services: Fine art, prints

Green Arc Bookstore

outdoor book kiosk on Union Square West at 16th Street
Hours: Mon.-Sun.: Noon to twilight (weather permitting)
Type of Store: Used
Subject Specialties: General
Owners: Scott Rogers, Richard Rogers
Sidelines and Services: CDs

Roger Gross Ltd.

15 W. 81st St. (bet. Second & Third Aves.)
New York, NY 10024 • (212) 759-2892 Fax: (212) 838-5425
Hours: By appointment only
Form of payment: Checks
Type of store: Antiquarian
Subject Specialties: Autographs/Manuscripts • Music • Opera
• Performing Arts • Dance • Ephemera
Owner: Roger Gross
Catalogs: 6/year

Cinema/Music 233 W 72 212 874 1588

Gryphon Bookshop

2246 Broadway (bet. 80th & 81st Sts.) New York, NY 10024

(212) 362-0706

Hours: Mon.-Sun. 10 A.M. to Midnight

Form of payment: Visa, MC

Type of store: Used, antiquarian, mail order

Subject Specialties: Art History • Children's/Juvenile
• Decorative Arts • Fiction - Fantasy/Horror • First Editions • Music
• Performing Arts • Theater/Drama • Wizard of Oz

Owner: Marc Lewis

Manager: Anthony De Pauw

Year Established: 1974

No. of Volumes: 50,000

Sidelines and Services: Search service, records, CDs, laser discs, books purchased

Solomon R. Guggenheim Museum Bookstore

1071 Fifth Ave. (bet. 88th & 89th Sts.) New York, NY 10128

(212) 423-3615

Hours: Sun.-Wed. 10 A.M. to 6 P.M.; Thu. 10 A.M. to 4 P.M.;
Fri. & Sat. 10 A.M. to 8 P.M.

Form of payment: Visa, MC, AMEX

Type of store: New

Subject Specialties: Art - Modern • Art - General

Manager: Ed Fuqua

Sidelines and Services: Gifts

Solomon R. Guggenheim Museum Soho Bookstore

575 Broadway (at Prince St.) New York, NY 10012

(212) 423-3876

Hours: Sun., Wed.-Fri. 11 A.M. to 6 P.M.; Sat. 11 A.M. to 8 P.M.

Form of payment: Visa, MC, AMEX

Type of store: New, periodicals

Subject Specialties: Art - Modern • Art - General

Year Established: 1992

Sidelines and Services: Gifts

The Gulack Collection— Theater and Cinema

250 Fort Washington Ave., #2H New York, NY 10032

(212) 923-5814

Hours: By appointment only

Type of store: Antiquarian, used

Subject Specialties: Cinema/Films • Theater/Drama

Owner: Max Gulack

No. of Volumes: 6,000

Sidelines and Services: Theater programs

HSA Bookstore

4 W. 43rd St. (bet. Fifth & Sixth Aves.) New York, NY 10036

(212) 997-0050 (ext. 250)

Hours: Mon-Fri: 10 A.M. to 6 P.M.

Form of payment: Visa, MC, AMEX

Type of store: New

Subject Specialties: Religion - Christianity • Spirituality

Sidelines and Services: Greeting cards

Comments: The store awning out front reads, "Unification Books."

Hacker Art Books

45 W. 57th St., 5th fl. (between Fifth and Sixth Aves.)

New York, NY 10019 • (212) 688-7600 Fax: (212) 754-2554

Hours: Mon.-Sat. 9:30 A.M. to 6 P.M. Closed Sat. during summer.

Form of payment: Visa, MC

Type of store: New, antiquarian, mail order

Subject Specialties: Fine Arts • Art - General • Applied Arts
• Prints/Drawings • Architecture • Design

President: Seymour Hacker

Manager: Pierre H. Colas

Year Established: 1946

No. of Volumes: 1,000,000 (50,000 titles)

Catalogs: 4/year

Hagstrom Map and Travel Center

57 W. 43rd St. (bet. Fifth & Sixth Aves.) New York, NY 10036

(212) 398-1222 Fax: (212) 398-9856

Hours: Mon.-Fri. 8:30 A.M. to 5:30 P.M.

Form of payment: Visa, MC, AMEX, Checks (with ID)

Type of store: New

Subject Specialties: Aviation • Maps/Atlases/Cartography
• Nautical/Maritime • Travel • Boating • Geography • New York City

• Hiking • Bicycling • Fishing
Manager: Leighton Warner
Year Established: 1910
No. of Volumes: 60,000
Sidelines and Services: Globes, maps, mounting service, world atlases

Charles Hamilton Autographs

166 E. 63rd St., Suite 18-A New York, NY 10021 • (212) 888-0338
Hours: By appointment only
Type of store: Mail order
Subject Specialties: Autographs/Manuscripts
Owner: Charles Hamilton
Year Established: 1949
Sidelines and Services: Buys autographs
Catalogs: 12/year

Carla Hanauer

**195 Bennett Ave. (bet. 189th & 190th Sts.) New York, NY 10040
(212) 942-6454**
Hours: By appointment only
Type of store: New, mail order, imports
Subject Specialties: Netherlands • Germany (including German Language and Literature) • Hebrew • Israel • Dutch Language
Owner: Carla Hanauer
Year Established: 1981
No. of Volumes: 200+

Sidelines and Services: Imports, exports, special orders, mail order, search service

Jim Hanley's Universe

14 W. 33rd St. (bet. Fifth Ave. & Broadway) New York, NY 10001 (212) 268-7088 Fax: (212) 268-7728

Hours: Mon.-Fri. 7:30 A.M. to 9:30 P.M.; Sat. 10 A.M. to 9 P.M.; Sun. 10 A.M. to 8 P.M.

Form of payment: Visa, MC, AMEX, Discover, Checks

Type of store: New, used, antiquarian, periodicals, mail order

Subject Specialties: Comic Books • Illustrated Books • Literature - General • Popular Culture • Fiction - Westerns • Posters • Fiction - Fantasy/Horror

Manager: David Alexander

Year Established: 1990

No. of Volumes: 100,000

Sidelines and Services: Videotapes, toys, games, posters, comic book supplies, trading cards

Hauswedell & Nolte (New York Office)

225 Central Park West, Suite 1518 (bet. 82nd & 83rd Sts.) New York, NY 10024 • (212) 595-0806 Fax: (212) 595-0832

Hours: Mon-Fri: 10 A.M. to 6 P.M.

Form of payment: Checks

Type of store: Auction house

Subject Specialties: Auction House

Director: Jeanne Hedstrom

Comments: This is the New York branch of German auction house. The address for the main headquarters is: Hauswedell & Nolte, Poseldorfer Weg 1, D 20148, Hamburg, Germany.

Hayden Planetarium Bookstore

81st St. and Central Park West New York, NY 10024
(212) 769-5910
Hours: Mon.-Fri. 9 A.M. to 5 P.M. Sat. & Sun. 10 A.M. to 5:30 P.M.
Form of payment: Visa, MC, AMEX
Type of store: New
Subject Specialties: Astronomy • Space Exploration

Hayden & Fandetta

P.O. Box 1549, Radio City Station New York, NY 10101
(212) 582-2505
Hours: By appointment only
Form of payment: Checks
Type of store: New, used, antiquarian, mail order
Subject Specialties: Ceramics • Glass • Antiques/Collectibles • Decorative Arts • Textiles • Jewelry • Applied Arts • Fashion/Costume/Clothing • Pottery • Porcelain
Owners: John-Peter Hayden Jr., David J. Fandetta
Year Established: 1988
No. of Volumes: 10,000
Sidelines and Services: Search service
Comments: This bookseller exhibits at 36 antiques shows annually.

Donald A. Heald Rare Books and Fine Art

124 E. 74th St. (bet. Park & Lexington Aves.)
New York, NY 10021 • (212) 744-3505 Fax: (212) 628-7847
E-mail address: heald@aol.com
Hours: By appointment only
Form of payment: Checks
Type of store: Antiquarian
Subject Specialties: Natural History • Exploration/Voyages
• Illustrated Books • Colorplate Books • Prints/Drawings
• Americana • First Editions • Watercolors • Sporting Books
Owner: Donald A. Heald
No. of Volumes: 2,000
Sidelines and Services: Appraise library collections, maps,
manuscripts, prints

Hebrew Union College Bookstore

1 W. Fourth St. (bet. Washington Square West & Sixth Ave.)
New York, NY 10012 • (212) 674-5300 Fax: (212) 533-0129
Hours: Mon-Thurs: 8:30 A.M. to 5:30 P.M.
Type of store: New
Subject Specialties: Judaica
Manager: Debra Stein-Davidson

Heller Audiobooks

30 Rockefeller Plaza (bet. 49th & 50th Sts., underground
Concourse Level) New York, NY 10112 • (212) 399-9300 or
(800) 218-8181 • E-mail address: audiobk@tiac.net

Hours: Mon.-Fri. 8:30 A.M. to 6 P.M.; Sat. 11 A.M. to 5 P.M.

Form of payment: Visa, MC, AMEX, Checks

Type of store: New

Subject Specialties: Self-Help • Business/Management • Foreign Language Instruction • Children's/Juvenile

Owner: Robert Heller

Manager: Jon Olsen

Year Established: 1993

No. of Volumes: 5,000+

Catalogs: Free annual catalog

Comments: For more information visit Heller's Web site at: http://www.helleraudiobooks.com

Heller Audiobooks

125 Maiden Lane (bet. Pearl & Water Sts., near Wall St.)
New York, NY 10038 • (212) 248-7800 or (800) 218-8181
E-mail address: audiobk@tiac.net

Hours: Mon.-Fri. 8:30 A.M. to 6 P.M.; Sat. 11 A.M. to 5 P.M.; Sun. Noon to 5 P.M.

Form of payment: Visa, MC, AMEX

Type of store: New

Subject Specialties: Business/Management • Children's/Juvenile • Fiction - Fantasy/Horror • Fiction - Westerns • Fiction - Crime/Mystery/Suspense • Self-Help • Literature - General • Foreign Language Instruction

Owner: Robert Heller

Manager: Jon Olsen

Year Established: 1993

No. of Volumes: 6,000 titles

Catalogs: Semiannual catalog

Comments: See above listing.

Hephzibah House Bookroom

51 W. 75th St. (bet. Columbus Ave. & Central Park West)

New York, NY 10023 • (212) 787-6150

Hours: Mon.-Fri. 8 A.M. to 10 P.M.

Form of payment: Checks

Type of store: New

Subject Specialties: Religion - Christianity

Manager: John Ewald

Year Established: 1924

Sidelines and Services: Religious goods

J. N. Herlin

40 Harrison St., Apt. 25D (at Greenwich St.) New York, NY 10013

(212) 732-1086

Hours: By appointment only

Form of payment: Checks

Type of store: Antiquarian

Subject Specialties: Art - Modern

Owner: Jean-Noël Herlin

Year Established: 1972

No. of Volumes: 5,000

Jonathan A. Hill Bookseller

325 West End Ave. (at 75th St.) New York, NY 10023
(212) 496-7856 Fax: (212) 496-9182 • E-mail address:
jonatha470@aol.com
Hours: By appointment only
Form of payment: Visa, MC, Checks
Type of store: Antiquarian
Subject Specialties: Science • Medicine • Books About Books/
Bibliography • Natural History • Fine Printing • Early Printed
Books
Owner: Jonathan A. Hill
No. of Volumes: 2,000+

Hispanic Society Bookshop

613 W. 155th St. (on Broadway) New York, NY 10032
(212) 926-2234
Hours: Tue.-Sat. 10 A.M. to 4:30 P.M.; Sun. 1 P.M. to 4 P.M.
Form of payment: Checks
Type of store: New
Subject Specialties: Spanish Language and Literature
• Portuguese • History - Latin America/Caribbean • Literature -
Latin American/Caribbean
Manager: George Moranda
Year Established: 1904
No. of Volumes: 50,000
Sidelines and Services: Gifts, greeting cards
Catalogs: Annual catalog

Peter Hlinka Historical Americana

P.O. Box 310 New York, NY 10028 • (718) 409-6407

Hours: Mail order only Mon.-Fri. 9 A.M. to 6 P.M.

Form of payment: Checks and money orders

Type of store: New, used, antiquarian, mail order

Subject Specialties: Military/War • History - America 20th c. • History - World Wars I and II • Holocaust • Espionage/ Intelligence • Nautical/Maritime • Numismatics • History - Russia & Soviet Union • Military Medals/Decorations/Orders • Military Uniforms/Insignia

Owner: Peter Hlinka

Year Established: 1963

No. of Volumes: 600

Sidelines and Services: Military medals, war relics

Catalogs: Semiannual catalog

Glenn Horowitz Bookseller

141 E. 44th St. (bet. Third & Lexington Aves.)
New York, NY 10017 • (212) 327-3538 Fax: (212) 327-3542

Hours: Mon.-Fri. 10 A.M. to 7 P.M.

Form of payment: Visa, MC, AMEX, Checks

Type of store: Antiquarian

Subject Specialties: Poetry • History - General • Literature - General • Limited Editions • Fiction - Historical

Owner: Glenn Horowitz

Year Established: 1979

Sidelines and Services: Appraise library collections, autographs, manuscripts, letters

Catalogs: 3-4/year
Comments: Also has a second location at 19 E. 76th St,
New York, NY 10021.

Housing Works Used Book Cafe

126 Crosby St. (bet. Houston & Prince Sts.,
1 block east of Broadway) New York, NY 10012
(212) 334-3324 Fax: (212) 334-3959
Hours: Mon.-Wed. 10 A.M. to 8 P.M.; Thu. & Fri. 10 A.M. to 9 P.M.;
Sat. Noon to 9 P.M.; Sun. Noon to 7 P.M.
Form of payment: Visa, MC, AMEX, Checks
Type of store: Antiquarian
Subject Specialties: Art - General • Gay/Lesbian Studies
• Cooking • Gardening • Theater/Drama • Poetry
Director: Cora Deutchman
Year Established: 1995
No. of Volumes: 100,000
Sidelines and Services: LP records, café

Huckleberry Designs

235 W. 76th St. (bet. Broadway & West End Ave.)
New York, NY 10023 • (212) 874-3631 Fax: (212) 721-6124
Hours: By appointment only
Form of payment: Visa, MC, AMEX
Type of store: Antiquarian, mail order
Subject Specialties: Arctic/Polar • Fiction - Science Fiction
• Design • Religion - General • Poetry • Humor • Arms and Armor

Owner: Janet MacAdam
Year Established: 1969
No. of Volumes: 250,000
Catalogs: Annual catalog

The Hudson Guild

441 W. 26th St. (bet. Ninth & Tenth Aves.) New York, NY 10001
(212) 760-9812
Hours: The Hudson Guild holds one sale each year in mid-October. It is not open during the rest of the year.
Form of payment: Checks (with 2 forms of ID)
Type of store: New, used, rare
Subject Specialties: General
No. of Volumes: 50,000
Sidelines and Services: Records
Comments: The Hudson Guild is a not-for-profit agency—not a store. It conducts one 4-day book sale per year, in mid-October. During the rest of the year it accepts donations—ONLY—of books. Contact the Development Office at the above phone number to make a donation.

Hudson News Bookstore

Type of store: New
Subject Specialties: General
Sidelines and Services: Gifts, greeting cards
Individual store locations are as follows:
265 E. 66th St. (at Second Ave.) New York, NY 10021

(212) 988-2683
Hours: Mon.-Fri. 8 A.M. to 10 P.M. Sat. 9 A.M. to Midnight;
Sun. 9 A.M. to 10 P.M.
Form of payment: Visa, MC, AMEX

753 Broadway (bet. W. 8th St. & Astor Pl.)
New York, NY 10003 • (212) 674-6655
Hours: Mon.-Thu. 8 A.M. to 11 P.M.; Fri.-Sat. 7 A.M. to Midnight;
Sun. 7 A.M. to 11 P.M.
Form of payment: Visa, MC, AMEX

Penn Station (bet. 31st & 33rd Sts. on Seventh Ave.)
New York, NY 10001 • (212) 971-6800 Fax: (212) 971-6142
Form of payment: Visa, MC, AMEX

Port Authority Bldg., North Wing
625 Eighth Ave. (42nd St. & Eighth Ave.)
New York, NY 10018 • (212) 563-1030
Hours: Mon.-Sun. 5:30 A.M. to 1 A.M.

Port Authority Bldg., South Wing
625 Eighth Ave. (42nd St. & Eighth Ave.)
New York, NY 10018 • (212) 563-1032
Hours: Mon.-Sun. 5:30 A.M. to 1 A.M.

Grand Central Station 89 E. 42nd St. (bet. Lexington &
Vanderbilt Aves., near Grand Central ticket lobby)
New York, NY 10017 • (212) 687-4580
Hours: Mon.-Sun. 5:30 A.M. to Midnight

1 World Trade Center New York, NY 10048 • (212) 432-9146
Hours: Mon.-Sun. open 24 hours
Form of payment: Visa, MC

Hunter College Bookstore

695 Park Ave. (entrance at 68th St. & Lexington Ave.)
New York, NY 10021 • (212) 650-3970 Fax: (212) 650-3743
Hours: Mon.-Thu. 9 A.M. to 7 P.M.; Fri. 9 A.M. to 4 P.M.
Form of payment: Visa, MC, AMEX, Discover, Checks
Type of store: New, used
Subject Specialties: General
Manager: Cosmo Olivieri
Sidelines and Services: Art and college supplies, office supplies, gifts, clothing
Comments: Operated by Barnes & Noble. Inc., this store carries primarily textbooks.

Idea Graphics Bookstore

1328 Broadway, Suite 645 (bet. 34th & 35th Sts.)
New York, NY 10001 • (212) 564-3954
Hours: Mon.-Thu. 9 A.M. to 6 P.M.; Fri. 9 A.M. to 5 P.M.
Form of payment: Visa, MC, AMEX, Diners Club, Discover, Company checks
Type of store: New, used
Subject Specialties: Graphics • Textiles • Trademarks • Knitting • Fashion/Costume/Clothing • Quilts
Owner: Allen Weinberg   **No. of Volumes:** 2,000+

Ideal Book Store

1125 Amsterdam Ave. (at 115th St.) New York, NY 10025
(212) 662-1909 Fax: (212) 662-1640
Hours: Mon.-Fri. 10 A.M. to 6 P.M.
Form of payment: Visa, MC, AMEX
Type of store: Antiquarian, used
Subject Specialties: Philosophy • Judaica • History - General
• Classical Studies
Owner: Aron Lutwak
Year Established: 1931
No. of Volumes: 45,000
Sidelines and Services: Appraisals
Catalogs: 4/year

Illustration House

96 Spring St., 7th fl. (bet. Broadway & Mercer St.)
New York, NY 10012 • (212) 966-9444 Fax: (212) 966-9425
Hours: Tue.-Sat. 10:30 A.M. to 5:30 P.M.
Form of payment: Visa, MC, Checks
Subject Specialties: Illustrated Books
Owners: Walt Reed, Roger Reed

Imperial Fine Books

790 Madison Ave., Rm. 200 (bet. 66th & 67th Sts.)
New York, NY 10021 • (212) 861-6620 Fax: (212) 249-0333
Hours: Mon.-Fri. 10 A.M. to 5:30 P.M.; Sat. 10 A.M. to 5 P.M.
Closed on Sat., June through August.

Form of payment: Visa, MC, AMEX, Checks
Type of store: Antiquarian
Subject Specialties: History - General • Poetry • Children's/Juvenile • Literature - General • Fine Bindings • Fore-edge Paintings • First Editions • Leatherbound Sets
Owner: Bibi T. Mohamed
Year Established: 1987
No. of Volumes: 5,000
Sidelines and Services: Search service, appraise library collections, bookbinding, restorations
Catalogs: Annual catalog ($3.00)

Integral Yoga Bookshop

227 W. 13th St. (bet. Seventh & Eighth Aves.)
New York, NY 10011 • (212) 929-0586
Hours: Mon.-Fri. 10 A.M. to 8:30 P.M.; Sat. 8:15 A.M. to 5:30 P.M.
Form of payment: Visa, MC, AMEX, Checks
Type of store: New
Subject Specialties: Yoga • Philosophy • Alternative Medicine • Holistics • Psychology/Psychiatry
Manager: Asa Kananda
Year Established: 1980
No. of Volumes: 5,000
Sidelines and Services: Literary magazines, posters, search service, religious goods, audio cassettes, incense

Interboro Institute Bookstore

450 W. 56th St., 3rd fl. (bet. Ninth & Tenth Aves.)
New York, NY 10019 • (212) 399-0091 Fax: (212) 765-5772
Hours: Open only for 3 weeks at the beginning of each semester
Form of payment: Visa, MC, Checks
Type of store: New
Subject Specialties: Business/Management • Accounting
• Optometry • Paralegalism • Secretarial Studies
Vice-President: Janny Chan
No. of Volumes: 300

International Bookstore & Cafe

552 Laguardia Place New York, NY 10012
(212) 260-1000 Fax: (212) 505-1517
Hours: Mon.-Sat. 10 A.M. to 8 P.M.; Sun. 11 A.M. to 6 P.M.
Form of payment: Visa, MC
Type of Store: New
Subject Specialties: International Affairs
Sidelines and Services: Magazines, newspapers, cafe

International Center of Photography

1130 Fifth Ave. (at 94th St.) New York, NY 10128
(212) 860-1751 Fax: (212) 360-6490
Hours: Tue. 11 A.M. to 8 P.M.; Wed.-Sun. 11 A.M. to 6 P.M.
Closed Mon.
Form of payment: Visa, MC, AMEX
Type of store: New

Subject Specialties: Photography
Manager: Edna Ghertler
Year Established: 1974
No. of Volumes: 700
Sidelines and Services: Posters, postcards, gifts, frames, albums

International Center of Photography

1133 Ave. of the Americas (at 43rd St.) New York, NY 10036
(212) 768-4684 Fax: (212) 768-4688
Hours: Tue. 11 A.M. to 8 P.M.; Wed.-Sun. 11 A.M. to 6 P.M.
Form of payment: Visa, MC, AMEX
Type of store: New
Subject Specialties: Photography

The Irish Bookshop

580 Broadway, Rm. 1103 (bet. Prince & Houston Sts.)
New York, NY 10012 • (212) 274-1923 Fax: (212) 431-5413
Hours: Mon.-Thu. 11 A.M. to 5 P.M.; Fri. 11 A.M. to 6:30 P.M.;
Sat. 1 P.M. to 4 P.M.
Form of payment: Visa, MC, Checks
Type of store: New, used, mail order
Subject Specialties: Ireland (including Irish Language
and Literature)
Owner: Angela Carter
Year Established: 1978
No. of Volumes: 15,000
Catalogs: Annual catalog

J. P. Medical Books

1800 Park Ave. (within New York College of Podiatric Medicine, at 124th St.) New York, NY 10035

(212) 410-0593 Fax: (212) 410-0421

Hours: Mon.-Thu. 7:30 A.M. to 2 P.M.

Form of payment: Visa, MC, Discover, Checks

Type of store: New

Subject Specialties: Medicine • Podiatry

Manager: Howard Granat

Sidelines and Services: Gifts, clothing, stationery, games

JBC Bookstore

3 E. 44th St. (bet. Madison & Fifth Aves.)
New York, NY 10017 • (212) 682-4521

Hours: Mon.-Fri. 10:30 A.M. to 8:30 P.M.; Sat. 10:30 A.M. to 7:30 P.M.; Sun. Noon to 6 P.M.

Form of payment: Checks

Type of store: Used

Subject Specialties: Japan (including Japanese Language and Literature)

JHM Video

711 Seventh Ave. (bet. 47th & 48th Sts.) New York, NY 10036
(212) 869-8845

Hours: Mon.-Sun. open 24 hours

Type of store: New

Subject Specialties: Adult

Jaffa Gate Bookshop

P.O. Box 464 New York, NY 10002 • (212) 260-3996

Subject Specialties: Judaica • Travel • Design • Children's/Juvenile

• Collectibles

Owner: Avram Weisberg

Java Joe's

SEE: Biblio's Cafe

150 28th St

Jay Bee Magazine Stores

134 W. 26th St. (bet. Sixth & Seventh Aves.)

New York, NY 10001 • (212) 675-1600

Hours: Mon.-Fri. 10 A.M. to 6 P.M.

Form of payment: Visa, MC

Type of store: New

Subject Specialties: Magazines/Journals/Newspapers

• Cinema/Films • Radio/Television

President: Henry Greenbaum

Year Established: 1957

No. of Volumes: 2,000,000 (2,000 titles)

Sidelines and Services: Magazine back issues, research

Catalogs: Semiannual catalog

Jewish Book Center of the Workmen's Circle

45 E. 33rd St. (bet. Park & Madison Aves.) New York, NY 10016

(212) 889-6800 ext. 285 or (800) 922-2558
Fax: (212) 532-7518
Hours: Mon.-Thu. 10 A.M. to 6 P.M.; Fri. 10 A.M. to 4:30 P.M.;
Sun. 11:30 A.M. to 3:30 P.M. Closed Sun. July through September.
Form of payment: Visa, MC, AMEX, Checks
Type of store: New, mail order
Subject Specialties: Judaica • Yiddish
Manager: Stephen Dowling
Year Established: 1910
No. of Volumes: 1,000 titles
Sidelines and Services: Videos, tapes, CDs, gifts, literary
magazines, search service
Catalogs: Annual catalog

Jewish Museum Book Shop

1109 Fifth Ave. (at 92nd St.) New York, NY 10128
(212) 423-3211 Fax: (212) 423-3232
Hours: Mon., Wed., Thu. 11 A.M. to 5:45 P.M.; Tue. 11 A.M. to 9 P.M.;
Fri. 11 A.M. to 3 P.M.; Sun. 10 A.M. to 5:45 P.M. Closed Sat.
Form of payment: Visa, MC, AMEX
Type of store: New, mail order
Subject Specialties: Art - General • Judaica • Women's Studies
• Children's/Juvenile • Cooking
Manager: Sara Abraham
Director: Robin Cramer
Year Established: 1965
No. of Volumes: 3,000
Sidelines and Services: Gifts, jewelry, catalog, hand-crafted

items, Jewish ceremonial items, graphics, museum reproductions
Catalogs: Annual catalog

John Jay College of Criminal Justice Bookstore

445 W. 59th St. (bet. Ninth & Tenth Aves.)
New York, NY 10019 • (212) 757-5030
Hours: Mon.-Thu. 9 A.M. to 7 P.M.; Fri. 10 A.M. to 3 P.M.
Form of payment: Visa, MC, AMEX, Checks
Type of store: New
Subject Specialties: Criminology
Manager: Dan Nitting
Sidelines and Services: College supplies, gifts, greeting cards, clothing
Comments: Operated by Barnes & Noble.

Harmer Johnson Books

21 E. 65th St., 4th fl. (bet. Fifth & Madison Aves.)
New York, NY 10021 • (212) 535-9364 Fax: (212) 861-9893
Hours: Mon.-Fri. 10:30 A.M. to 5 P.M.
Form of payment: Checks
Type of store: New, used, periodicals, mail order
Subject Specialties: Art History • Colorplate Books • Art - Ancient/Classical • Art - African • Art - Oceania • Art - Native American • Art - Pre-Columbian • Archaeology • History - Australia/Oceania • Native Americans
Owners: Harmer Johnson, Peter Sharrer

Year Established: 1977
No. of Volumes: 10,000
Sidelines and Services: Appraise library and private collections
Catalogs: 4/year

Jonah's Whale

935 Eighth Ave. (bet. 55th & 56th Sts.) New York, NY 10019
(212) 581-8181 or (212) 534-5999 Fax: (212) 315-0554
Hours: Sun.-Thu. 11 A.M. to 6:30 P.M. Summer hours: Mon.-Fri.
11 A.M. to 6:30 P.M. Additional hours by previous appointment.
Form of payment: Checks (with I.D.)
Type of store: Used, antiquarian, mail order
Subject Specialties: Ephemera • Art - General • Music
• Poetry • Theater/Drama • Cinema/Films • Sports
• Transportation • Biography/Autobiography • History - General
• Literature - General
Owner: Ann Abrams
No. of Volumes: 100,000
Sidelines and Services: Collections purchased, prints
Catalogs: Catalog to be published

Arnold B. Joseph

1140 Broadway, Rm. 701 (bet. 26th & 27th Sts.)
New York, NY 10001 • (212) 532-0019
Hours: By appointment only
Type of store: New, used, antiquarian, periodicals, mail order
Subject Specialties: Trains/Railways • Nautical/Maritime

Owner: Arnold B. Joseph
Year Established: 1968
No. of Volumes: 5,500

Sidelines and Services: All kinds of railroadiana (e.g., timetables, passes, calendars, etc.), collections purchased

Judaica Experience

208 W. 72nd St. (bet. Amsterdam & West End Aves.)
New York, NY 10023 • (212) 724-2424
Hours: Mon.-Wed. 10 A.M. to 7 P.M.; Thu. 10 A.M. to 7:30 P.M.;
Fri. 10 A.M. to 3 P.M.; Sun. 10:30 A.M. to 5:30 P.M. Closed Sat.
Form of payment: Visa, MC, AMEX, Discover, Checks
Subject Specialties: Judaica

Juilliard School Bookstore

60 Lincoln Center Plaza New York, NY 10023
(212) 799-5000 ext. 237 Fax: (212) 724-0263
Hours: Mon.-Wed. 9 A.M. to 7 P.M.; Thu.-Sat. 9 A.M. to 5 P.M.
Form of payment: Visa, MC, AMEX, Checks
Type of store: New
Subject Specialties: Dance • Theater/Drama • Music • Opera
Manager: Jay Johnson
Year Established: 1971
No. of Volumes: 15,000
Sidelines and Services: College supplies, sheet muscis, stationery, audio cassettes, compact discs, musical instrument supplies

C. G. Jung Foundation Book Service

28 E. 39th St. (bet. Park & Madison Aves.) New York, NY 10016
(212) 697-6433 or (800) 356-5864 [356-JUNG]
Fax: (212) 953-3989
Hours: Mon.-Wed. 10 A.M. to 4 P.M.; Thu. 10:30 A.M. to 7 P.M.;
Fri. 10 A.M. to 4 P.M. Closed Fri. from Memorial Day through
Labor Day.
Form of payment: Visa, MC, Checks
Type of store: New, mail order
Subject Specialties: Psychology/Psychiatry • Folklore/Mythology
• Anthropology • Women's Studies • New Age • Astrology
• Religion - General • Sexuality • Psychology - Jungian • Dreams
• Men's Studies • Tarot
Manager: Arnold De Vera
Year Established: 1977
No. of Volumes: 5,000 (1,700 titles)
Sidelines and Services: Greeting cards, bookmarks, games,
audiotapes, videotapes
Catalogs: Annual catalog

Jung Ku Books and Stationery

8 Pell St. (west of Bowery, 2 blocks south of Canal St.)
New York, NY 10013 • (212) 732-1030
Hours: Mon.-Sun. 10 A.M. to 7 P.M.
Form of payment: AMEX
Subject Specialties: China (including Chinese Language
and Literature)

Julian's Books
939-3620
110 W 25th
Chelsea Antiques Bldg.
10 - 6
9th Floor

Gallagher's
126 E 12th ST
11 - 6:30 M → SaT
Fashion, CrafTs

K & M Camera

377 E. 23rd St. (bet. First & Second Aves.) New York, NY 10010
(212) 532-1106 Fax: (212) 532-4403
Hours: Mon.-Fri. 8:30 A.M. to 7 P.M.; Sat. 9 A.M. to 6 P.M.
Form of payment: Visa, MC, AMEX (min. charge $30)
Type of store: New
Subject Specialties: Photography
Manager: Jaimie Gordon

Victor Kamkin

925 Broadway (bet. 21st & 22nd Sts.) New York, NY 10010
(212) 673-0776 Fax: (212) 881-1637
Hours: Mon.-Fri. 9:30 A.M. to 5:30 P.M.; Sat. 10 A.M. to 5 P.M.
Form of payment: Visa, MC, AMEX, Discover, Checks
Type of store: New
Subject Specialties: Russia (including Russian Language
and Literature)
Owner: Elena Kamkin
Year Established: 1953
Sidelines and Services: Gifts, maps, teaching supplies, magazine
subscriptions

L. Kaplan Magazine and Book Search

P.O. Box 384, Cathedral Station New York, NY 10025
(212) 222-8028 • E-mail address: lkaplan310@aol.com
Form of payment: Checks
Type of store: Periodicals, mail order

Subject Specialties: Magazines/Journals/Newspapers
Owner: Larry Kaplan
Year Established: 1987
No. of Volumes: 2,000,000
Sidelines and Services: Search service
Comments: Specializes in vintage magazines from 1900
to the present.

Kauffman International Ltd.

P.O. Box 1672 New York, NY 10021
(212) 838-1080 Fax: (212) 755-3111
Hours: Mail order only
Form of payment: Visa, MC, Checks
Type of store: New
Subject Specialties: Equestrian • Riding
Manager: Charles Kauffman
Year Established: 1875
No. of Volumes: 1,000
Sidelines and Services: Videotapes, supplies for horses and riders

Kennedy Galleries Book Department

730 Fifth Ave. (bet. 56th & 57th Sts.) New York, NY 10019
(212) 541-9600 Fax: (212) 977-3833
Hours: Tue.-Sat. 10 A.M. to 6 P.M. Summer hours:
Mon.-Fri. 9:30 A.M. to 5:30 P.M.
Form of payment: Checks
Subject Specialties: Art - American

Manager: Lillian Brenwasser
Year Established: 1874
Sidelines and Services: Original art, prints
Catalogs: 6/year

Kinokuniya Bookstore

10 W. 49th St. (across from Rockefeller Plaza)
New York, NY 10020 • (212) 765-1461 Fax: (212) 541-9335
E-mail address: kinokuniya@kinokuniya.com
Hours: Mon.-Sun. 10 A.M. to 7:30 P.M.
Form of payment: Visa, MC, AMEX, Discover, JCB, Checks
Type of store: New
Subject Specialties: Japan (including Japanese Language
and Literature) • Martial Arts
General Manager: Eiichi Ichihashi
Sales Manager: John Fuller
Year Established: 1981
Sidelines and Services: CDs, stationery, greeting cards,
videotapes in Japanese
Catalogs: Annual catalog

Kitchen Arts and Letters

1435 Lexington Ave. (bet. 93rd & 94th Sts.)
New York, NY 10128 • (212) 876-5550 Fax: (212) 876-3584
Hours: Mon. 1 P.M. to 6 P.M.; Tue.-Fri. 10 A.M. to 6:30 P.M.;
Sat. 11 A.M. to 6 P.M. Closed Sat. during July & August.
During Summer, call to confirm hours.

Form of payment: Visa, MC (with $40 min. purchase), Checks
Type of store: New, antiquarian, mail order
Subject Specialties: Cooking • Wine • Health/Nutrition • Agriculture
Owner: Nahum Waxman
Year Established: 1983
No. of Volumes: 10,000 titles
Sidelines and Services: Free search service
Catalogs: 2-3/year (annotated list of new arrivals) free with self-addressed, stamped envelope

Judith and Peter Klemperer

400 Second Ave. (bet. 23rd & 24th Sts.)
New York, NY 10010 • (212) 684-5970 Fax: (212) 689-1499
Hours: By appointment only
Form of payment: Checks
Type of store: Antiquarian
Subject Specialties: New York City • Ephemera • New York State
Owners: Peter Klemperer, Judith Klemperer
Year Established: 1975
No. of Volumes: 5,000
Sidelines and Services: Sheet music, magazines, ephemera, postcards
Catalogs: Annual catalog (New York City books & ephemera)

Kolwyck-Jones Books on Art

588 Broadway, Suite 905 (bet. Prince & Houston Sts.)
New York, NY • (212) 663-3465

Hours: Mon. Noon to 5 P.M.; Tue.-Fri. Noon to 6 P.M.;
Sat. Noon to 5 P.M. August hours may vary.
Form of payment: Visa, MC, AMEX, Discover, Checks
Type of store: Antiquarian, mail order
Subject Specialties: Art - Modern • Art - American • Art - European
20th c. • Design • Art History • Architecture • Art - Reference
Owners: David Kolwyck, Dwight Owsley
Year Established: 1988
No. of Volumes: 20,000
Sidelines and Services: Books purchased
Catalogs: 4/year
Comments: Specializes in books about post-World War II
American and European painting and sculpture.

Koryo Books

35 W. 32nd St. (bet. Fifth & Sixth Aves.)
New York, NY 10001 • (212) 564-1844
Hours: Mon.-Sat. 9 A.M. to 8 P.M.; Sun. 12:30 P.M. to 7 P.M.
Form of payment: Visa, MC, AMEX, Checks
Type of store: New
Subject Specialties: Korea • Cooking • Alternative Medicine
• Religion - Oriental • Acupuncture
Owner: Eung Choi
Year Established: 1979
No. of Volumes: 50,000

Kosciuszko Foundation

15 E. 56th St. (bet. Madison & Fifth Aves.) New York, NY 10022
(212) 734-2130 or (800) 287-9956 Fax: (212) 628-4552
Hours: Mon.-Fri. 9 A.M. to 5 P.M.
Form of payment: Visa, MC, Checks
Type of store: New
Subject Specialties: Poland
Manager: Krystyna Gutt
Sidelines and Services: Art gallery
Catalogs: Free annual catalog
Comments: Sells books in English (primarily) about Poland,
as well as English translations of Polish authors.

H. P. Kraus Rare Books and Manuscripts

16 E. 46th St. (bet. Madison & Fifth Aves.) New York, NY 10017
(212) 687-4808 Fax: (212) 983-4790 • E-mail address:
hpkraus@maestro.com
Hours: Mon.-Fri. 9:30 A.M. to 5 P.M.
Form of payment: Visa, MC, AMEX
Type of store: Antiquarian
Subject Specialties: Early Printed Books • Incunabula • Americana
• Science • Books About Books/Bibliography • Illuminated
Manuscripts • Autographs/Manuscripts - Medieval
Year Established: 1932
No. of Volumes: 10,000
Catalogs: 3-4/year

Kendra Krienke

230 Central Park West (bet. 83rd & 84th Sts.)
New York, NY 10024 • (212) 580-6516 Fax: (201) 930-9765
Hours: By appointment only (call in advance)
Subject Specialties: Children's/Juvenile • llustrated Books
Managers: Kendra Krienke, Allan Daniel
Comments: Sells primarily original artwork—oils, watercolors, drawings—used in children's books from 1880 to 1950.

Madeline Kripke Books

317 W. 11th St. New York, NY 10014 • (212) 989-6832
Hours: By appointment only
Form of payment: Checks
Type of store: Antiquarian
Subject Specialties: Dictionaries/Encyclopedias • Linguistics
Owner: Madeline Kripke

Kubies

1227 Lexington Ave. (at 83rd St.) New York, NY 10021
(212) 744-3292
Hours: Mon-Fri: 9 A.M. to 7 P.M. / Sat: 9 A.M. to 6 P.M.
Form of payment: Visa, MC, AMEX, Discover, Diners Club, Checks
Type of store: New
Subject Specialties: Cooking • Environment/Conservation/Ecology • Health/Nutrition • Nature
Comments: This store is a branch of Good Earth Foods (see separate listing).

Kyobo Bookstore

22 W. 32nd St. (bet. Fifth & Sixth Aves.) New York, NY 10001
(212) 465-0923
Hours: Mon.-Sat. 9 A.M. to 8 P.M.
Form of payment: Visa, MC, AMEX, Checks
Type of store: New
Subject Specialties: Korea • Religion - Christianity • Bibles
Owner: James Ahn
Manager: Young Ahn
Year Established: 1980
No. of Volumes: 20,000
Sidelines and Services: Greeting cards, religious goods, maps
Catalogs: Semiannual catalog

La Bohemia Bookstore

3441 Broadway (bet. 140th & 141st Sts.) New York, NY 10031
(212) 862-5500
Hours: Mon.-Sun. 8 A.M. to 4 P.M.
Type of store: New
Subject Specialties: Spanish Language and Literature
Owner: V. Chinea
Sidelines and Services: Gifts, greeting cards, magazines, games

Lafayette Books

552 La Guardia Pl. (bet. Bleecker & W. 3rd Sts.)
New York, NY 10012 • (212) 260-1000 Fax: (212) 505-1517
Hours: Mon-Sat: 10 A.M. to 8 P.M.; Sun: 11 A.M. to 6 P.M.

Form of payment: Visa, MC
Type of store: New
Subject Specialties: International Affairs
Owner: Gerard Hamon
Sidelines and Services: Special orders

Landy Fine Judaica

80 Fifth Ave., #1206 (bet. 13th & 14th Sts.)
New York, NY 10011 • (212) 647-0743 Fax: (212) 647-0745
Hours: By appointment only
Form of payment: AMEX, Checks
Type of store: Antiquarian
Subject Specialties: Judaica • Art - Judaica
Owner: Michael Landy
Year Established: 1985

Last Word Used Books and Records

1181 Amsterdam Ave. (at corner of 118th St.)
New York, NY 10027 • (212) 864-0013
Hours: Mon.-Sat. 10 A.M. to 8 P.M.; Sun. 11 A.M. to 6 P.M.
Form of payment: Visa, MC, AMEX
Type of store: Used
Subject Specialties: African-American Studies • Literature -
General • Philosophy • History - General • Theology • Literary
Criticism • Psychology/Psychiatry • Classical Studies • Sociology
Owners: Dondi Clark, Karen Clark
Year Established: 1993   **No. of Volumes:** 15,000

Larry Lawrence Rare Sports

150 Fifth Ave., Rm 842 (at 20th St.) New York, NY 10024

(212) 362-8593 or (212) 255-9230

Hours: By appointment only

Form of payment: Checks

Type of store: Antiquarian, mail order

Subject Specialties: Sports • Golf • Sports Ephemera

Owner: Larry Lawrence

Year Established: 1978

No. of Volumes: 500

Catalogs: 8/year

Comments: Mailing address: P.O. Box 756, New York, NY 10024

Lectorum Publications

137 W. 14th St. (bet. Sixth & Seventh Aves.) New York, NY 10011

(212) 741-0220 or (212) 929-2833 Fax: (212) 727-3035

Hours: Mon.-Sat. 9:30 A.M. to 6:15 P.M.; Sun. Noon to 5 P.M.

Form of payment: Visa, MC, AMEX

Type of store: New, periodicals

Subject Specialties: Spanish Language and Literature • Foreign Language Instruction • Parapsychology • Cooking

Year Established: 1960

No. of Volumes: 60,000

Catalogs: Occasional catalogs

Janet Lehr

891 Park Ave. (at 79th St.) New York, NY 10021

(212) 288-1802 Fax: (212) 288-6234
Hours: By appointment only
Form of payment: Visa, MC, AMEX, Discover, Checks
Type of store: New, used, antiquarian
Subject Specialties: Photography • Asian Studies • Western Americana • Fashion/Costume/Clothing
Owner: Janet Lehr
Year Established: 1966
Sidelines and Services: Manuscripts, search service, journals
Catalogs: 4/year
Comments: Mailing address: P.O. Box 617, Gracie Station, New York, NY 10028

Barbara Leibowits Graphics Ltd.

E-mail address: artbooks@aol.com
Hours: By appointment only
Form of payment: Checks
Type of store: Antiquarian
Subject Specialties: Art - Art Deco • Art - Art Nouveau • Art - Russian/Soviet • Art - Modern • Art - Russian Avant-Garde • Art - Dadaism • Art - Surrealism • Art - Futurism • Art - Cubism • Book Arts • Livres d'Artiste • Illustrated Books • Prints/Drawings • Photography
Owner: Barbara Leibowits
Year Established: 1978
Sidelines and Services: Posters, drawings, prints
Catalogs: Annual catalog

Lenox Hill Bookstore

1018 Lexington Ave. (bet. 72nd & 73rd Sts.) New York, NY 10021
(212) 472-7170 Fax: (212) 772-1790
Hours: Mon.-Fri. 9:30 A.M. to 7 P.M. Sat. & Sun. 11 A.M. to 6 P.M.
Form of payment: Visa, MC, AMEX, Checks
Type of store: New
Subject Specialties: Biography/Autobiography • Art - General
• Literature - General • Children's/Juvenile • Travel
Manager: Lenny Golay
Year Established: 1995
Sidelines and Services: Free delivery in neighborhood, special orders
Catalogs: Free newsletter issued 4 times a year

J. Levine Books and Judaica

5 W. 30th St. (bet. Fifth Ave. and Broadway) New York, NY 10001
(212) 695-6888 or (800) 5-JEWISH Fax: (212) 643-1044
Hours: Sun. 10 A.M. to 5 P.M. except July; Mon.-Wed. 9 A.M.
to 6 P.M.; Thu. 9 A.M. to 7 P.M.; Fri. 9 A.M. to 2 P.M.
Form of payment: Visa, MC, AMEX, Discover
Type of store: New
Subject Specialties: Judaica • Bibles • Holocaust • Hebrew • Yiddish
Owner: Daniel Levine
Manager: Philip Kastel
Year Established: 1890
No. of Volumes: 500,000 (50,000 titles)
Sidelines and Services: Gifts, religious goods, school supplies,
Sunday school supplies, posters, prints, wholesale, video rentals
Comments: The entire inventory of this store is computerized.

Mona Levine

165 Park Row, #12F New York, NY 10038 • (212) 732-9878

Hours: By appointment only

Form of payment: Checks

Type of store: Antiquarian, mail order

Subject Specialties: Art History • Art - General • Art - Medieval • Art - Renaissance • Art - Modern • Art - Ancient • Art - Classical • Art - American • Architecture • Photography

Owners: Mona Levine, Bernard Levine

Year Established: 1990

Sidelines and Services: Maintains want lists

Liberation Bookstore, Inc.

421 Lenox Ave. (at 131st St.) New York, NY 10037
(212) 281-4615

Hours: Mon.-Fri. 11 A.M. to 7 P.M.; Sat. 11:30 A.M. to 6 P.M.

Type of store: New, periodicals, mail order

Subject Specialties: History - Africa • History - Latin America/ Caribbean • African-American Studies • Children's/Juvenile - Afrocentric • Cooking • Literature - African • Native Americans • Sociology - Afrocentric • Biography/Autobiography • Alternative Medicine • Anthropology • Art - African • Dictionaries/ Encyclopedias • Economics • Fiction - Crime/Mystery/Suspense • History - America - Civil War

Manager: Una G. Mulzac

Year Established: 1967   **No. of Volumes:** 5,000

Sidelines and Services: Greeting cards, maps, magazines, posters, tapes

Librairie Francaise

27 W. 20th St. New York, NY 10011 • (212) 463-9644
Hours: Mon.-Fri. 9 A.M. to 5 P.M. Mail and phone orders only.
Form of payment: Visa, MC, Checks
Type of store: Mail order
Subject Specialties: France (including French Language and Literature)
Manager: Philippe Lahmani

Librairie de France

SEE: French and European Publications

Libreria Hispanica

SEE: French and European Publications

LifeVisions

150-2 W. 10th St. (bet. Greenwich Ave. & Waverly Pl.)
New York, NY 10014 • (212) 691-6775 Fax: (212) 691-7314
E-mail address: lifevisions@pipeline.com
Hours: Mon.-Sat. Noon to 7:30 P.M.; Sun. 1 P.M. to 6 P.M.
Form of payment: Visa, MC, AMEX
Type of store: New
Subject Specialties: Astrology • Recovery • Personal Growth
Owner: Jim Stewart
Year Established: 1995   **No. of Volumes:** 2,000+
Sidelines and Services: Equinox horoscopes and interpretations

Lion Heart Autographs, Inc.

470 Park Ave. South, Penthouse (bet. 31st & 32nd Sts.)
New York, NY 10016 • (212) 779-7050 or (800) 969-1310
Fax: (212) 779-7066 • E-mail address: lhaautog@aol.com
Hours: By appointment only (Mon.-Fri. 9 A.M. to 6 P.M.)
Form of payment: Visa, MC, AMEX, Checks
Type of store: Antiquarian, mail order
Subject Specialties: Autographs/Manuscripts • Art - General
• History - General • Literature - General • Music • Science
• Signed Editions
President: David Lowenherz
Associate: Marcie S. Gitlin
Year Established: 1978
Sidelines and Services: Auction representation, appraisals, corporate and personal gifts
Catalogs: Semiannual (spring & autumn) catalog
Comments: Signed editions in stock are usually first editions. This store's Web site can be found at: http://www.lionheartinc.com

Lion's Den

230 E. 53rd St. (bet. Second & Third Aves.) New York, NY 10022
(212) 753-7800
Hours: Mon.-Thu. 9 A.M. to 12:30 A.M.; Fri.-Sat. 9 A.M.
to 1:30 A.M.; Sun. Noon to 11:30 P.M.
Form of payment: Visa, MC, AMEX
Type of store: New
Subject Specialties: Adult

Living Word Books

62 Thomas St. New York, NY 10013 • (212) 571-2644
Hours: Mon.-Thu. 10 A.M. to 6 P.M.; Fri. 10 A.M. to 7 P.M.;
Sat. 10 A.M. to 4 P.M.
Type of store: New
Subject Specialties: Religion - Christianity • Bibles

Logos Bookstore

1575 York Ave. (bet. 83rd & 84th Sts.) New York, NY 10028
(212) 517-7292 Fax: (212) 517-7399
Hours: Mon.-Fri. 8 A.M. to 6 P.M.; Sat. 10 A.M. to 6 P.M.;
Sun. Noon to 6 P.M.
Form of payment: Visa, MC, AMEX, Checks
Type of store: New
Subject Specialties: Religion - Christianity • Theology • Spirituality
• Bibles • General • Self-Help
Manager: Harris Healy III
Year Established: 1975
No. of Volumes: 8,000
Sidelines and Services: Greeting cards

James Lowe Autographs, Ltd.

30 E. 60th St., Suite 304 (bet. Madison & Park Aves.)
New York, NY 10022 • (212) 759-0775 Fax: (212) 759-2503
Hours: Mon.-Fri. 9:30 A.M. to 4:30 P.M.
Also open Sat. by appointment only.
Form of payment: Checks

Type of store: Antiquarian
Subject Specialties: Autographs/Manuscripts • First Editions
• Limited Editions • History - America - Colonial/Revolution
• History - America - Civil War • History - America - 19th c.
• Music • Signed Editions • Photography - 19th c. • Royalty
President: James Lowe
Gallery Manager: Sal Alberti
Year Established: 1970
Catalogs: 4/year
Comments: Specializes in autographs and manuscripts in the fields of music, art, science, literature, politics, Black history, and women's studies.

MJS Books and Graphics

9 E. 82nd St., Suite 3A (bet. Fifth & Madison Aves.)
New York, NY 10028 • (212) 517-8565 or (212) 535-4865
Fax: (212) 650-9561
Hours: By appointment only (Tue.-Sat.)
Form of payment: Checks
Type of store: Antiquarian
Subject Specialties: Prints/Drawings • Illustrated Books • Fine Printing • Art - European 20th c. • Art - Russian • Art - German Avant-Garde • Art - Dutch • Typography • Ephemera
Owner: Monica J. Strauss
Year Established: 1987
Catalogs: Free annual catalog
Comments: Books on Dutch art pertaining primarily to the early 20th century.

Macondo Books

221 W. 14th St. (bet. Seventh & Eighth Aves.)
New York, NY 10011 • (212) 741-3108
Hours: Mon.-Sat.: 10 A.M. to 6 P.M.
Subject Specialties: Spanish Language and Literature

Macy's Department Store
Book Department

151 W. 34th St., 7th fl. (bet. Broadway & Seventh Av.)
New York, NY 10001 • (212) 695-4400 ext. 2027
Hours: Mon.-Sat. 10 A.M. to 8:30 P.M. Sun. 11 A.M. to 7 P.M.
Form of payment: All major credit cards (+ Macy's), Checks
Type of store: New
Subject Specialties: General
Sidelines and Services: Videotapes

Madison Avenue Bookshop

833 Madison Ave. (bet. 69th & 70th Sts.) New York, NY 10021
(212) 535-6130 Fax: (212) 794-5231
Hours: Mon.-Sat. 10 A.M. to 6 P.M. Closed Sat. during summer.
Form of payment: Checks
Type of store: New
Subject Specialties: General • Art - American • First Editions
• History - General • Literature - General • Photography
• Signed Editions
Manager: Perry Haberman
Year Established: 1973

Sidelines and Services: Special order
Catalogs: Monthly newsletter
Comments: Also hosts author receptions and offers free delivery.

Magazine Center

1133 Broadway (bet. 25th & 26th Sts.) New York, NY 10010
(212) 929-5255 Fax: (212) 243-3609 • E-mail address:
quoyoon@dorsai.org
Hours: Mon.-Fri. 10 A.M. to 7 P.M.
Form of payment: Visa, MC, AMEX, Discover, Checks
Type of store: Mail order, antiquarian
Subject Specialties: Magazines/Journals/Newspapers
Owner: H. B. Quoyoon
Year Established: 1974
Sidelines and Services: Sheet music
Catalogs: Semiannual catalog
Comments: Specializes in general magazines from 1850 to 1990.

Andrew Makowsky Fine Books

63 Downing St., #7B (bet. Sixth & Seventh Aves., just north
of W. Houston St.) New York, NY 10014 • (212) 675-7789
Hours: By appointment only (Mon.-Sat. 10 A.M. to 6 P.M.)
Form of payment: Checks
Type of store: Used, used, mail order
Subject Specialties: Photography
Owner: Andrew Makowsky
Year Established: 1990

No. of Volumes: 2,000
Sidelines and Services: Maintains want lists
Catalogs: 4/year (free)

David Malamud Books

382 Central Park West, Suite 11-P (on 97th St., bet. Central Park West & Columbus Ave.) New York, NY 10025 • (212) 866-8478
Hours: By appointment only
Type of store: Antiquarian, used
Subject Specialties: Art - General • First Editions • New York City • Politics/Political Science
Owner: David Malamud
Year Established: 1989
No. of Volumes: 1000+
Sidelines and Services: Accepts want lists

Manhattan Comics and Cards

228 W. 23rd St. (bet. Seventh & Eighth Aves.)
New York, NY 10011 • (212) 243-9349
Hours: Mon.-Tue. 10 A.M. to 7 P.M.; Wed.-Thu., Sat. 10 A.M. to 9 P.M.; Fri. 10 A.M. to 9:30 P.M.; Sun. Noon to 8 P.M.
Form of payment: Visa, MC
Type of store: New
Subject Specialties: Comic Books
Owner: Jeff Rosoff

Manhattan Gaming Co.

66 W. 39th St. New York, NY 10018 • (212) 997-0880
Hours: Mon.-Fri. 10:30 A.M. to 7:30 P.M.
Subject Specialties: Games/Gambling

Isaac H. Mann

240 W. 98th St. (at Broadway) New York, NY 10025
(212) 423-6712 or (212) 666-1149
Hours: By appointment only
Form of payment: Checks
Type of store: Used, mail order
Subject Specialties: Judaica • Holocaust • Hebraica
Owner: Isaac H. Mann
Year Established: 1984
No. of Volumes: 10,000
Sidelines and Services: Search service (within specialties above)
Catalogs: Occasional lists

Martayan Lan

48 E. 57th St., 4th fl. (bet. Park & Madison Aves.)
New York, NY 10022 • (212) 308-0018 Fax: (212) 308-0074
E-mail address: martlan@aol.com
Hours: Mon.-Fri. 9:30 A.M. to 5:30 P.M. Other times by appointment.
Type of store: Antiquarian
Subject Specialties: Medicine • Architecture • Americana • Travel
• Maps/Atlases/Cartography • Science • Technology • Early Printed
Books • Fine Bindings

Owners: Richard Lan, Seyla Martayan
Year Established: 1985
No. of Volumes: 400
Catalogs: 4/year

Matchless Gifts

26 Second Ave. (corner of 1st St.) New York, NY 10003
(212) 420-1130
Subject Specialties: Religion - Oriental • Spirituality
• Vedic Scriptures
Manager: Kathleen Anderson
Year Established: 1966
No. of Volumes: 80 titles
Catalogs: Annual catalog

McGraw-Hill Bookstore

1221 Avenue of the Americas (at 49th St., lower plaza of the
McGraw-Hill bldg.) New York, NY 10020
(212) 512-4100 or (800) 352-3566 Fax: (212) 512-4105
E-mail address: mghbookstore@attmail.com
Hours: Mon.-Sat. 10 A.M. to 5:45 P.M.
Form of payment: Visa, MC, AMEX, Discover, Checks
Type of store: New
Subject Specialties: Business/Management • Computers
• Engineering • Science • Technology • Architecture • Design
Manager: Jason Pollock
Year Established: 1961

No. of Volumes: 150,000
Sidelines and Services: Computer software, calculators, CD-ROMs, audiotapes, author appearances

Isaac Mendoza Book Company

77 W. 85th St., Apt. 6F New York, NY 10024 • (212) 362-1129
Hours: By appointment only
Type of store: Antiquarian
Subject Specialties: Fiction - Crime/Mystery/Suspense • Fiction - Science Fiction
Owner: Walter Caron

Mercer Street Books and Records

206 Mercer St. (bet. Bleecker & Houston Sts.)
New York, NY 10012 • (212) 505-8615
Hours: Mon.-Thu. 10 A.M. to 10 P.M.; Fri.-Sat. 10 A.M. to Midnight; Sun. 11 A.M. to 10 P.M.
Form of payment: Visa, MC, Discover, Checks
Type of store: Used
Subject Specialties: Art - General • Cinema/Films • Literature - General • Performing Arts • Philosophy • Poetry • Psychoanalysis/Psychotherapy • Social Science/Cultural History
Owners: Wayne Conti, Stan Fogel
Year Established: 1990
No. of Volumes: 30,000
Sidelines and Services: CDs, books, and records purchased

Metropolis Comics and Collectibles

873 Broadway, Suite 201 New York, NY 10003

(212) 627-9691 Fax: (212) 627-5947

Hours: Mail order only

Form of payment: Visa, MC, AMEX, Checks

Type of store: Mail order

Subject Specialties: Comic Books • Posters • Cinema/Films

Owner: Steven Fishler

Year Established: 1988

No. of Volumes: 60,000

Catalogs: Semiannual catalog ($5.00 subscription)

Metropolitan Book Auction

123 W. 18th St., 4th fl. (bet. Sixth & Seventh Aves.)
New York, NY 10011 • (212) 463-0200 or (212) 929-4488
Fax: (212) 463-7099

Hours: Mon.-Fri. 10 A.M. to 5 P.M.

Type of store: Auction house

Subject Specialties: Auction House • Ephemera

Auction Manager: Arby Rolband

Sidelines and Services: Also holds auctions of postage stamps and fabric swatches

Catalogs: Monthly catalog ($75 for 1-year subscription)

Comments: Book auctions are held here once a month.

Metropolitan Book Center

123 W. 18th St., 4th fl. (bet. Sixth & Seventh Aves.)

New York, NY 10011 • (212) 929-4477
Hours: Tue.-Sat. 11 A.M. to 7 P.M. Closed Sun. & Mon.
Type of store: Antiquarian
Subject Specialties: Fine Bindings • Exploration/Voyages
• Colorplate Books • Americana • Books About Books/
Bibliography • Antiques/Collectibles
Director: Rebecca Myers
Year Established: 1996
No. of Volumes: 25,000
Sidelines and Services: Search service, archival supplies, seminars for collectors and dealers, book readings and signings

Metropolitan Book Kiosks

(3 locations, see below)
Hours: Mon.-Sun. 10 A.M. to Dusk (Weather Permitting)
Type of store: New, rare
Subject Specialties: General
Manager: Arby Rolband
Sidelines and Services: Prints, maps, postcards, CDs, LPs
Comments: 3 locations: 1) Roosevelt Tram Plaza (Second Ave., bet. 59th & 60th Sts.); 2) Fifth Ave., bet. 60th & 61st Sts., on Central Park sidewalk; 3) Columbus Circle, on sidewalk outside the Coliseum

Metropolitan Museum of Art Bookshop

1000 Fifth Ave. (bet. 82nd & 84th Sts.) New York, NY 10028
(212) 650-2911 Fax: (212) 794-2152

Hours: Sun., Tue.-Thu. 9:30 A.M. to 5:15 P.M.;
Fri. & Sat. 9:30 A.M. to 8:45 P.M. Closed Mon.
Form of payment: Visa, MC, AMEX, JCB, Discover, Checks
Type of store: New, periodicals, mail order
Subject Specialties: Classical Studies • Art - General
• Architecture • Arms and Armour • Fashion/Costume/Clothing
• Photography • Textiles • History - General • History - Ancient
• University Presses
Manager: Kathryn Wiebusch
Asst. Manager: Jeffrey Johnson
Year Established: 1979
No. of Volumes: 11,000
Sidelines and Services: Magazines, prints, art reproductions,
stationery

Metropolitan Museum of Art Bookshop—Cloisters Branch

Fort Tryon Park (at end of Ft. Washington Ave., near 192nd St.)
New York, NY 10040 • (212) 923-3700
Hours: Tue.-Sat. 9:30 A.M. to 5:15 P.M.
Form of payment: Visa, MC, AMEX, Checks
Type of store: New
Subject Specialties: History - Medieval/Renaissance • Art - Medieval/Renaissance
Manager: Carmen C. Lugay

Metropolitan Museum of Art Bookshop at Rockefeller Center

15 W. 49th St. (west of Fifth Ave., on south side of Rockefeller Center Promenade) New York, NY 10020 • (212) 332-1360
Fax: (212) 332-1390
Hours: Mon.-Fri. 10 A.M. to 7 P.M.; Sat. & Sun. 10 A.M. to 6 P.M.
Form of payment: Visa, MC, AMEX, JCB, Discover, Diners Club, Checks
Type of store: New
Subject Specialties: Art - General • New York City • Posters
• Children's/Juvenile • Gardening • Religion - Christianity • Judaica
• Scholarly Publications • Exhibition Catalogs
No. of Volumes: 300 titles

Metropolitan Opera Gift Shop

Lincoln Center
136 W. 65th St. (Columbus Ave. at 63rd St., inside lobby of Metropolitan Opera House) New York, NY 10023
(212) 580-4090
Hours: Mon.-Sat. 10 A.M. to 9:30 P.M.; Sun. Noon to 6 P.M.
Form of payment: Visa, MC, AMEX, Discover, Checks
Type of store: New
Subject Specialties: Opera • Music • Theater/Drama • Dance
Director: Meg Galea
Year Established: 1980
No. of Volumes: 3,500
Sidelines and Services: Cds, audiotapes, gifts, posters, games, videotapes
Catalogs: Semiannual catalog

Metropolitan Opera Gift Shop

835 Madison Ave. (bet. 69th & 70th Sts.) New York, NY 10021

(212) 734-8406

Hours: Mon.-Sat. 10 A.M. to 6 P.M.; Sun. Noon to 6 P.M.

Closed Sun. during the summer.

Form of payment: Visa, MC, AMEX, Checks

Type of store: New

Subject Specialties: Opera • Music • Theater/Drama • Dance

Jeryl Metz

697 West End Ave., #13A New York, NY 10025

(212) 864-3055 Fax: (212) 222-8048

Hours: Mon.-Fri. 12.30 P.M. to 5.30 P.M. (some Sats.)

Type of store: Used, antiquarian, mail order

Subject Specialties: Children's/Juvenile • Illustrated Books

Owner: Jeryl Metz

Year Established: 1989

No. of Volumes: 1,400

Catalogs: 5-6/year

The Military Bookman

29 E. 93rd St. (bet. Madison and Fifth Aves.)

New York, NY 10128 • (212) 348-1280

Hours: Tues-Sat: 10:30 A.M. to 5:30 P.M. Closed Sun. & Mon.

Form of payment: Visa, MC ($50 minimum), Checks

Type of store: Used, mail order

Subject Specialties: Military/War • Aviation • Nautical/Maritime

• Espionage/Intelligence • History - World Wars I and II
• Holocaust • Arms and Armor • Americana
Owners: Margaretta Colt, Harris Colt
Year Established: 1976
No. of Volumes: 12,000
Sidelines and Services: Prints, original World War II art
Catalogs: 4/year ($20 for 2 years; $25 foreign subscription)

The Mill Store

SEE: Dieu Donne Papermill

Millers

**117 E. 24th St. (bet. Park & Lexington Aves.) New York, NY 10010
(212) 673-1400**
Hours: Mon.-Wed., Fri., Sat.: 10 A.M. to 6 P.M.;
Thu. 10 A.M. to 7 P.M.
Form of payment: Visa, MC, AMEX, Discover, Checks
Type of store: New, used
Subject Specialties: Equestrian
Manager: Robert MacCury
Year Established: 1912

Monographs Ltd.

**124 W. 25th St. (bet. Sixth & Seventh Aves.)
New York, NY 10001 • (212) 604-9510 Fax: (212) 604-0959
E-mail address: monographs@msn.com**

Hours: Tue.-Sun. 11 A.M. to 6 P.M.
Form of payment: Visa, MC, AMEX, Checks
Type of store: New, used
Subject Specialties: Photography
Owners: Lawrence Lesman, Joyce Hoffman

Moria Libreria

628 W. 207th St. (bet. Broadway & Cooper Sts.)
New York, NY 10034 • (212) 304-2197
Hours: Mon.-Sat. 10 A.M. to 7 P.M.
Subject Specialties: Spanish Language and Literature

Morton: The Interior Design Bookshop

989 Third Ave. (bet. 58th & 59th Sts.) New York, NY 10022
(212) 421-9025
Hours: Mon.-Thu., Sat. 11 A.M. to 7 P.M.; Fri. 11 A.M. to 6 P.M.
Form of payment: Visa, MC, AMEX
Type of store: New
Subject Specialties: Design • Architecture
Owner: Morton Dosik

Mount Sinai Medical Bookstore

1 Gustave Levy Pl. (100th St. & Madison Ave., inside lobby of
Mount Sinai Hospital) New York, NY 10029
(212) 241-2665 Fax: (212) 534-1499
Hours: Mon.-Fri. 9 A.M. to 5 P.M.

Form of payment: Visa, MC, AMEX, Checks
Type of store: New
Subject Specialties: Medicine
Manager: Stephen Underberg
Year Established: 1975
No. of Volumes: 6,000
Sidelines and Services: Stationery, computer software, computer accessories, video rentals, medical equipment

Murder Ink

1467 Second Ave. (bet. 76th & 77th Sts.)
New York, NY 10021 • (212) 517-3222
Hours: Mon.-Sat. 10 A.M. to 10 P.M.; Sun. 11 A.M. to 9 P.M.
Form of payment: Visa, MC, AMEX
Type of store: New, used, antiquarian, periodicals, mail order
Subject Specialties: Fiction - Crime/Mystery/Suspense
• Children's/Juvenile - Mysteries • Writer's Guides
Manager: Margot Liddell
Year Established: 1985
No. of Volumes: 5,000
Sidelines and Services: Gift book baskets, free delivery in neighborhood, book signings
Catalogs: 4/year

Murder Ink

2486 Broadway (bet. 92nd & 93rd Sts.) New York, NY 10025
(212) 362-8905 or (800) 488-8123

Hours: Mon.-Sat. 10 A.M. to 7:30 P.M.; Sun. 11 A.M. to 6 P.M.
Form of payment: Visa, MC, AMEX, Checks
Type of store: New, used
Subject Specialties: Fiction - Crime/Mystery/Suspense
• Espionage/Intelligence • First Editions • Sherlock Holmes
Owner: Jay Pearsall
Year Established: 1972
No. of Volumes: 25,000
Sidelines and Services: Games, posters, records, stationery
Catalogs: 4/year

Museum of American Folk Art Museum Shop

**62 W. 50th St. (bet. Fifth & Sixth Aves.) New York, NY 10020
(212) 247-5611**
Hours: Mon.-Sat. 10:30 A.M. to 5:30 P.M.
Form of payment: Visa, MC, AMEX
Type of store: New
Subject Specialties: Folk Art • Art - American
Manager: Rita Pollett
Sidelines and Services: Greeting cards

Museum of American Folk Art Museum Shop

**2 Lincoln Square (Columbus Ave., bet. 65th & 66th Sts.)
New York, NY 10023 • (212) 496-2966**
Hours: Mon. 11 A.M. to 6 P.M.; Tue.-Fri. 11 A.M. to 7:30 P.M.;

Sat. 11 A.M. to 7 P.M.; Sun. 11 A.M. to 6 P.M.

Form of payment: Visa, MC, AMEX

Type of store: New

Subject Specialties: Folk Art • Art - American

Manager: Marie DiManno

Sidelines and Services: Greeting cards

Museum of Modern Art Bookstore

11 W. 53rd St. (bet. Fifth & Sixth Aves.) New York, NY 10019

(212) 708-9700

Hours: Mon.-Tue., Sat.-Sun. 11 A.M. to 6:30 P.M.;
Thu.-Fri. 11 A.M. to 9 P.M. Closed Wed.

Form of payment: Visa, MC, AMEX

Type of store: New

Subject Specialties: Art - Modern • Design • Photography
• Architecture • Cinema/Films • Sculpture

Manager: John Weatherman

Year Established: 1939

No. of Volumes: 3,500 titles

Sidelines and Services: Games, gifts, greeting cards, art reproductions, posters, videotapes, design objects

Museum of Television and Radio Gift Shop

25 W. 52nd St. (bet. Fifth & Sixth Aves.) New York, NY 10019

(212) 621-6880

Hours: Tue.-Wed. Noon to 6 P.M.; Thu. Noon to 8 P.M.;

Fri. Noon to 9 P.M.; Sat.-Sun. Noon to 6 P.M. Closed Mon.

Form of payment: Visa, MC, AMEX, Checks

Type of store: New

Subject Specialties: Radio/Television

Manager: John Horvath

Year Established: 1991

No. of Volumes: 700

Sidelines and Services: Videotapes, audio cassettes, TV and radio memorabilia

Museum of the City of New York Museum Shop

1220 Fifth Ave. (at 103rd St.) New York, NY 10029

(212) 534-1672 ext. 230 or 227 Fax: (212) 534-5974

Hours: Wed.-Sat. 10 A.M. to 5 P.M.; Sun. 1 P.M. to 5 P.M. Closed Mon. & Tue.

Form of payment: Visa, MC, AMEX

Type of store: New

Subject Specialties: New York City • Fashion/Costume/Clothing • Theater/Drama • Decorative Arts • Architecture • Children's/ Juvenile • Exhibition Catalogs

Manager: Ann B. Goldsmith

Year Established: 1923

No. of Volumes: 600 titles

Sidelines and Services: Prints, toys (including antique replicas), posters, postcards, dolls, stationery, videotapes, jewelry, original photographic reproductions

Comments: Includes New York City art and exhibition catalogs.

Music Inn

169 W. Fourth St. (bet. Sixth & Seventh Aves.)
New York, NY 10014 • (212) 243-5715
Hours: Tue.-Sat. 1 P.M. to 7 P.M.
Type of store: New, used
Subject Specialties: Music • Art - General • Ethnic Studies
Owner: G. Halpern
Sidelines and Services: Instruction books

The Mysterious Bookshop

129 W. 56th St. (bet. Sixth & Seventh Aves.) New York, NY 10019
(212) 765-0900 or (800) 352-2840 Fax: (212) 265-5478
Hours: Mon.-Sat. 11 A.M. to 7 P.M. Closed the week of July 4th.
Form of payment: Visa, MC, AMEX, Discover
Type of store: New, used, antiquarian, mail order
Subject Specialties: Fiction Crime/Mystery/Suspense
• Espionage/Intelligence • Sherlock Holmes
President: Otto Penzler
Manager: Diane Plumley
Year Established: 1979
No. of Volumes: 40,000 (15,000 titles)
Sidelines and Services: Autographed books, search service,
mail order
Catalogs: 2-3/year

National Academy of Design Bookshop

1083 Fifth Ave. (bet. 89th & 90th Sts.) New York, NY 10128

(212) 369-4880

Hours: Wed.-Thu. 10 A.M. to 5 P.M.; Fri. Noon to 8 P.M.;
Sat.-Sun. Noon to 5 P.M. Closed Mon. & Tue.

Form of payment: Visa, MC, AMEX, Checks

Type of store: New

Subject Specialties: Design

National Museum of the American Indian (Smithsonian Institution) Bookshop

1 Bowling Green (4 blocks north of Staten Island Ferry terminal)
New York, NY 10004 • (212) 825-8093/8094 Fax: (212) 825-8083

Hours: Mon.-Sun. 10 A.M. to 4:45 P.M. Closed Christmas Day.

Form of payment: Visa, MC, AMEX, Discover, Checks

Type of store: New

Subject Specialties: Native Americans • History - General • Crafts
• Jewelry • Maps/Atlases/Cartography • Design • Children's/Juvenile
• Art - Native American

Manager: Mercedes Reyes

Asst. Manager: Holly Seal

Year Established: 1922

No. of Volumes: 1,500 titles

Naturalist's Bookshelf

540 W. 114th St. (bet. Broadway & Amsterdam Ave.)
New York, NY 10025 • (212) 865-6202 Fax: (212) 865-2718

Hours: Mon.-Fri. 9 A.M. to 6 P.M.

Form of payment: Checks

Type of store: Antiquarian, used, periodicals, mail order
Subject Specialties: Natural History • Exploration/Voyages
• Fine Bindings • Incunabula • Illustrated Books • Birds
Owner: Herman W. Kitchen
Year Established: 1972
No. of Volumes: 6,000
Sidelines and Services: Appraise library collections, prints
Catalogs: Semiannual catalog

The New Museum of Contemporary Art Bookshop

583 Broadway (bet. Prince & Houston Sts.)
New York, NY 10012 • (212) 219-1222 Fax: (212) 431-5328
Hours: Wed.-Fri., Sun. Noon to 6 P.M.; Sat. Noon to 8 P.M.
Closed Mon. & Tue.
Form of payment: Visa, MC, Checks
Type of store: New
Subject Specialties: Art - Modern • Art - Post Modern
Director: Marcia Tucker
Year Established: 1983
No. of Volumes: 38

New York Astrology Center

124 E. 40th St., Suite 402 (bet. Lexington & Park Aves.)
New York, NY 10016 • (212) 949-7211 Fax: (212) 949-7274
E-mail address: afund@aol.com
Hours: Wed.-Fri. 11 A.M. to 6:30 P.M.; Sat. 11 A.M. to 5 P.M.;

Mon.-Tue. by appointment
Form of payment: Visa, MC, AMEX
Type of store: New, mail order
Subject Specialties: Astrology
President: Henry Weingarten
Year Established: 1968
No. of Volumes: 5,000
Sidelines and Services: Computer software, computer-calculated astrology charts, astrology classes, consultations
Catalogs: Annual catalog ($2 subscription)

New York Bible Society

139 W. 57th St. (bet. Sixth & Seventh Aves.)
New York, NY 10019 • (212) 315-0230 Fax: (212) 974-1945
Hours: Mon., Wed. 10 A.M. to 7 P.M.; Tue., Thu.-Fri. 10 A.M. to 6 P.M.
Form of payment: Visa, MC
Type of store: New
Subject Specialties: Bibles

New York Bound Bookshop

50 Rockefeller Plaza (bet. 50th & 51st Sts., inside "AP" bldg.)
New York, NY 10020 • (212) 245-8503 Fax: (212) 245-8701
Hours: Mon.-Fri. 10 A.M. to 5:30 P.M.; Sat. Noon to 4 P.M.
Closed Sat. during summer.
Form of payment: Visa, MC, AMEX
Type of store: New, used, antiquarian
Subject Specialties: New York City • New York State

Owners: Barbara L. Cohen, Judith Stonehill
Year Established: 1976
No. of Volumes: 4,000
Sidelines and Services: Prints, photographs, search service
Catalogs: Annual catalog

New-York Historical Society Museum Shop

170 Central Park West (at 76th St.) New York, NY 10024
(212) 873-3400
Hours: Wed.-Sun. Noon to 5 P.M.
Form of payment: Visa, MC
Type of store: New
Subject Specialties: New York City • History - America 19th c.

New York Institute of Technology Bookstore

1855 Broadway (bet. 60th & 61st Sts.)
New York, NY 10023 • (212) 261-1551
Hours: Mon.-Thu. 10 A.M. to 4 P.M.; Fri. 10 A.M. to 3 P.M.
Form of payment: Visa, MC, AMEX, Checks
Type of store: New
Subject Specialties: Technology
Manager: John Femia
Comments: Operated by Barnes & Noble.

New York Is Book Country Fair

Outdoor annual book fair on Fifth Avenue, below 57th Street.
On a Sun. in mid-September. Predominantly book publishers'
exhibits; but the "Antiquarian Row" section of the fair brings
together about 20 or 30 used and antiquarian dealers.

New York Law School Bookstore

57 Worth St. (bet. Church St. & West Broadway)
New York, NY 10013 • (212) 431-2315
Hours: Mon.-Thu. Noon to 6:30 P.M.; Fri. 10 A.M. to 3 P.M.
Form of payment: Visa, MC, AMEX, Discover
Type of store: New
Subject Specialties: Law
Manager: Dan Nedding
Comments: Operated by Barnes & Noble.

New York Nautical Instrument and Service Corp.

140 West Broadway (at Thomas St.) New York, NY 10013
(212) 962-4522 Fax: (212) 406-8420
Hours: Mon.-Fri. 9 A.M. to 5 P.M.; Sat. 9 A.M. to Noon.
Closed Sat. June through August.
Form of payment: Visa, MC, AMEX
Type of store: New, used, periodicals, mail order
Subject Specialties: Nautical/Maritime • Boating • Navigation
• Ships • Cruising Guides (boating)
Owners: Herbert Maisler, Kenneth Maisler

Year Established: 1965
No. of Volumes: 5,000
Sidelines and Services: Nautical charts, government publications, stationery, ships' clocks, barometers, binoculars

New York Open Center Bookstore

83 Spring St. (bet. Broadway and Crosby St.) New York, NY 10012 • (212) 219-2527 ext. 109 Fax: (212) 219-1347
Hours: Mon.-Fri. 11:30 A.M. to 7:20 P.M.; Sat. 11 A.M. to 7:30 P.M.; Sun. Noon to 6 P.M.
Form of payment: Visa, MC, AMEX
Type of store: New, periodicals, mail order
Subject Specialties: New Age • Health/Nutrition • Psychology/Psychiatry • Religion - General • Religion - Oriental • Women's Studies • Alternative Medicine • Native Americans • Metaphysics • Holistics
Manager: Alyssa Bonilla
Year Established: 1985
Sidelines and Services: Special order, jewelry, incense, video-tapes, greeting cards, audiotapes, music
Catalogs: Gift catalog + course catalog (3 times/year)

The Book Store of the New York Psychoanalytic Institute

247 E. 82nd St. (bet. Second & Third Aves.)
New York, NY 10028 • (212) 772-8282 Fax: (212) 879-0588
E-mail address: mvu@pipeline.com

Hours: Mon.-Thu. 9 A.M. to 8 P.M.; Fri. 9 A.M. to 4 P.M.
Form of payment: Visa, MC, AMEX
Type of store: New, used, mail order
Subject Specialties: Psychoanalysis/Psychotherapy
• Psychology/Psychiatry
Manager: Richard Schweitzer
Year Established: 1989
No. of Volumes: 1,500

New York Public Library Bookstore

Fifth Ave. & 42nd St. New York, NY 10018
(212) 930-0641 Fax: (212) 930-0849
Hours: Mon., Thu.-Sat. 10 A.M. to 5:45 P.M.;
Tue.-Wed. 11 A.M. to 6 P.M.
Form of payment: Visa, MC, AMEX, Checks
Type of store: New, mail order
Subject Specialties: Literature - General • Books About
Books/Bibliography • Children's/Juvenile • Reference • New York
City • Literature - General • Poetry • Fine Printing • Art - General
• New York Public Library
Manager: Hope Van Winkle
Sidelines and Services: Gifts, posters, toys, tickets to library
lectures, note cards, exhibition merchandise
Catalogs: Journal "Biblion" ($60 per year)
Comments: The Library Bookstore carries publications of the
New York Public Library, as well as catalogs of the many
exhibitons held at the library.

New York Theological Seminary Bookstore

5 W. 29th St., 8th fl. (bet. Fifth Ave. & Broadway)
New York, NY 10001 • (212) 532-4012 Fax: (212) 684-0757
Hours: Mon.-Thu. Noon to 7:30 P.M.; Fri. Noon to 6:30 P.M.;
Sat. 10 A.M. to 3 P.M.
Form of payment: Visa, MC, AMEX, Discover, Checks
Type of store: New
Subject Specialties: Religion - Christianity • Theology
Manager: Brenda L. Harris
No. of Volumes: 10,000
Sidelines and Services: School supplies

New York University Book Center— Main Branch

18 Washington Pl. (1/2 block east of Washington Square Park)
New York, NY 10003 • (212) 998-4667 Fax: (212) 995-4118
Hours: Mon.-Thu. 10 A.M. to 7:15 P.M.; Fri. 10 A.M. to 6 P.M.;
Sat. 10 A.M. to 6 P.M. Summer hours vary.
Form of payment: Visa, MC, AMEX, Checks
Type of store: New, used, periodicals, mail order
Subject Specialties: Academic • University Presses • Cinema/Films
• Literary Criticism • Literature - General • Women's Studies
Manager: Jo Ann McGreevy
Year Established: 1930
No. of Volumes: 25,000
Sidelines and Services: Stationery supplies, consumer electronics, school-related clothing and gifts

New York University Book Store— Computer Store

242 Greene St. (bet. W. 4th St. & Washington Pl.)

New York, NY 10003 • (212) 998-4672 Fax: (212) 995-3779

Hours: Mon.-Sat. 10 A.M. to 6 P.M.

Form of payment: Visa, MC, AMEX

Type of store: New

Subject Specialties: Computers • Mathematics • Physics
• Electronics

Manager: Kathy Bear

Year Established: 1992

No. of Volumes: 6,000

New York University Book Store— Health Sciences Bookstore

333 E. 29th St. (bet. First & Second Aves.)

New York, NY 10016 • (212) 998-9990 Fax: (212) 725-9296

E-mail address: health.books@nyu.edu

Hours: Mon.-Thu. 10 A.M. to 7 P.M.; Fri. 10 A.M. to 6 P.M.;
Sat. 11 A.M. to 5 P.M.

Form of payment: Visa, MC, AMEX, Checks

Type of store: New

Subject Specialties: Dentistry • Medicine • Health/Nutrition • Nursing

Manager: Bruno Plate

Year Established: 1995

No. of Volumes: 5,000 titles

Sidelines and Services: Stationery, medical instruments

New York University Book Center— Professional Bookstore

530 La Guardia Pl. (bet. West 3rd & Bleecker Sts.)
New York, NY 10012 • (212) 998-4680
Hours: Mon.-Thu. 10 A.M. to 7 P.M.; Fri. 10 A.M. to 6 P.M.;
Sat. Noon to 6 P.M.
Form of payment: Visa, MC, AMEX, Checks
Type of store: New
Subject Specialties: Business/Management • Public Service
Manager: Wendy Myers

Nudel Books

135 Spring St. (bet. Wooster & Green Sts.) New York, NY 10012
(212) 966-5624
Hours: By appointment only
Form of payment: Checks
Type of store: Antiquarian
Subject Specialties: Photography • Art - Reference • First Editions
• Limited Editions • Illustrated Books • Design • Holocaust
• Literature - African-American
Owner: Harry Nudel
Year Established: 1981
No. of Volumes: 30,000
Sidelines and Services: Appraise library collections, original art
Catalogs: Occasionally

Nur Al-Haqq Book Store

1711 Third Ave. (bet. 96th & 97th Sts., inside mosque)
New York, NY 10029 • (212) 996-7323
Hours: Mon.-Sun. Noon to 10 P.M.
Type of store: New
Subject Specialties: Religion - Islam

OAN / Oceanie Afrique Noire Art Books

15 W. 39th St., 2nd fl. (bet. Fifth & Sixth Aves.)
New York, NY 10018 • (212) 840-8844 Fax: (212) 840-3304
Hours: Mon.-Fri. 10 P.M. to 5:30 P.M. Other hours by appointment.
Form of payment: Visa, MC, AMEX, Discover
Type of store: New, used, rare
Subject Specialties: Art - African • Art - Australia/Oceania
• Art - Pre-Columbian • Art - Native American • Art - Caribbean
• Art - Southeast Asian • Ethnology • Architecture - African
• Architecture - Australia/Oceania • Architecture - Pre-Columbian
• Architecture - Native American • Architecture - Caribbean
• Architecture - Southeast Asian • Textiles • Anthropology
President: G. M. Feher
Year Established: 1967
No. of Volumes: 100,000
Sidelines and Services: Appraisals, auction catalogs
Catalogs: Free semiannual catalog

Irving Oaklander Books

547 W. 27th St., Rm. 540 (bet. Tenth & Eleventh Aves.)

New York, NY 10001 • (212) 594-4210
Hours: Mon.-Sat. 9:30 A.M. to 4:30 P.M. by previous
appointment only.
Form of payment: Checks
Type of store: Used, antiquarian, periodicals, mail order
Subject Specialties: Books About Books/Bibliography • Graphic
Arts • Art - Modern • Typography • Publishing • Calligraphy
• Private Press • Advertising Art • Poster Books • Book Collecting
• Book Plates
Owner: Irving Oaklander
Manager: Lenore Oaklander
Year Established: 1989
No. of Volumes: 7,000
Catalogs: Periodic catalogs
Comments: Also stocks books about vintage advertising art
of the 20th century.

Old Paper Archive

122 W. 25th St. (bet. Sixth & Seventh Aves.)
New York, NY 10001 • (212) 645-3983
Hours: Mon-Sun: 10 A.M. to 6 P.M.
Form of payment: Visa, MC, AMEX, Checks
Type of store: Used, antiquarian, periodicals
Subject Specialties: Opera • Ballet • Theatre/Drama • Cinema/Films
• Children's/Juvenile • Prints/Drawings • Woodcuts
No. of Volumes: 4,000
Comments: The Archive has approximately 30,000 prints in stock.

The Old Print Shop

150 Lexington Ave. (bet. 29th & 30th Sts.) New York, NY 10016
(212) 683-3950 Fax: (212) 779-8040
Hours: Mon.-Thu. 9 A.M. to 5 P.M.; Fri.-Sat. 9 A.M. to 4 P.M.
Closed on Sat., June through September.
Type of store: Antiquarian
Subject Specialties: Americana • Prints/Drawings
• Maps/Atlases/Cartography
Owner: Kenneth M. Newman

Oriental Culture Enterprises

13-17 Elizabeth St., 2nd fl. (south of Canal St.)
New York, NY 10013 • (212) 226-8461 Fax: (212) 431-6695
Hours: Mon.-Sun. 10 A.M. to 7 P.M.
Type of store: New
Subject Specialties: China (including Chinese Language
and Literature)
Sidelines and Services: Periodicals, paintings, stationery, CDs,
audiotapes

Oscar Wilde Memorial Bookshop

15 Christopher St. (bet. Sixth & Seventh Aves., near Gay St.)
New York, NY 10014 • (212) 255-8097
Hours: Mon.-Fri. 11:30 A.M. to 8:30 P.M.; Sat. Noon to 7 P.M.
Form of payment: Checks, Visa, MC, AMEX, Discover
Type of store: New, used, periodicals, mail order
Subject Specialties: Gay/Lesbian Studies

Owner: William Offenbaker
Manager: Marli Higa
Year Established: 1967
No. of Volumes: 5,000
Sidelines and Services: Greeting cards, magazines, posters, video rentals, pamphlets, buttons, flags, gay liberation paraphernalia, lesbian/gay music
Catalogs: 10/year (lifetime subscription, $5.00; overseas, $10.00)
Comments: Founded by Craig Rodwell in 1967, this shop also carries books and literature with pertinent community information.

Pace University Bookstore

1 Pace Plaza (bet. Spruce St. & Park Row)
New York, NY 10038 • (212) 349-8580 Fax: (212) 374-1317
Hours: Mon.-Thu. 9 A.M. to 7 P.M.; Fri. 9 A.M. to 3 P.M.
Form of payment: Visa, MC, AMEX, Discover, Checks
Type of store: New
Subject Specialties: Literature - General • Accounting
• Business/Management • Reference
Manager: Robert J. Masto
Year Established: 1990
No. of Volumes: 75,000 (6,000 titles)
Comments: Operated by Barnes & Noble.

Pageant Book and Print Shop

114 W. Houston St. (bet. Sullivan & Thompson Sts.)
New York, NY 10012 • (212) 674-5296 Fax: (212) 674-2609

Hours: Tue.-Sat. Noon to 8 P.M.; Sun. Noon to 7 P.M.
Form of payment: Visa, MC, AMEX, Checks
Type of store: Antiquarian, rare, used
Subject Specialties: Art - General • Literature - General
• Prints/Drawings • History - General • Americana
• Maps/Atlases/Cartography • Incunabula • Ephemera
Owner: Shirley Solomon
Year Established: 1945
No. of Volumes: 250,000

Fred and Elizabeth Pajerski

250 W. 24th St., #4-GE (bet. Seventh & Eighth Aves.)
New York, NY 10011 • (212) 255-6501 Fax: (212) 255-6501
Hours: By appointment only
Form of payment: Checks
Type of store: New, used, antiquarian, mail order
Subject Specialties: Photography • Photography - 19th c.
• Photography - History
Owners: Fred Pajerski, Elizabeth Pajerski
Year Established: 1984
No. of Volumes: 8,000 (3,500 titles)
Catalogs: 4-5/year (free)

Paperback Discounter—Video 83

2517 Broadway (bet. 93rd & 94th Sts.) New York, NY 10025
(212) 662-1718
Hours: Mon.-Sun. 11 A.M. to 11 P.M.

Type of store: New
Subject Specialties: Fiction - Crime/Mystery/Suspense

Papyrus Booksellers

2915 Broadway (at 114th St.) New York, NY 10025 *[handwritten: 112th Street btwn Broadway and Amsterdam]*
(212) 222-3350 Fax: (212) 316-7832
Hours: Mon.-Sun. 10 A.M. to 11 P.M.
Form of payment: Visa, MC, AMEX, Checks
Type of store: New, used
Subject Specialties: Psychology/Psychiatry • Computers
• Literature - General
Owner: Siggy Caban
Sidelines and Services: College supplies, magazines, posters

Paraclete Book Center

146 E. 74th St. (bet. Third & Lexington Aves.)
New York, NY 10021 • (212) 535-4050
Hours: Tue.-Fri. 10 A.M. to 6 P.M.; Sat. 10 A.M. to 5 P.M.
Closed Sun. & Mon.
Form of payment: Visa, MC, Checks
Type of store: New
Subject Specialties: Theology • Academic
Manager: Mary C. Butler
Year Established: 1951
Sidelines and Services: Shipping worldwide, gift wrapping,
special orders

Partners & Crime Mystery Booksellers

44 Greenwich Ave. (bet. Sixth & Seventh Aves.)
New York, NY 10011 • (212) 243-0440
E-mail address: partners@mail.gw.com
Hours: Mon.-Thu. Noon to 10 P.M.; Fri.-Sat. Noon to 11 P.M.;
Sun. 12 Noon to 8 P.M.
Form of payment: Visa, MC, AMEX
Type of store: New, used, antiquarian, periodicals, mail order
Subject Specialties: Fiction - Crime/Mystery/Suspense • First
Editions • Espionage/Intelligence • Magazines/Journals/
Newspapers • Prints/Drawings • Gay/Lesbian Studies • Children's/
Juvenile • Criminology • Sherlock Holmes
Partner: John Douglas
Year Established: 1994
No. of Volumes: 20,000
Sidelines and Services: Original crime-book cover art, puzzles and
games, mysterious events, rental library, vintage mystery radio
show performances, readings, writers' forum, crime-writing classes
Catalogs: Free catalog, first-editions catalog

Joseph Patelson Music House, Ltd.

160 W. 56th St. (bet. Sixth & Seventh Aves.) New York, NY 10019
(212) 757-5587 or (212) 582-5840 Fax: (212) 246-5633
Hours: Mon.-Sat. 9 A.M. to 6 P.M. Summer hours:
Mon.-Fri. 9 A.M. to 6 P.M. Closed Sat. July & August.
Form of payment: Visa, MC, AMEX, Discover, Checks (with I.D.)
Type of store: New, used, mail order, periodicals
Subject Specialties: Music • Opera • Biography/Autobiography

• Performing Arts • Music Theory
Owner: Daniel Patelson
Manager: Carlos Vazquez
Year Established: 1929
No. of Volumes: 7,500 (2,000 titles)
Sidelines and Services: Sheet music, metronomes, music stands, tuning forks, composers' portraits, batons
Catalogs: Semiannual catalog

Pathfinder Books

214 Avenue A (bet. 13th & 14th Sts.) New York, NY 10009
(212) 388-9346 Fax: (212) 388-1659
Hours: Tue.-Fri. 5:30 P.M. to 9:30 P.M.; Sat.-Sun. 11 A.M. to 6 P.M.
Form of payment: Checks
Type of store: New, mail order
Subject Specialties: Spanish Language and Literature • Industry • France (including French Language and Literature) • African-American Studies • Women's Studies • History - General • Latin America • Politics/Political Science • Marxism
Manager: Wendy Lyons
Year Established: 1994
No. of Volumes: 10,000
Sidelines and Services: Fri. evening programs
Catalogs: Free annual catalog
Comments: Mailing address: P.O. Box 2652, New York, NY 10009

Paths Untrodden Book Service

P.O. Box 3245, Grand Central Station
New York, NY 10163 • (212) 661-5997 Fax: (212) 661-5997
E-mail address: 75143.1664@compuserve.com
Hours: Mail order only
Type of store: New, used, antiquarian, mail order
Subject Specialties: Gay/Lesbian Studies • Erotica/Curiosa
• Transvestitism • Men's Studies
Owner: Walter J. Phillips
Year Established: 1979
No. of Volumes: 3,000
Sidelines and Services: Magazine back issues, search service,
videotapes
Catalogs: Annual catalog; booklist
Comments: Also specializes in books specifically related to male
homosexuality.

Pauline Books & Media

150 E. 52nd St. (bet. Lexington & Third Aves.)
New York, NY 10022 • (212) 754-1110 Fax: (212) 754-2268
E-mail address: fspnyc@aol.com
Hours: Mon.-Thu. 9:30-5:30 P.M.; Fri. 9:30 A.M. to 6 P.M.;
Sat. 10 A.M. to 5:30 P.M.
Form of payment: Visa, MC, AMEX
Type of store: New, periodicals, mail order
Subject Specialties: Religion - Christianity • Biography/
Autobiography • Children's/Juvenile • Christmas • Spanish
Language and Literature • Metaphysics • Radio/Television

• Theology • Spirituality
Manager: Sister Denise Cecilia
Year Established: 1976
No. of Volumes: 10,000
Sidelines and Services: Video rentals, monthly lecture series, audiotapes, CDs, chapel
Catalogs: Free annual catalog
Comments: Formerly known as the St. Paul Book & Media Center/Daughters of St. Paul Bookstore, this store also has a chapel on the premises.

Paulist Book and Gift Shop

SEE: Church of St. Paul the Apostle Book and Gift Shop

Evelyn Pearl

219 W. 81st St., Apt. 5A New York, NY 10024
(212) 877-1704 Fax: (212) 787-3466
Hours: By appointment only (Please call first)
Form of payment: Checks
Type of store: Used, mail order
Subject Specialties: Holocaust • Judaica • Literary Criticism
• Children's/Juvenile
Owner: Evelyn Pearl
Catalogs: 2-3/year

Penn Books

**1 Penn Plaza (Penn Station, 32nd St. & Seventh Ave.,
Long Island Railroad Level) New York, NY 10119
(212) 239-0311 or (212) 239-7433**
Hours: Mon.-Fri. 7:30 A.M. to 10 P.M.; Sat. 10 A.M. to 8 P.M.;
Sun. 11 A.M. to 7 P.M.
Form of payment: Visa, MC, AMEX, Discover
Type of store: New
Subject Specialties: General • Trains/Railways • Computers
Owner: Craig Newman
Manager: Richard Frey
Year Established: 1963
No. of Volumes: 7,000
Sidelines and Services: Special orders, greeting cards, book
accessories (bookmarks, bookends, etc.), maps
Comments: Mailing address: Penn Concessions, Inc., 371 Seventh
Ave., New York, NY 10001

Penn Station Book Store

**1 Penn Plaza (Penn Station, Concourse Level, Seventh Ave. side)
New York, NY 10119 • (212) 594-9572**
Hours: Mon.-Sun. open 24 hours
Type of store: New
Subject Specialties: General

Penn Station Book Store

1 Penn Plaza (Penn Station, Concourse Level, Eighth Ave. side)

New York, NY 10119 • (212) 594-9572
Hours: Mon.-Sun. 7 A.M. to Midnight
Type of store: New
Subject Specialties: General

Perimeter
21 Cleveland Place

146 Sullivan St. (bet. Houston & Prince Sts.)
New York, NY 10012 • (212) 529-2275 Fax: (212) 274-9809
334 6560   334 6560
Hours: Mon.-Sat. Noon to 7 P.M.
Form of payment: Visa, MC, AMEX, Checks
Type of store: New, mail order
Subject Specialties: Architecture • Design
Manager: Kazumi Futagawa
Year Established: 1986   **No. of Volumes:** 3,000
Sidelines and Services: Posters, greeting cards, postcards
Catalogs: 4/year

Les Perline & Co.

630 First Ave. (at 36th St.) New York, NY 10016
(212) 725-0123 or (800) 567-2014 Fax: (212) 725-0124
Hours: By appointment only
Form of payment: AMEX, Checks
Type of store: Antiquarian
Subject Specialties: Autographs/Manuscripts
Owner: Les Perline
Year Established: 1991
Sidelines and Services: Appraisals

Phillips Auctioneers

406 E. 79th St. (bet. First & York Aves.) New York, NY 10021
(212) 570-4830 or (800) 825-ART1 Fax: (212) 570-2207
Hours: Mon-Fri: 9 A.M. to 5 P.M.
Form of Payment: Visa, MC, Checks
Type of store: Auction house
Subject Specialties: Auction House • Art - European 20th c.
• Art - European, 1600-1900 • Autographs/Manuscripts • Philately
Vice-President (NY): Claudia Florian
Book Specialist: Elizabeth Merry
Year Established: 1796
Sidelines and Services: Appraisals
Catalogs: Auction catalogs (subscription of 10 catalogs for £85)
Comments: Branch of London-based auction company

Elizabeth Phillips

215 W. 90th St., Apt. 2D New York, NY 10024 • (212) 579-3302
Fax: (212) 579-3328 • E-mail address: ejpbooks@aol.com
Hours: By appointment only
Type of store: Antiquarian
Subject Specialties: Illustrated Books • Fine Bindings • Art -
Modern • Livres d'Artiste • Art - Surrealism • Art - Dadaism
• Art - Russian Avant-Garde
Owner: Elizabeth Phillips
Year Established: 1982
No. of Volumes: 200
Sidelines and Services: Appraisals for insurance purposes
Catalogs: Free semiannual catalog

A Photographers Place

133 Mercer St. (bet. Prince & Spring Sts.) New York, NY 10012
(212) 431-9358 Fax: (212) 941-7920
Hours: Mon.-Sat. 11 A.M. to 8 P.M.; Sun. Noon to 6 P.M. February
through April: Mon.-Sat. 11 A.M. to 6 P.M.; Sun. Noon to 6 P.M.
Form of payment: Visa, MC, Discover, AMEX. For mail order, Visa,
MC, and Discover only.
Type of store: New, used
Subject Specialties: Photography • Photography - 19th c.
Owner: Harvey S. Zucker
Year Established: 1979
No. of Volumes: 9,000 (4,000 titles)
Sidelines and Services: Books purchased, libraries evaluated,
photographic estates evaluated
Catalogs: 5/year (free subscription upon request)

The Photographic Arts Center

163 Amsterdam Ave. New York, NY 10023
(212) 838-8640 Fax: (212) 873-7065
Hours: Mail order only
Form of payment: Visa, MC, AMEX, Checks
Type of store: New, mail order
Subject Specialties: Photography
• Art - General • Business/Management
Owner: Robert Persky
Year Established: 1983
No. of Volumes: 33,000
Sidelines and Services: Subscription agency for "The Photograph

Collector" and "The Linked Ring Letter" newsletters

Catalogs: Semiannual catalog

Pierpont Morgan Library Book Shop

29 E. 36th St. (at Madison Ave., with second entrance at Madison Ave. & 37th St.) New York, NY 10016

(212) 685-0008 ext. 358 or (800) 861-0001 Fax: (212) 685-4740

E-mail address: book shop@P.M.l.org

Hours: Tue.-Fri. 10:30 A.M. to 4:45 P.M.; Sat. 10:30 A.M. to 5:45 P.M.; Sun. Noon to 5:45 P.M. Between Thanksgiving and Christmas open Mon. 10:30 A.M. to 4:45 P.M.

Form of payment: Visa, MC, AMEX

Type of store: New

Subject Specialties: Art - Medieval/Renaissance • Art - European, 1600-1900 • History - Medieval/Renaissance • Illuminated Manuscripts • Books About Books/Bibliography • Literature - General • Early Printed Books • Autographs/Manuscripts • Art - Master Drawings • Music • Children's/Juvenile

Manager: John Frazier

Year Established: 1974

No. of Volumes: 10,000

Sidelines and Services: Gifts, note cards, postcards, posters

Pomander Books

211 W. 92nd St., Box 30 New York, NY 10025 • (212) 749-5906

E-mail address: szavv@aol.com

Hours: By appointment only

Form of payment: Checks
Type of store: Antiquarian
Subject Specialties: Literature - Modern • Poetry
• Children's/Juvenile
Owner: Suzanne Zavrian
Year Established: 1974
No. of Volumes: 3,000
Sidelines and Services: Search service
Catalogs: 4/year

Posman Books

**1 University Pl. (corner of Waverly Pl., north of Washington
Square Park) New York, NY 10003 • (212) 533-2665**
Fax: (212) 533-2681 • E-mail address: posmanbook@aol.com
Hours: Mon.-Thu. 10 A.M. to 9 P.M.; Fri.-Sat. 11 A.M. to 10 P.M.; Sun.
Noon to 8 P.M.
Form of payment: Visa, MC, AMEX, Discover
Type of store: New
Subject Specialties: Literature - General • Philosophy
• Psychology/Psychiatry • Poetry • Literary Criticism • University
Presses • Art - General • Theater/Drama • Cultural Studies
Vice-President: Raymond Fiechter
Year Established: 1993
No. of Volumes: 60,000
Sidelines and Services: Will special order any book in print.

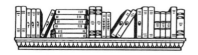

Posman Books Annex

31 Waverly Pl. (bet. University Pl. & Greene St.)
New York, NY 10003 • (212) 529-8555
E-mail address: posmanbook@aol.com
Hours: Mon.-Thu. 8 A.M. to 8 P.M.; Fri. 8 A.M. to 7 P.M.;
Sat.-Sun. 10 A.M. to 5 P.M.
Type of store: New
Subject Specialties: Literature - General • Philosophy
• Psychology/Psychiatry • Poetry • Literary Criticism • University
Presses • Art - General • Theater/Drama
Vice-President: Raymond Fiechter
Sidelines and Services: Will special order any book in print.

Posman Books at Barnard College

2955 Broadway (bet. 115th & 116th Sts.) New York, NY 10025
(212) 961-1527 or (212) 961-9140 • E-mail address:
posmanbook@aol.com
Hours: Mon.-Fri. 10 A.M. to 9 P.M.; Sat.-Sun. 11 A.M. to 7 P.M.
Form of payment: Visa, MC, AMEX, Checks
Type of store: New
Subject Specialties: Literary Criticism • Chess • Philosophy
• Poetry • Literature - Modern • Women's Studies • University
Presses • Academic • International Affairs • Politics/Political
Science • Classical Studies
Owner: Gene Posman
Manager: Robert Fader
Sidelines and Services: Scholarly journals

Potala

9 E. 36th St. (bet. Madison & Fifth Aves.) New York, NY 10016
(212) 251-0360
Hours: Mon.-Fri. 10 A.M. to 5 P.M.; Sat. Noon to 5 P.M.
Form of payment: Visa, MC, AMEX, Checks
Type of store: New
Subject Specialties: Religion - Oriental • Orient • History - Asia
• Spirituality
Manager: Nyima Wangyal
Year Established: 1977
Catalogs: Free annual catalog

535 West 22nd

Printed Matter

77 Wooster St. (bet. Spring & Broome Sts.) New York, NY 10012
(212) 925-0325 Fax: (212) 925-0464
Hours: Tue.-Fri. 10 A.M. to 6 P.M.; Sat. 11 A.M. to 7 P.M.
Form of payment: Visa, MC
Type of store: New, mail order
Subject Specialties: Art - General • Livres d'Artiste
Director: David Dean
Manager: Max Schumann
Year Established: 1976
No. of Volumes: 25,000 (5,000 titles)
Sidelines and Services: Wholesale, consultant to collections
Catalogs: Free mail-order catalog

Pryor & Johnson Booksellers

360 E. 65th St. (at First Ave.) New York, NY 10021 • (212) 879-1853

Type of store: New, antiquarian

Subject Specialties: First Editions • Autographs/Manuscripts
• Books About Books/Bibliography • Exploration/Voyages • Art
• Photography • Literature - British • Literature - American
• Signed Editions

Owners: David Johnson, Barbara Pryor

Year Established: 1993

No. of Volumes: 8,000-10,000

Sidelines and Services: Appraisals, collection
development, literary research

Catalogs: Free occasional catalogs

Puski-Corvin Hungarian Books

217 E. 83rd St. (bet. First & Second Aves.)
New York, NY 10028 • (212) 879-8893 Fax: (212) 734-3848

Hours: Mon.-Sat. 10 A.M. to 6:30 P.M.

Form of payment: Visa, MC, AMEX

Type of store: New, used

Subject Specialties: Hungary (including Hungarian
Language and Literature)

Owner: Istvan Puski

Year Established: 1960

No. of Volumes: 120,000 (15,000 titles)

Sidelines and Services: Music CDs & tapes, magazines, maps,
posters, wholesale

Catalogs: Annual catalog

Quest Bookshop

240 E. 53rd St. (bet. Second & Third Aves.)
New York, NY 10022 • (212) 758-5521 Fax: (212) 758-4679
Hours: Mon., Wed., Fri. 10 A.M. to 6 P.M.;
Tue., Thu. 10 A.M. to 8 P.M.
Form of payment: Visa, MC, Checks
Type of store: New
Subject Specialties: Astrology • Alternative Medicine • Yoga
• Metaphysics • Occult/Mysticism • Theosophy • Tarot • Healing
Managers: William Lyle, Michele Lidofsky
Year Established: 1968
No. of Volumes: 12,000
Sidelines and Services: Incense, greeting cards, gift wrapping,
tarot cards, mail orders, astrology charts done

Bruce J. Ramer, Experimenta Old and Rare Books

401 E. 80th St., Suite 24-J (bet. York & First Aves.)
New York, NY 10021 • (212) 772-6211 or (212) 772-6212
Fax: (212) 650-9032 • E-mail address: 6763925@mcimail.com
Hours: By appointment only
Type of store: Antiquarian
Subject Specialties: Medicine • Mathematics • Natural History
• Science • Early Printed Books • Astronomy • Occult/Mysticism
Owner: Bruce J. Ramer
Year Established: 1981
No. of Volumes: 4,000
Sidelines and Services: Appraise library collections, search service

Catalogs: Semiannual catalog plus specialized lists
Comments: Also specializes in bibliography related to medicine, mathematics, natural history, science, early printed books, astronomy and occult/mysticsim.

Richard C. Ramer Old and Rare Books

225 E. 70th St. (bet. Second & Third Aves.)
New York, NY 10021 • (212) 737-0222 or (212) 737-0223
Fax: (212) 288-4169 • E-mail address: 5222386@mcimail.com
Hours: By appointment only
Form of payment: Checks
Type of store: Antiquarian, mail order
Subject Specialties: Americana • Asian Studies • Latin America • Nautical/Maritime • Spanish Language and Literature • Exploration/ Voyages • Maps/Atlases/Cartography • Portuguese • Brazil
Owner: Richard C. Ramer
Year Established: 1969
No. of Volumes: 10,000
Sidelines and Services: Appraisals, manuscripts, search service, auction representative
Catalogs: Annual catalog; bulletins of current books published in Portugal (issued several times/year)

Rand McNally, The Map and Travel Store

150 E. 52nd St. (bet. Third & Lexington Aves.)
New York, NY 10022 • (212) 758-7488
Hours: Mon.-Fri. 9 A.M. to 6 P.M.; Sat. Noon to 5 P.M.;

December: Mon.-Fri. 9 A.M. to 7 P.M.; Sat. 10 A.M. to 5 P.M.
Form of payment: Visa, MC, AMEX, Discover, Personal
and company checks accepted
Type of store: New, mail order
Subject Specialties: Travel • Maps/Atlases/Cartography
• Dictionaries/Encyclopedias • Foreign Language Instruction
• Travel Guides
Manager: Maria Haritopoulos
Year Established: 1940
No. of Volumes: 5,000
Sidelines and Services: Globes, U.S.G.S. topographic maps,
videotapes, language tapes, framed maps, gifts, travel acces-
sories, geographic games and toys
Catalogs: Semiannual gift catalog

Reborn—14th St. Bookstore

238 E. 14th St. (bet. Second & Third Aves.) New York, NY 10003
(212) 529-7370
Hours: Mon.-Sun. 11:30 A.M. to 10 P.M.
Form of payment: Checks
Type of store: Used
Subject Specialties: General
Comments: A great place to find out-of-print economics,
accounting, and sociology textbooks. Also stocks comic books
and records.

Dan Redmon

400 W. 43rd St., #42-0 New York, NY 10036 • (212) 947-6357
Hours: By appointment only
Subject Specialties: Illustrated Books • First Editions • Private
Press • Prints/Drawings

Reference Book Center

175 Fifth Ave., Rm. 701 (at 23rd St., inside the Flatiron Bldg.)
New York, NY 10010 • (212) 677-2160 Fax: (212) 533-0826
Hours: Mon.-Fri. 10 A.M. to 4 P.M.
Form of payment: Checks
Type of store: New, used, mail order
Subject Specialties: Dictionaries/Encyclopedias • Reference
• Sets of Books
Owners: Saul Shine, Margery Shine
Year Established: 1961
No. of Volumes: 7,000
Catalogs: Semiannual catalog

Reinhold-Brown Gallery

26 E. 78th St. (bet. Madison & Fifth Aves.) New York, NY 10021
(212) 734-7999 Fax: (212) 734-7044
Hours: Tue.-Sat. 10:30 A.M. to 5 P.M. Summer hours:
Mon.-Fri. 10:30 A.M. to 5 P.M.
Form of payment: Checks
Type of store: New, antiquarian
Subject Specialties: Art - General • Graphic Arts • Livres d'Artiste

• Graphic Design • Poster Art
Owners: Robert Brown, Susan Reinhold
Year Established: 1975
No. of Volumes: 500
Sidelines and Services: Appraise library collections, prints, fine art

Kenneth W. Rendell Gallery

989 Madison Ave. (bet. 76th & 77th Sts.) New York, NY 10021
(212) 717-1776 or (800) 376-1776 Fax: (212) 717-1492
Hours: Mon.-Sat. 10 A.M. to 6 P.M.
Form of payment: Visa, MC, AMEX, Checks
Type of store: Antiquarian
Subject Specialties: Autographs/Manuscripts • Illuminated
Manuscripts • Signed Editions
Owner: Kenneth W. Rendell
Manager: Paul Poster
Year Established: 1986
No. of Volumes: 70,000
Sidelines and Services: Appraisals
Catalogs: 9/year
Comments: Headquarters are located in South Natick,
Massachusetts.

Revolution Books

9 W. 19th St. (bet. Fifth & Sixth Aves.) New York, NY 10011
(212) 691-3345 Fax: (212) 645-1952
Hours: Mon.-Sat. 10 A.M. to 7 P.M.; Sun. Noon to 5 P.M.

Form of payment:
Visa, MC, AMEX, Discover, Checks
Type of store:
New, used, periodicals
Subject Specialties: Politics/Political Science • Radical Issues
• Economics • History - General • Women's Studies • African-
American Studies • Middle Eastern Languages and Literature
• Poetry • Marxism • Leninism • Maoism • Literature - Revolution
• Progressivism
Manager: Joan Hirsch
Year Established: 1979
No. of Volumes: 15,000

Rhyme & Reason

117 E. 14th St. (off Irving Pl.) New York, NY 10003
Fax: (212) 260-3612
Hours: Mon.-Fri. 7 A.M. to 8 P.M.; Sat. 11 A.M. to 7:30 P.M.;
Sun. 11 A.M. to 7:30 P.M.
Form of payment: Visa, MC, AMEX, Discover
Type of store: New
Subject Specialties: General • Cooking • Fiction - Crime/Mystery/
Suspense • Fiction - Romance • Humor
Manager: Roger Young
Year Established: 1993
Sidelines and Services: Gifts, cards, magazines, coffee, snacks

Rizzoli Bookstore

31 W. 57th St. (bet. Fifth & Sixth Aves.) New York, NY 10019

(212) 759-2424 or (800) 52-BOOKS Fax: (212) 826-9754

Hours: Mon.-Sat. 9 A.M. to 8 P.M.; Sun. 11 A.M. to 7 P.M.

Form of payment: Visa, MC, AMEX, Checks

Type of store: New

Subject Specialties: Architecture • Art - General • Design
• Graphic Arts • Italy (including Italian Language and Literature)
• Photography • Fashion/Costume/Clothing

Manager: John Deen

Year Established: 1964

No. of Volumes: 5,000 titles

Sidelines and Services: Music recordings, art objects, international periodicals

Catalogs: Semiannual catalog (spring & fall)

Rizzoli Bookstore

**3 World Financial Center (inside the Winter Garden
shopping complex) New York, NY 10281**

(212) 385-1400 or (800) 52-BOOKS Fax: (212) 608-7905

Hours: Mon.-Fri. 10 A.M. to 7 P.M.; Sat.-Sun. Noon to 5 P.M.

Form of payment: Visa, MC, AMEX, Checks

Type of store: New

Subject Specialties: Architecture • Art - General • Design
• Graphic Arts • Italy (including Italian Language and Literature)
• Photography • Business/Management

Manager: Monique Strong

Catalogs: Semiannual catalog (spring & fall)

Rizzoli Bookstore and Art Boutique

454 West Broadway (bet. Prince & Houston Sts.)
New York, NY 10012 • (212) 674-1616 or (800) 52-BOOKS
Fax: (212) 979-9504
Hours: Mon.-Sat. 10:30 A.M. to 9 P.M.; Sun. Noon to 7 P.M.
Form of payment: Visa, MC, AMEX, Discover, Diners Club, Checks
Type of store: New
Subject Specialties: Architecture • Art - General • Design
• Graphic Arts • Italy (including Italian Language and Literature)
• Photography • Fashion/Costume/Clothing
Manager: John Wall
No. of Volumes: 5,000
Sidelines and Services: Gift items, stationery
Catalogs: Semiannual catalog (spring & fall)

Roig Spanish Books

29 W. 19th St. (bet. Fifth & Sixth Aves.) New York, NY 10011
(212) 675-1047 Fax: (212) 229-0160
Hours: By appointment only
Type of store: New, periodicals
Subject Specialties: Spanish Language and Literature
Manager: Diane Mahiques
Sidelines and Services: Spanish periodicals and newspapers

Theodore Roosevelt Birthplace National Historic Site Bookstore

28 E. 20th St. (bet. Broadway & Park Ave. South)

New York, NY 10003 • (212) 260-1616 (212) 260-0536
Hours: Wed.-Sun. 9 A.M. to 5 P.M. Closed Federal holidays.
Form of payment: Checks and money orders accepted;
no credit cards
Type of store: New
Subject Specialties: History - America 20th c. • History - America
19th c. • Antiques/Collectibles • Architecture • Biography/
Autobiography • Theodore Roosevelt
Site Manager: Kathryn Gross
Year Established: 1923
No. of Volumes: 60
Catalogs: Price list available

Paulette Rose Fine and Rare Books

10 E. 70th St., Rm. 8C New York, NY 10021 • (212) 861-5607
Fax: (212) 861-5619 • E-mail address: prose326@aol.com
Hours: By appointment only
Type of store: Antiquarian
Subject Specialties: Women's Studies • France (including French
Language and Literature) • Literature - British • Literature -
American
Owner: Paulette Rose
Year Established: 1978
No. of Volumes: 2,000 (1,000 titles)
Catalogs: Annual catalog plus
occasional lists

Mary S. Rosenberg, Inc.
SEE: German Book Center N.A.

Leona Rostenberg and Madeleine B. Stern Rare Books

40 E. 88th St. New York, NY 10128

(212) 831-6628 Fax: (212) 831-1961

Hours: By appointment only

Form of payment: Checks

Type of store: Antiquarian, mail order

Subject Specialties: History - Europe • Politics/Political Science • History - Medieval/Renaissance • Literature - Medieval/ Renaissance • Early Printed Books

Owners: Leona Rostenberg, Madeleine B. Stern

Year Established: 1944

No. of Volumes: 3,000

Sidelines and Services: Appraise library collections

Catalogs: Approximately 4/year (free)

Ruby's Book Sale

119 Chambers St. (bet. Church St. and West Broadway, west of City Hall) New York, NY 10007 • (212) 732-8676

Hours: Mon.-Fri. 10 A.M. to 6 P.M.; Sat. 10 A.M. to 5:30 P.M.

Form of payment: Visa, MC, AMEX, Discover, Traveler's checks

Type of store: New, used, periodicals

Subject Specialties: Computers • Art - General • Children's/Juvenile • Cooking • Military/War • Crafts • Gardening • Sports

• Architecture • Home Repair • Health/Nutrition • Religion
• Reference • Photography • Art Instruction • Travel • Automobiles
• Aviation

Owners: Martin Sadofsky, Roberta Sadofsky

Year Established: 1970

Sidelines and Services: Magazine back issues

Comments: All new paperbacks and computer books are 20 percent off; hardcover books are remainders.

Russian House

253 Fifth Ave. (bet. 28th & 29th Sts.) New York, NY 10016

(212) 685-1010

Hours: Mon.-Sat. 10 A.M. to 6 P.M.

Form of payment: Visa, MC, AMEX, Discover, Checks

Type of store: New

Subject Specialties: Russia (including Russian Language and Literature)

Sidelines and Services: Art, gifts, Russian imports

Russica Book and Art Shop

799 Broadway, 3rd fl. (at 11th St.) New York, NY 10003

(212) 473-7480

Subject Specialties: Russia (incl. Russian language and literature)

Charlotte F. Safir Books

1349 Lexington Ave., Apt. 9B (at 90th St.) New York, NY 10128

(212) 534-7933
Hours: Primarily mail order, but also by appointment
Type of store: Antiquarian, mail order, used
Subject Specialties: Cooking • Children's/Juvenile • Judaica
• Art History • Literature - General • Biography/Autobiography
• Books About Books/Bibliography • Ephemera
Owner: Charlotte F. Safir
Year Established: 1980
No. of Volumes: 5,000
Sidelines and Services: Free search service, antique greeting
cards, guidance in forming subject collections
Catalogs: Will issue custom-made lists about specific subject
requests.

Saint Francis Bookstore

131 W. 31st St. (bet. Sixth & Seventh Aves.) New York, NY 10001
(212) 736-8500 ext. 324 Fax: (212) 947-0890
Hours: Tue.-Sat. 10 A.M. to 5:30 P.M. Closed Sun. & Mon.
Form of payment: Visa, MC, Checks
Type of store: New, periodicals, mail order
Subject Specialties: Religion - Christianity • Spirituality • Bibles
• Theology • Catholicism
Manager: Brother William P. Mann
Year Established: 1969
No. of Volumes: 8,000
Sidelines and Services: Religious goods,
religious music, audio cassettes, CDs, videos
Catalogs: Free semiannual catalog

Saint Mark's Bookshop

31 Third Ave. (at 9th St.) New York, NY 10003

(212) 260-7853 or (212) 260-0443 Fax: (212) 598-4950

Hours: Mon.-Sat. 10 A.M. to Midnight; Sun. 11 A.M. to Midnight

Form of payment: Visa, MC, AMEX, Discover, Checks

Type of store: New, periodicals, mail order

Subject Specialties: Philosophy • Poetry • Politics/Political Science
• Women's Studies • University Presses • Literature - General
• Small Press • Cultural Studies

Owners: Robert Contant, Terence McCoy

Year Established: 1977

No. of Volumes: 50,000

Sidelines and Services: Greeting cards, literary magazines, poetry audiotapes, CDs

Saint Mark's Comics

11 St. Mark's Place (bet. Second & Third Aves.)

New York, NY 10003 • (212) 598-9439 Fax: (212) 477-1294

Hours: Mon. 10 A.M. to 11 P.M.; Tue.-Sat. 10 A.M. to 1 A.M.;
Sun. 11 A.M. to 11 P.M. Closed on Christmas Day only.

Form of payment: Visa, MC, AMEX, Traveler's Checks

Type of store: New, used, periodicals, mail order

Subject Specialties: Comic Books • Magazines/Journals/
Newspapers • Fiction - Science Fiction • Fiction - Fantasy/Horror
• Posters • Cinema/Films

Manager: Mitch Cutler

Year Established: 1983

Sidelines and Services: Comic book-related products, toys,

posters, shirts, games

Catalogs: Several catalogs available

Saint Paul Book and Media Center

SEE: Pauline Books & Media

St. Paul the Apostle Book and Gift Shop

SEE: Church of St. Paul the Apostle Book & Gift Shop

William H. Schab Gallery

24 W. 57th St., Suite 301 (bet. Fifth & Sixth Aves.)

New York, NY 10019 • (212) 410-2366 Fax: (212) 974-0339

Hours: Tue.-Sat. 9:30 A.M. to 5:30 P.M. Summer hours:
Mon.-Fri. 9:30 A.M. to 5:30 P.M.

Form of payment: Checks

Type of store: Antiquarian

Subject Specialties: Incunabula • Illustrated Books • History -
Ancient • Literature - Ancient • Humanities • History of Science
• Art History

Owner: Frederick G. Schab

Year Established: 1940

Sidelines and Services: Manuscripts, prints, drawings

Catalogs: Annual catalog

Howard Schickler

52 E. 76th St. (bet. Park & Madison Aves.) New York, NY 10021
(212) 737-6647 Fax: (212) 737-2534 • E-mail address:
hsart@interport.net
Hours: Tue.-Sat. 11 A.M. to 6 P.M.
Type of store: Antiquarian
Subject Specialties: Art - Modern • Art - Avant-Garde
Owner: Howard Schickler
Comments: For further information, visit this shop's Web site at:
http://colophon.com/schickler

Justin G. Schiller Ltd.

135 E. 57th St., 12th fl. (corner of Lexington Ave.)
New York, NY 10022 • (212) 832-8231 or (914) 331-3309
Fax: (212) 688-1139 • E-mail address: childlit@maestro.com
Hours: By appointment only (Mon.-Fri. 10 A.M. to 5 P.M.)
Form of payment: Visa, MC, AMEX, Checks
Type of store: Antiquarian
Subject Specialties: Children's/Juvenile • Graphic Arts • Illustrated
Books • Autographs/Manuscripts
Owners: Justin Schiller, Raymond Wapner
Manager: Greg Gillert
Year Established: 1969
Sidelines and Services: Appraise library collections, original art,
prints
Catalogs: Annual catalog; catalog also available online at Web
site (see below)
Comments: Most of the inventory here consists of rare children's

books from the 17th through the 20th century. The Web site can be found on the Internet at: http://www.abaa-booknet/alldrs/ma/10022jus.html

Schomburg Center for Research in Black Culture—Shop

515 Malcolm X Blvd. (Lenox Ave. at 135th St.)
New York, NY 10037 • (212) 491-2206 Fax: (212) 491-6760
Hours: Mon.-Fri. 11 A.M. to 6 P.M.
Form of payment: Visa, MC, AMEX, Checks
Type of store: New
Subject Specialties: African-American Studies
Year Established: 1991
Sidelines and Services: Posters, cards, gift items
Catalogs: Free catalog available

School of Visual Arts Bookstore

207 E. 23rd St. (at Third Ave.) New York, NY 10010
(212) 685-7140
Hours: Mon.-Thu. 9:30 A.M. to 6 P.M.; Fri. 9 A.M. to 3 P.M.; Sat. 10 A.M. to 2 P.M.
Form of payment: Visa, MC, AMEX, Discover, Checks
Type of store: New
Subject Specialties: Visual Arts
Manager: Kimberly Feeney
Comments: Operated by Barnes & Noble.

E. K. Schreiber Rare Books

(phone for address) New York, NY • (212) 873-3180

Fax: (212) 873-3190 • E-mail address: ekslibris@aol.com

Hours: By appointment only

Form of payment: Visa, MC, Checks

Type of store: Antiquarian

Subject Specialties: Incunabula • Early Printed Books • Literature - Medieval/Renaissance • Classical Studies • History - Medieval/Renaissance • Humanism

Owners: Fred Schreiber, Ellen Schreiber

Year Established: 1971   **No. of Volumes:** 2,000

Sidelines and Services: Appraise library collections, manuscripts

Catalogs: 4/year (no charge for first catalog)

David Schulson Autographs

11 E. 68th St., Suite 2E (at Madison Ave.) New York, NY 10021

(212) 517-8300 Fax: (212) 517-2014 • E-mail address: clstrauss@aol.com

Hours: Mon.-Fri. 10 A.M. to 6 P.M. (best to phone first)

Form of payment: Visa, MC, AMEX, Checks

Type of store: Antiquarian, mail order

Subject Specialties: Autographs/Manuscripts • Photography • Science • Art - General • Literature - General • Music

Owners: David Schulson, Claudia Strauss Schulson

Year Established: 1975

Catalogs: 5-7/year

Comments: Their Web site can be found at: http://home.navi-soft.com/schulson/index.html

F.A.O. Schwarz Book Department

767 Fifth Ave., 2nd fl. (at 58th St.) New York, NY 10153

(212) 644-9400 Fax: (212) 826-1826

Hours: Mon.-Sat. 10 A.M. to 7 P.M.; Sun. 11 A.M. to 6 P.M.

Form of payment: Major credit cards, Checks

Type of store: New

Subject Specialties: Children's/Juvenile

Manager: William Miller

Sidelines and Services: Gifts, toys

Comments: Also stocks children's books in French, German, Italian, and Spanish.

Science Fiction Mysteries & More!

140 Chambers St. (bet. West Broadway & Greenwich St., 5 blocks north of World Trade Center) New York, NY 10007

(212) 385-8798 • E-mail address: sfmm@interport.net

Hours: Mon.-Fri. 11:30 A.M. to 7 P.M.; Sat. 2:30 P.M. to 6:30 P.M.

Form of payment: Visa, MC, AMEX, Diners Club, Discover

Type of store: New, used, antiquarian, periodicals, mail order

Subject Specialties: Fiction - Science Fiction • Fiction - Crime/Mystery/Suspense • Fiction - Fantasy/Horror • Comic Books • Environment/Conservation/Ecology • Espionage/Intelligence • Military/War • Politics/Political Science • Fiction - Romance

Owner: Alan Zimmerman

Year Established: 1992

No. of Volumes: 13,000 (used) + 6,000 (new)

Sidelines and Services: Coffee mugs, tee-shirts, posters, audio tapes, videotapes, software, magazines, courses in science fic-

tion and mystery writing
Comments: Their World Wide Web address is:
http://www.interport.net/~sfmm

The Science Fiction Shop
214 Sullivan St., Rm. 2D (bet. Bleecker & W. 3rd Sts.)
New York, NY 10012 • (212) 473-3010 Fax: (212) 473-4384
Hours: Mon.-Fri. Noon to 7 P.M.; Sat. 11 A.M. to 7 P.M.;
Sun. Noon to 6 P.M.
Form of payment: Visa, MC, AMEX, Discover, JCB, Checks
Type of store: New, used, periodicals, mail order
Subject Specialties: Fiction - Science Fiction • Fiction -
Fantasy/Horror • First Editions • Signed Editions
Owner: Joe Lihach
Manager: Michael Franklin
Year Established: 1973   **No. of Volumes:** 6,000 titles
Sidelines and Services: Science fiction magazines, international
mail order, books on CD-ROM, books on tape
Catalogs: 3/year (free)

Scientific & Medical Publications
of France
100 E. 42nd St., Suite 1002 New York, NY 10017
(212) 983-6278 Fax: (212) 687-1407
Subject Specialties: Medicine • France (including French
Language and Literature)
President: Gerard G. Juery

Israel Sefer

SEE: Gozlan's Sefer Israel Inc.

Shakespeare & Co.

1 Whitehall St. (1 block south of Bowling Green, behind the U.S. Custom House) New York, NY 10004 • (212) 742-7025 Fax: (212) 742-7023 • E-mail address: bill@panix.com

Hours: Mon.-Fri. 8 A.M. to 6:30 P.M.

Form of payment: Visa, MC, AMEX, Checks

Type of store: New, used

Subject Specialties: Fiction - Crime/Mystery/Suspense
• Literature - General

Manager: Lori Istok

Year Established: 1996

Shakespeare & Co.

716 Broadway (at Washington Place, 1 block north of W. 4th St.) New York, NY 10003 • (212) 529-1330 Fax: (212) 979-5711 E-mail address: bill@panix.com

Hours: Sun.-Thu. 10 A.M. to 11 P.M.; Fri.-Sat. 10 A.M. to Midnight

Form of payment: Visa, MC, AMEX, NYCE debit cards, Checks

Type of store: New

Subject Specialties: Philosophy • Fiction - Science Fiction
• Psychology/Psychiatry • Theater/Drama • Travel • Poetry
• Literature - General • Occult/Mysticism • Theater/Drama
• Cultural Studies

Manager: Chris Peterson

Year Established: 1987
Sidelines and Services: Search service, special orders
Comments: This store also carries a selection of textbooks.

Shakespeare & Co.

939 Lexington Ave. (bet. 68th & 69th Sts.)
New York, NY 10021 • (212) 570-0201 Fax: (212) 570-0369
Hours: Mon.-Fri. 9 A.M. to 8:30 P.M.; Sat. 10 A.M. to 7:30 P.M.;
Sun. 10 A.M. to 6 P.M.
Form of payment: Visa, MC, AMEX, Checks
Type of store: New
Subject Specialties: Literature - General • Fiction - Crime/Mystery/
Suspense • Travel • Poetry • Children's/Juvenile • Health/Nutrition
Manager: Delia Kurland
Year Established: 1995
Sidelines and Services: Magazines, cards, blank books
Comments: This branch also carries textbooks.

Marsha J. Shapiro Books

355 W. 85th St., #77 New York, NY 10024 • (212) 595-4219
Hours: By appointment only
Form of payment: Checks
Type of store: Used, mail order
Subject Specialties: Literature - British • History - General
Owner: Marsha J. Shapiro
Year Established: 1988   **No. of Volumes:** 2,500
Sidelines and Services: Search service

Myrna Shinbaum Books & Book Themes

P.O. Box 1170, Madison Square Station New York, NY 10159

(212) 982-5749 • E-mail address: popuplady@aol.com

Hours: By appointment only

Form of payment: Checks

Type of store: Antiquarian

Subject Specialties: Children's/Juvenile • Etiquette • Cooking • Art - General • New York City • Books About Books/Bibliography • Judaica • J. M. Barrie • Moveables

Owner: Myrna Shinbaum

Manager: Ellen Rubin

Year Established: 1982

Sidelines and Services: Ephemera, prints, bookends

Sidewalk Book Dealers

There are an indeterminate number of booksellers who sell books and magazines of all descriptions from tables, stands, and booths set up on sidewalks throughout Manhattan. These vendors are impossible to count, let alone list. With a few exceptions, such as the Metropolitan Book kiosks, these are generally cash-only operations run by booksellers who may or may not be at the same location the following week or even the next day.

With that caveat in mind, you can find some great bargains. The best place to hunt for this breed of bookseller is along any busy avenue or cross street. Some of the more popular areas include:

• Along Third, Lexington, Madison, and Fifth Avenues in midtown (roughly south of 60th Street)

- Along 42nd Street
- In the vicinity of most colleges and universities
- Union Square

6 Rays of Gold

230 Mulberry St. (bet. Spring & Prince Sts.)
New York, NY 10012 • (212) 431-8348
E-mail address: 73552.2022@compuserve.com
Hours: Mon.-Wed. 5:30 P.M. to 8:30 P.M.;
Thu.-Sun. 3 P.M. to 8:30 P.M.
Form of payment: Visa, MC, AMEX
Subject Specialties: Astrology • Metaphysics • Occult/Mysticism
Owner: Meri Winston
Year Established: 1996
Sidelines and Services: Astrology charts, amulets, bells, runes,
tarot cards, pendulums, crystal balls, aromatic oils, qabala magick

Skyline Books & Records

13 W. 18th St. (bet. Fifth & Sixth Aves.) New York, NY 10011
(212) 759-5463 or (212) 675-4773
Hours: Mon.-Sat. 9:30 A.M. to 8 P.M.; Sun. 11 A.M. to 7 P.M.
Form of payment: Visa, MC, AMEX, Checks
Type of store: Used
Subject Specialties: Music • Art - General • Architecture • Germany
(including German Language and Literature) • Literature -
Modern • Fiction - Science Fiction • Fiction - Crime/Mystery/
Suspense • First Editions

Owner: Rob Warren
Year Established: 1990
No. of Volumes: 50,000
Sidelines and Services: Records (jazz, R&B), search service
Catalogs: 4/year

R. M. Smythe and Co.

26 Broadway, Suite 271 New York, NY 10004
(212) 943-1880 Fax: (212) 908-4047
Hours: By appointment only
Type of store: Auction house
Subject Specialties: Auction House
President: Diane Herzog
Comments: Deals only in autographs, and collectible documents, stocks, and bonds.

Soho Books

351 W. Broadway (bet. Broome & Grand Sts.)
New York, NY 10013 • (212) 226-3395
Hours: Mon.-Sun. 10:30 A.M. to 11 P.M.
Form of payment: Visa, MC, AMEX, Checks
Type of store: New, used
Owner: Paul Valluzzi

80 Nassau ST.

Sotheby's Book and Manuscripts Department

1334 York Ave. (at 72nd St.) New York, NY 10021

(212) 606-7385 or (212) 606-7000 Fax: (212) 606-7041

Hours: Mon.-Fri. 9 A.M. to 5:30 P.M. Summer hours:
Mon.-Fri. 9 A.M. to 5 P.M.

Form of payment: Visa, MC, AMEX, Checks

Type of store: Auction house

Subject Specialties: Auction House • Americana
• Autographs/ Manuscripts • Colorplate Books • Early Printed
Books • Fine Bindings • First Editions • Illuminated Manuscripts
• Maps/ Atlases/Cartography • Fine Printing • Illustrated Books
• Incunabula

International Head: David N. Redden

Head of N.Y. division: Paul Needham

Year Established: 1744

Sidelines and Services: Appraisals

Catalogs: Catalogs for all auctions; subscriptions can be purchased by calling 1-800-444-8709.

South Street Seaport Museum Bookstore

14 Fulton St. (east of Water St.) New York, NY 10038

(212) 748-8600 ext. 663 Fax: (212) 748-8610

Hours: Mon.-Wed. 10 A.M. to 6 P.M.; Thu.-Sun. 10 A.M. to 8 P.M.

Form of payment: Visa, MC, AMEX, Checks

Type of store: New, periodicals, mail order

Subject Specialties: Nautical/Maritime • New York City • Boating
• Exploration/Voyages • Crafts • Oceanography • History - America

19th c. • Arctic/Polar
Manager: Jack Putnam
Year Established: 1970
No. of Volumes: 4,000
Sidelines and Services: Boating magazines, gifts, prints, stationery, audiotapes, videotapes, museum publications, navigational charts, nautical prints and posters
Comments: Mailing address: 207 Front St., New York, NY 10038

Spoken Word

285 West Broadway (just south of Canal St.)
New York, NY 10013 • (212) 431-6121 Fax: (212) 226-1057
E-mail address: spokie285@aol.com
Hours: Mon-Sat: 11 A.M. to 7 P.M.
Form of payment: Visa, MC, AMEX
Type of store: Audio books
Subject Specialties: Audio Books
Owners: Gene Coppola, Michael Pagnotta
Catalogs: Free catalog available

SportsWords Ltd.

1475 Third Ave. (bet. 83rd & 84th Sts.) New York, NY 10028
(212) 772-8729 or (800) 778-7937 Fax: (212) 772-8809
E-mail address: sportswds@aol.com
Hours: Mon.-Fri. 11 A.M. to 6 P.M.; Sat. 10:30 A.M. to 6 P.M.
Check for special hours during the holidays.
Form of payment: Visa, MC, AMEX

Type of store: New, used, mail order
Subject Specialties: Sports • Automobiles • Fishing • Golf • Skiing
• Signed Editions • Automobile Racing
President: Marty Laufer
Year Established: 1993
No. of Volumes: 3,000
Sidelines and Services: Search service

Spring Street Books

169 Spring St. (bet. W. Broadway & Thompson St.)
New York, NY 10012 • (212) 219-3033 Fax: (212) 431-8441
Hours: Mon.-Thu. 10 A.M. to 11 P.M.; Fri. 10 A.M. to Midnight;
Sat. 10 A.M. to 1 A.M.; Sun. 11 A.M. to 10 P.M.
Form of payment: Visa, MC, Discover, AMEX, Checks
Type of store: New
Subject Specialties: General • Literature - General • Judaica
• Belles Lettres
Owner: Israel Jaronowski
Year Established: 1983
No. of Volumes: 20,000
Sidelines and Services: Magazines, foreign periodicals, greeting cards

Stavsky Hebrew Bookstore

147 Essex St. (bet. Rivington & Stanton Sts.,
1 block north of Delancey St.) New York, NY 10002
(212) 674-1289 Fax: (212) 674-3430
Hours: Sun.-Thu. 9:15 A.M. to 5 P.M.

Form of payment: Checks
Type of store: New
Subject Specialties: Judaica
President: Himan Stavsky
Year Established: 1931

No. of Volumes: 2,000
Sidelines and Services: Religious goods, audio cassettes, videotapes, Jewish music

Rudolf Steiner Bookstore

138 W. 15th St. (bet. Sixth & Seventh Aves.) New York, NY 10011
(212) 242-8945
Subject Specialties: Metaphysics

4/1 Union Square 9th fl # 937

Richard Stoddard Performing Arts Books

18 E. 16th St., Rm. 305 (bet. Fifth Ave. & Union Sq.)
New York, NY 10003 • (212) 645-9576
Hours: Mon.-Tue., Thu.-Sat. 11 A.M. to 6 P.M. Closed Wed. and Sun.
Form of payment: AMEX, Checks
Type of store: Used, antiquarian
Subject Specialties: Performing Arts • Circus • Dance • Cinema/ Films • Music • Theater/Drama • Autographs/Manuscripts • Ephemera
Owner: Richard Stoddard
Year Established: 1975
No. of Volumes: 15,000
Sidelines and Services: Appraise library collections, original art, playbills (12,000 in stock), search service

Catalogs: Occasional catalog
Comments: Richard Stoddard boasts the largest stock of Broadway playbills in the world.

Strand Bookstore

828 Broadway (corner of 12th St.) New York, NY 10003
(212) 473-1452 Fax: (212) 473-2591 • E-mail address:
strand@strandbooks.com
Hours: Mon.-Sat. 9:30 A.M. to 9:30 P.M.; Sun. 11 A.M. to 9:30 P.M.
Form of payment: Visa, MC, AMEX, Discover, JCB, Checks (over $15)
Type of store: New, used, antiquarian, mail order
Subject Specialties: Americana • Architecture • Art - General • First Editions • History - General • Humanities • Literature - General • Fine Bindings
Owner: Fred Bass
Manager: Nancy Bass
Year Established: 1929
No. of Volumes: 2,500,000
Sidelines and Services: Search service, appraise library collections, gift certificates, libraries purchased, supply books by the foot to decorators and prop stylists
Catalogs: 8/year (free)
Comments: All new paperbacks are 50 percent off.

Strand Bookstore Rare Book Department

826 Broadway, 2nd fl. (bet. 12th & 13th Sts., next door to main Strand Bookstore) New York, NY 10003 • (212) 473-1452

Fax: (212) 473-2591 • **E-mail address: strand@strandbooks.com**
Hours: Mon-Sat: 9:30 A.M. to 6:30 P.M. / Sat: 11 A.M. to 6:30 P.M.
Form of payment: Visa, MC, AMEX, Discover, JCB, Checks (over $15)
Type of store: Antiquarian
Subject Specialties: Art - General • Photography • Books About Books/Bibliography • Americana
Vice-President: Marvin Mondlin
Manager: Craig Anderson
Sidelines and Services: Search service, appraise library collections, libraries purchased

Strand Bookstore

88 Fulton St. (bet. William & Gold Sts.) New York, NY 10038
(212) 732-6070 • E-mail address: strand@strandbooks.com
Hours: Mon.-Sat. 10 A.M. to 9 P.M.; Sun. 10 A.M. to 8 P.M.
Form of payment: Visa, MC, AMEX, Discover, Checks
Type of store: New
Subject Specialties: Americana • Architecture • Art - General • Children's/Juvenile • History - General • Humanities • Literature - General • Music • Performing Arts • Photography
Owner: Fred Bass
Manager: Steven Maine
Year Established: 1996
No. of Volumes: 500,000

Stress Less Step

48 E. 61st St. (bet. Park & Madison Aves.) New York, NY 10021
(212) 826-6222
Hours: Mon.-Sun. 8 A.M. to 10 P.M.
Form of payment: Visa, MC, Diners Club, Discover
Type of store: New
Subject Specialties: Self-Help • Yoga • Health/Nutrition
Manager: Connie Cox
Year Established: 1985
No. of Volumes: 50 titles
Sidelines and Services: Audiotapes, massages, stress reduction, facials

Stubbs Books and Prints

153 E. 70th St. (bet. Lexington & Third Aves.)
New York, NY 10021 • (212) 772-3120 Fax: (212) 794-9071
E-mail address: jkstubbs@aol.com
Hours: Mon.-Sat. 11 A.M. to 6 P.M.
Form of payment: Visa, MC, AMEX, Checks
Type of store: Antiquarian
Subject Specialties: Architecture • Cooking • Decorative Arts
• Literature - British • Prints/Drawings • Fashion/Costume/Clothing
• Social History
Owners: John H. Stubbs, Jane K. Stubbs
Year Established: 1981
No. of Volumes: 6,000
Sidelines and Services: Gallery of original
art, prints, architectural drawings

Studio Museum in Harlem Store

144 W. 125th St. (bet. Lenox Ave. & Adam Clayton Powell Jr. Blvd.) New York, NY 10027 • (212) 864-4500 ext. 237

Fax: (212) 666-5753

Hours: Wed.-Fri. 10 A.M. to 4:45 P.M.; Sat.-Sun. 1 P.M. to 5:45 P.M.

Form of payment: Visa, MC, AMEX

Type of store: New, mail order

Subject Specialties: Art - American • Art - African • African-American Studies • Diaspora - African

Manager: Sheila Singleton

Year Established: 1982

No. of Volumes: 230

Sidelines and Services: Games, gifts, greeting cards, posters

Catalogs: Annual catalog

Comments: Stocks art books related to the African diaspora.

Sufi Books

227 West Broadway (bet. White & Franklin Sts.) New York, NY 10013 • (212) 334-5212 Fax: (212) 334-5214

Hours: Mon.-Fri. 11 A.M. to 7 P.M.; Sat. 11 A.M. to 6:30 P.M.

Form of payment: Visa, MC, AMEX, Checks

Type of store: New

Subject Specialties: Religion - Islam • Spirituality • Art - Middle Eastern • Health/Nutrition • Sufism • Mysticism • Traditional Healing

Owner: Pir Publications

Manager: Ann Everus

Year Established: 1992

No. of Volumes: 2,600 titles

Catalogs: "Sufi Review" (4/year; free by calling 800-925-3449)

Superintendant of Documents Bookstore

SEE: United States Government Printing Office

Supersnipe Comic Book Euphorium

P.O. Box 502, Planetarium Station New York, NY 10024

(212) 580-8843 Fax: (212) 580-8843 • E-mail address:

supersnipe@juno.com

Hours: By appointment only

Form of payment: Checks

Type of store: New, used

Subject Specialties: Comic Books • Fiction - Fantasy/Horror

• Animation

Owner: Edward Summer

Year Established: 1970

No. of Volumes: 300,000

Sidelines and Services: Appraisals, filling want lists

Catalogs: Semiannual catalog

Comments: Also stocks comic-strip anthologies and books on the history of comic books.

Surma Book and Music Co.

11 E. 7th St. (bet. Second & Third Aves.) New York, NY 10003

(212) 477-0729 Fax: (212) 473-0439

Hours: Mon.-Sat. 11 A.M. to 6 P.M.; Sun. 11 A.M. to 2 P.M.
Closed Sun. & Mon. June through August.
Form of payment: Visa, MC, AMEX, Checks
Subject Specialties: Ukraine (including Ukrainian Language
and Literature)
Owner: Myron Surmach
Year Established: 1918
Sidelines and Services: Crafts, magazines, prints, sheet music
Comments: Speciales in Ukranian fiction and books on Ukranian
music and history.

Swann Galleries

104 E. 25th St. (bet. Lexington & Park Aves.)
New York, NY 10010 • (212) 254-4710 Fax: (212) 979-1017
E-mail address: swannsales@aol.com
Hours: Mon.-Fri. 9 A.M. to 6 P.M.; Sat. by appointment
Type of store: Auction house, antiquarian, mail order
Subject Specialties: Auction House • Autographs/Manuscripts
• Prints/Drawings • Photography • Maps/Atlases/Cartography
• Americana • Literature - Modern • Early Printed Books
President: George S. Lowry
Year Established: 1942
Sidelines and Services: Works of art on paper, appraisal services
Catalogs: 35/year, plus quarterly newsletter and free brochure

Swedish Book Nook

P.O. Box 1353 New York, NY 10028 • (212) 744-8224

Hours: Mail order only
Form of payment: Checks
Type of store: Mail order
Subject Specialties: Sweden (including Swedish
Language & Literature) • Scandinavia
Owner: Alvalene Karlsson
Year Established: 1974
No. of Volumes: 1,500
Sidelines and Services: Gifts, greeting cards, maps, sheet music, toys

Synod Bookstore

75 E. 93rd St. (corner of Park Ave. and 93rd St.)
New York, NY 10128 • (212) 369-0288
Hours: Irregular hours. Phone ahead before coming.
Form of payment: Checks
Type of store: New, periodicals, mail order
Subject Specialties: Religion - Christianity
Catalogs: Issued irregularly ($1.25 postpaid)

Talas

568 Broadway (at Prince St.) New York, NY 10012
(212) 219-0770 Fax: (212) 219-0735
Hours: Mon.-Fri. 9 A.M. to 5 P.M.; open only first & third Sats.
of every month 10 A.M. to 3 P.M.
Type of store: New, mail order
Subject Specialties: Book Arts • Art Restoration • Bookbinding
• Marbling

Owners: Marge Salik, Jake Salik

Year Established: 1962

No. of Volumes: 100 titles

Sidelines and Services: Bookbinding and conservation supplies, wholesale section

Catalogs: Current price list available ($5 for catalog and price list)

Target Books and Music

outdoor kiosk on Madison Square Park (southwest corner of Madison Square Park, at Fifth Ave. & 23rd St.)

Hours: Mon.-Sun. 10 A.M. to twilight (weather permitting)

Form of payment: AMEX, checks

Type of Store: Used

Subject Specialties: General

Owner: Mark Rogers

Year Established: 1996

Sidelines and Services: CDs (classical and jazz), vintage postcards

Teachers College Bookstore (Columbia University Graduate School of Education)

1224 Amsterdam Ave. (at 120th St.) New York, NY 10027

(212) 678-3920 Fax: (212) 678-3985

E-mail address: tcbkstore@msmailhub.tc.columbia.edu

Hours: Mon.-Thu. 10 A.M. to 7:30 P.M.; Fri. 10 A.M. to 5 P.M.; Sat. 11 A.M. to 4 P.M.

Form of payment: Visa, MC, AMEX, Discover, Checks

Type of store: New

Subject Specialties: Education • Children's/Juvenile
Manager: Cathleen Mithaug
No. of Volumes: 25,000 titles
Sidelines and Services: College and school supplies, gifts, greeting cards, posters, games, computer software, teacher supplies, children's story hours
Comments: The general public is welcome and children's books are discounted at this store, which is operated by Barnes & Noble.

Technical Career Institute Bookstore

320 W. 31st St. (bet. Eighth & Ninth Aves.) New York, NY 10001
(212) 594-4000 ext. 213 Fax: (212) 330-0896
Hours: Mon.-Thu. 8:45 A.M. to 6:30 P.M. Fri. 8:30 A.M. to 4:30 P.M.
Form of payment: Visa, MC, AMEX, Checks
Type of store: New
Subject Specialties: Science • Technology
• Computers • Secretarial Studies
Manager: Lida Samson
Year Established: 1974
Sidelines and Services: Calculators, school supplies

Textbook Express

SEE: Corporate Book Express

Three Lives and Co.

154 W. Tenth St. (at the corner of Waverly Place)

New York, NY 10014

(212) 741-2069 Fax: (212) 741-4565

Hours: Mon.-Tue. 1 P.M. to 8 P.M.; Wed.-Sat. 11 A.M. to 8:30 P.M.;
Sun. 1 P.M. to 7 P.M.

Form of payment: Visa, MC, AMEX

Type of store: New, mail order

Subject Specialties: Architecture • Art - General • Design
• Literature - General • Humanities • Gay/Lesbian Studies

Owners: J. A. Feder, Jill Dunbar

Year Established: 1978

No. of Volumes: 15,000

Sidelines and Services: Greeting cards, special orders, reading
series, shipping within the U.S.

Tollett and Harman Autographs

175 W. 76th St. (at Amsterdam Ave.) New York, NY 10023

(212) 877-1566 Fax: (212) 877-0433

Hours: By appointment only

Form of payment: Checks

Type of store: Antiquarian

Subject Specialties: Autographs/Manuscripts • Photography
• Signed Editions

Owner: Robert Tollett

Year Established: 1984

Catalogs: Semiannual catalog

Comments: Also stocks cabinet and carte-de-visite photographs.

Tompkins Square Books

111 E. 7th St. (bet. Avenue A & First Ave.) New York, NY 10009

(212) 979-8958

Hours: Mon.-Sun. Noon to 11 P.M.

Form of payment: Checks

Type of store: New, used

Subject Specialties: Art - Modern • Literature - General

Owner: Gani Remorca

Comments: Also stocks books in Spanish, German, and French.

Tootsie's Children's Books

554 Hudson St. (bet. Perry & W. 11th Sts.) New York, NY 10014

(212) 242-0182

Hours: Mon.-Sat. 11 A.M. to 6 P.M. Open 7 days a week
in December.

Form of payment: Visa, MC, AMEX

Type of store: New

Subject Specialties: Children's/Juvenile • Christmas • Animals
• Toys • Folklore/Mythology • Science • Trains/Railways • Spanish
Language and Literature

Owner: Kathleen M. Solomon

Year Established: 1994

No. of Volumes: 4,000

Sidelines and Services: Educational CD-ROMs, musical recordings,
videotapes, puppets, games & puzzles, book-character dolls,
shipping service, free gift wrapping, book search service

Catalogs: Free newsletter 4 times/year

Touba Khassyitt Books & Tapes

243 W. 116th St. (bet. Adam Clayton Powell Jr. Blvd. & Frederick Douglass Blvd.) New York, NY 10026

(212) 280-0827 Fax: (212) 280-0827

Hours: Mon.-Sun. 10 A.M. to 10 P.M.

Subject Specialties: Religion - Islam • Koran

Manager: Amadou Sarr

Year Established: 1995

Sidelines and Services: Posters, videos, gift items

Comments: Stocks books in English, French, and Arabic.

Touro College Bookstore

240 E. 123rd St. (bet. Second & Third Aves.) New York, NY 10035

(212) 722-1575 (ext. 453) Fax: (212) 348-6971

Hours: Mon.-Thu. 10 A.M. to 6 P.M.; Fri. 10 A.M. to 2 P.M.

Form of payment: Visa, MC, Checks

Type of store: New

Subject Specialties: General

Manager: Clifford Anuforoh

Sidelines and Services: Stationery, clothing

Tower Books

383 Lafayette St. (at 4th St.) New York, NY 10003

(212) 228-5100 Fax: (212) 228-5338

Hours: Mon.-Sun. 11 A.M. to 11 P.M.

Form of payment: Visa, MC, AMEX, Discover, Checks

Type of store: New

Subject Specialties: Literature - General • Popular Culture
• Art - General • Music • New York City • General
Manager: Jonathan Glenn
Year Established: 1990
No. of Volumes: 250,000
Sidelines and Services: Maps, books on tape, magazines
(domestic & foreign)

Traveler's Choice Bookstore

111 Greene St. (bet. Prince & Spring Sts.)
New York, NY 10012 • (212) 941-1535 Fax: (212) 219-1865
Hours: Mon.-Fri. 9 A.M. to 6 P.M.; Sat. 10 A.M. to 5 P.M.
Form of payment: Visa, MC, AMEX
Type of store: New
Subject Specialties: Travel
Manager: Nicholas Christopher
Year Established: 1995
No. of Volumes: 5,000
Sidelines and Services: Maps, travel accessories, camera bags

Traveller's Bookstore

22 W. 52nd St. (bet. Fifth & Sixth Aves., in lobby of Time-
Warner Bldg.) New York, NY 10019 • (212) 664-0995 or
(800) 755-8728 Fax: (212) 397-3984
Hours: Mon.-Fri. 9 A.M. to 6 P.M.; Sat. 11 A.M. to 5 P.M.
Form of payment: Visa, MC, AMEX, Checks
Type of store: New, mail order

Subject Specialties: Travel • Maps/Atlases/Cartography • Foreign Language Instruction • Natural History • Sports • Travel • Memoirs
Owner: Diana Wells
Year Established: 1982
No. of Volumes: 30,000
Sidelines and Services: Maps, guides, language tapes, historical & archaeological background material, free giftwrap, special orders, bulk corporate orders
Catalogs: Annual catalog ($2 to be on mailing list; free with an order), quarterly newsletter

Trinity Bookstore

74 Trinity Pl. (bet. Rector and Thames Sts., behind Trinity Church) New York, NY 10006 • (212) 602-9689 or (800) 551-1220
Fax: (212) 602-0727
Hours: Mon.-Thu. 8:30 A.M. to 6 P.M.; Fri. 8:30 A.M. to 5:30 P.M.
Form of payment: Visa, MC, AMEX
Type of store: New, mail order
Subject Specialties: Religion - Christianity • Bibles • Banking • Religion - General • Spirituality • Theology
Manager: Arlene E. Bullard
Year Established: 1983
Sidelines and Services: Special orders, gifts
Catalogs: Free annual catalog
Comments: Store will bill churches.

Peter Tumarkin Fine Books

409 W. 21st St. (bet. Ninth & Tenth Aves.) New York, NY 10011
(212) 741-7237 Fax: (212) 741-1861
Hours: By appointment only
Type of store: Antiquaria
Subject specialties: Germany (including German Language
and Literature) • Judaica • Incunabula • Illustrated Books
• Books About Books/Bibliography
Owner: Peter Tumarkin
Year Established: 1973
Sidelines and Services: Appraise library collections

David Tunick

12 E. 81st St. (bet. Madison & Fifth Aves.) New York, NY 10028
(212) 570-0090 Fax: (212) 744-8931
Hours: Appointment advisable (Mon.-Fri.: 10 A.M. to 5 P.M.)
Type of store: Antiquarian
Subject Specialties: Prints/Drawings
President: David P. Tunick
Year Established: 1966

TwoSixtyOne Arts

261 Broadway, Suite 8A (at Chambers St.) New York, NY 10007
(212) 619-0869
Hours: Mon.-Fri. 10 A.M. to 5 P.M. (best to call ahead before coming)
Form of payment: Checks
Subject Specialties: Art - Modern • Illustration - Modern

Owner: Richard Gardner
No. of Volumes: 7,000

UNICEF House Gift Shop

3 UN Plaza (44th St. & First Ave.) New York, NY 10017
(212) 326-7054 Fax: (212) 759-0767
Hours: Mon.-Fri. 10 A.M. to 6 P.M.; Sat. 10 A.M. to 3 P.M.
Form of payment: Visa, MC, AMEX, Discover, Checks
Type of store: New, periodicals
Subject Specialties: International Affairs • Cooking
Year Established: 1985
No. of Volumes: 50
Sidelines and Services: Greeting cards, gifts

Unification Books

SEE: HSA Bookstore

Union Square Art Books

33 Union Square West New York, NY 10003 • (212) 989-3083
Hours: By appointment only
Type of store: Mail order, new, rare
Subject Specialties: Art - General
Owners: Rita Di Pace, Alfredo de Palchi
Year Established: 1980
No. of Volumes: 3,000

Union Theological Seminary Bookstore

3041 Broadway (bet. 120th & 121st Sts.) New York, NY 10027
(212) 280-1554 Fax: (212) 280-1416 • E-mail address:
ennassef@uts.columbia.edu
Hours: Mon., Wed.-Fri. 9:30 A.M. to 5 P.M.; Tue. 9:30 A.M. to 7 P.M.
Form of payment: Visa, MC, AMEX, Checks
Type of store: New
Subject Specialties: Religion - Christianity • Theology • Philosophy
• Bibles • Women's Studies • African-American Studies
Manager: Henry Moren
Sidelines and Services: Stationery, greeting cards

United Nations Bookshop

General Assembly Bldg., Rm. 32; United Nations (46th St.
at First Ave.) New York, NY 10017 • (212) 963-7680 or
(800) 553-3210 Fax: (212) 963-4910
Hours: Mon.-Fri. 9:15 A.M. to 4:45 P.M.; Sat.-Sun. 9:15 A.M. to 4:45
P.M. Closed Sat. and Sun. during January and February.
Form of payment: Visa, MC, AMEX
Type of store: New
Subject Specialties: International Affairs • Foreign Language
Instruction • Travel • Economics • Women's Studies • Politics/
Political Science • Children's/Juvenile • Environment/Conservation/
Ecology • Human Rights • United Nations
Manager: Cathe Lotter
Year Established: 1948
No. of Volumes: 16,000
Sidelines and Services: Videotapes, postcards, calendars,

UN souvenirs

Catalogs: Annual catalog

Comments: Also stocks publications of the United Nations.

United States Government Printing Office Bookstore

26 Federal Plaza, Rm. 110 (Foley Square, on Broadway bet. Duane & Worth Sts.)

New York, NY 10278

(212) 264-3825 Fax: (212) 264-9318

Hours: Mon.-Fri. 8:15 A.M. to 4:15 P.M.

Form of payment: Visa, MC, Checks (with I.D.)

Type of store: New, periodicals, mail order

Subject Specialties: Government Publications • Health/Nutrition • Business/Management • Nautical/Maritime • Military/War • Reference • History - 20th c. • Environment/Conservation/Ecology

Manager: Alexander Wilson

Year Established: 1971

No. of Volumes: 1,800 titles

Sidelines and Services: Posters, decals

Catalogs: Free semiannual catalog

Comments: Also known as "Superintendent of Documents Bookstore" or "U.S. Government Bookstore"

United Synagogue Book Service

155 Fifth Ave. (bet. 20th & 21st Sts.) New York, NY 10010

(212) 533-7800 (ext. 2003) Fax: (212) 353-9439

E-mail address: 71263.333@compuserve.com

Hours: By appointment only (primarily a mail-order business)

Form of payment: Visa, MC (min. charge $25), Checks

Type of store: New, mail order

Subject Specialties: Judaica

Director: Joseph Sandler

No. of Volumes: 200 titles

Catalogs: Free annual catalog

Unity Book Center

237 W. 23rd St. (bet. Seventh & Eighth Aves.)

New York, NY 10011 • (212) 242-2934

Hours: Mon.-Fri. 10:30 A.M. to 5:30 P.M.; Sat. 11 A.M. to 4 P.M.

Form of payment: Checks

Type of store: New

Subject Specialties: African-American Studies • Industry • Poetry
• Politics/Political Science • Labor

Manager: Mavis N. Ueberall

Year Established: 1978

Sidelines and Services: Gifts, magazines, CDs, audio cassettes

Unity Center of Practical Christianity Bookstore

213 W. 58th St. (bet. Seventh Ave. & Broadway)

New York, NY 10019 • (212) 582-1300 Fax: (212) 582-2158

Hours: Tue.-Wed. 11 A.M. to 7 P.M.; Thu. 11 A.M. to 5 P.M.;

Fri. 11 A.M. to 4 P.M.

Form of payment: Checks

Type of store: New

Subject Specialties: Religion - Christianity • Self-Help
• Metaphysics • Occult/Mysticism

Manager: Olga Butterworth

Sidelines and Services: Audio cassettes

Untitled/Fine Art in Print

159 Prince St. (bet. Thompson St. & West Broadway)
New York, NY 10012 • (212) 982-2088 Fax: (212) 925-5533
E-mail address: bdavies@gnn.com
Hours: Mon.-Sat. 10 A.M. to 10 P.M.; Sun. 11 A.M. to 7 P.M.

Form of payment: Visa, MC, AMEX, Discover, Checks

Type of store: New

Subject Specialties: Art - General • Design • Architecture
• Photography

Owner: Michelle Davies

Year Established: 1984

No. of Volumes: 1,000 titles

Sidelines and Services: Art cards and postcards

Catalogs: Monthly catalog

Urban Center Books

457 Madison Ave. (bet. 50th & 51st Sts., in courtyard of the
Villard Houses) New York, NY 10022 • (212) 935-3592
Fax: (212) 223-2887 • E-mail address: uc_books@usa.pipeline.com

Hours: Mon.-Thu. 10 A.M. to 7 P.M.; Fri. 10 A.M. to 6 P.M.; Sat. 10 A.M. to 5:30 P.M. Open Sun. during Christmas season.

Form of payment: Visa, MC, Checks

Type of store: New, periodicals, mail order

Subject Specialties: Architecture • Design • Preservation • History • Urban Planning • Landscape Architecture

Manager: Ken Tracy

Year Established: 1980

No. of Volumes: 16,000

Sidelines and Services: Magazines (current & back issues), search service

Catalogs: Free annual catalog

Ursus Art Books in Soho

375 West Broadway, 3rd fl. (bet. Broome & Spring Sts.)
New York, NY 10012 • (212) 226-7858 Fax: (212) 226-7955
E-mail address: ursus@panix.com

Hours: Mon.-Fri. 10 A.M. to 6 P.M.; Sat. 11 A.M. to 5 P.M.

Form of payment: Visa, MC, AMEX, Checks

Type of store: New

Subject Specialties: Art - General • Fine Arts • Architecture • Art - Modern • Illustrated Books • Exhibition Catalogs • Art - Artists' Monographs

Owner: Peter Kraus

Year Established: 1991

No. of Volumes: 25,000

Sidelines and Services: Search service

Catalogs: 8/year (free)

Comments: This is a branch of Ursus Books' main store at 981 Madison Avenue.

Ursus Books and Prints

981 Madison Ave., Mezzanine Level (bet. 76th & 77th Sts.)
New York, NY 10021 • (212) 772-8787 Fax: (212) 737-9306
E-mail address: ursus@panix.com
Hours: Mon.-Fri. 10 A.M. to 6 P.M.; Sat. 11 A.M. to 5 P.M.
Form of payment: Visa, MC, AMEX, Checks
Type of store: New, antiquarian, mail order
Subject Specialties: Art - General • Prints/Drawings • Fine Arts
• Architecture • Art - Modern • Illustrated Books • Natural History
• Literature - General
Owner: Peter Kraus
Year Established: 1972
No. of Volumes: 50,000
Sidelines and Services: Appraise library collections
Catalogs: 8/year

Used Book Cafe

SEE: Housing Works Used Book Cafe

H. Valentine Books

211 E. 11th St. New York, NY 10003 • (212) 533-3883
Hours: Mail order only
Form of payment: Visa, MC, AMEX, Checks

Type of store: Antiquarian
Subject Specialties: First Editions • Fiction - Crime/Mystery/ Suspense
Owner: Joshua Mrvos
Year Established: 1993
Sidelines and Services: Search service
Catalogs: 4/year (free)

S. F. Vanni

30 W. 12th St. (bet. Fifth & Sixth Aves.)
New York, NY 10011 • (212) 675-6336
Hours: Mon.-Fri. 10 A.M. to 5:30 P.M.; Sat. 10 A.M. to 4 P.M.
Form of payment: Checks
Type of store: New
Subject Specialties: Italy (including Italian Language and Literature)
Owners: O. Ragusa, I. Ragusa
Year Established: 1884
No. of Volumes: 100,000
Catalogs: Annual catalog

Viewpoint Gallery

41 Union Square West, Penthouse New York, NY 10003
(212) 242-5478 Fax: (212) 979-8806
Hours: Mon.-Fri. 1 P.M. to 6 P.M. (call ahead first).
Open Sat. by appointment only.
Form of payment: Checks

Type of store: Antiquarian
Subject Specialties: History - General • Literature - General
• Art - General
Owner: Robert H. Pettit
Year Established: 1981
No. of Volumes: 2,000
Sidelines and Services: Music recordings, art gallery, search service
Comments: Mailing address: 111 E. 14th St., Suite. 125, New
York, NY 10003

Village Comics

214 Sullivan St. (bet. Bleecker & W. 3rd Sts.)
New York, NY 10012 • (212) 777-2770 Fax: (212) 475-9727
Hours: Mon.-Tue. 10 A.M. to 8 P.M.; Wed. 9:30 A.M. to 9 P.M.;
Thu.-Sat. 10 A.M. to 9 P.M.; Sun. 10:30 A.M. to 7:30 P.M.
Form of payment: Visa, MC, AMEX, Discover, JVC, Checks
Type of store: New, used, periodicals, mail order
Subject Specialties: Comic Books • Graphic Arts • Humor
• Signed Editions • Posters • Prints/Drawings
• Magazines/Journals/ Newspapers • Toys
Owner: Joseph Lihach
Year Established: 1978
Sidelines and Services: Models, model kits, trading cards,
tee-shirts, collectibles, Japanimation

Virgin Megastore Book Department

1540 Broadway, Level B-2 (bet. 45th & 46th Sts.)

New York, NY 10036 • (212) 921-1020 (ext. 296)
Hours: Sun.-Thu. 8 A.M. to 1 A.M.; Fri.-Sat. 8 A.M. to 2 A.M.
Form of payment: Visa, MC, AMEX, Discover, Checks
Type of store: New
Subject Specialties: Music • Popular Culture • Art - General
• Photography
Senior Sales: Danielle Bottinger
Year Established: 1996

Waldenbooks

57 Broadway (bet. Rector St. & Exchange Pl., just south of Wall
St.) New York, NY 10006 • (212) 269-1139 Fax: (212) 809-2433
Hours: Mon.-Fri. 8 A.M. to 6 P.M.
Form of payment: Visa, MC, AMEX, Discover, Checks
Type of store: New
Subject Specialties: Business/Management
Manager: Melissa Glowski

Andrew D. Washton Books on the Fine Arts

88 Lexington Ave., Ste. 10G New York, NY 10016
(212) 481-0479 Fax: (212) 861-0588
Hours: By appointment only
Form of payment: Checks
Type of store: Antiquarian, used, mail order
Subject Specialties: Art - European, 1600-1900 • Art - General
• Art - Reference • Art - Medieval/Renaissance

Owner: Andrew D. Washton
Year Established: 1981
No. of Volumes: 3,000
Sidelines and Services: Appraise library collections
Catalogs: 4-6/year (free)

Weitz, Weitz & Coleman

1377 Lexington Ave. (bet. 90th & 91st Sts.)
New York, NY 10128 • (212) 831-2213 Fax: (212) 427-5718
Hours: Mon.-Thu. 9 A.M. to 7 P.M.; Fri. 9 A.M. to 5 P.M.;
Sat. Noon to 5 P.M.
Form of payment: Checks
Type of store: Antiquarian, used
Subject Specialties: Americana • Art - General • Books About
Books/Bibliography • History - General • Fine Bindings
• Colorplate Books
Owners: H. Weitz, Elspeth Coleman
Year Established: 1909
No. of Volumes: 15,000
Sidelines and Services: Bookbinding on the premises, folding
boxes, book restoration

West Side Judaica

2412 Broadway (bet. 88th & 89th Sts.) New York, NY 10024
(212) 362-7846 Fax: (212) 787-4202
Hours: Mon.-Thu. 10:30 A.M. to 7:30 P.M.; Fri. 10:30 A.M. to 3 P.M.
(closes at 1 P.M. on Fri. in winter); Sun. 10:30 A.M. to 6 P.M.

Form of payment: Visa, MC, Checks
Type of store: New, mail order
Subject Specialties: Judaica
Owner: Y. Salczer
Manager: Carla Hanauer
Year Established: 1981
No. of Volumes: 15,000

Sidelines and Services: Games, gifts, greeting cards, religious goods, toys, videotapes, special orders, decorative art
Comments: Also carries publications from Israel.

Jonathan White

98 Riverside Dr., #10G (entrance on W. 82nd St.)
New York, NY 10024 • (212) 496-8854
Hours: By appointment only
Type of store: Used, antiquarian, mail order, periodicals
Subject Specialties: Fiction - Science Fiction • Fiction - Fantasy/Horror
Owner: Jonathan White
No. of Volumes: 10,000
Sidelines and Services: Magazine back issues, original art
Catalogs: 1-2/year
Comments: Stock includes vintage paperbacks and pulp magazines.

Whitney Museum of American Art Bookstore

945 Madison Ave. (at 75th St.) New York, NY 10021

(212) 570-3614 Fax: (212) 570-1807
Hours: Tue. 10 A.M. to 5 P.M.; Wed., Fri.-Sun.: 11 A.M. to 6 P.M.;
Thu. 1 P.M. to 8 P.M. Closed Mon.
Form of payment: Visa, MC, AMEX, Checks
Type of store: New
Subject Specialties: Art - American
Manager: Michael Lagios
Year Established: 1966
No. of Volumes: 500
Sidelines and Services: Posters, postcards, notecards, video-
tapes, exhibition catalogs, tee-shirts

Whitney Museum of American Art Store Next Door

943 Madison Ave. (bet. 74th & 75th Sts.)
New York, NY 10021 • (212) 606-0600
Hours: Tue.-Wed., Fri.-Sat. 10 A.M. to 6 P.M.; Thu. 10 A.M.
to 8 P.M.; Sun. 11 A.M. to 6 P.M. Closed Mon.
Form of payment: Visa, MC, AMEX, Checks
Type of store: New
Subject Specialties: Art - American
Manager: Megan Russell
Sidelines and Services: Calendars, jewelry, stationery, video-
tapes, glassware, American crafts, children's merchandise

Philip Williams Posters

60 Grand St. (bet. W. Broadway & Wooster St.)

New York, NY 10013 • (212) 226-7830
E-mail address: vintagepostr@earthlink.com
Hours: Mon.-Sun. 11 A.M. to 7 P.M.
Form of payment: Visa, MC, AMEX, Checks
Type of store: New, used
Subject Specialties: Art - General • Posters
Owner: Philip Williams
Year Established: 1973
No. of Volumes: 100 titles
Sidelines and Services: Appraise library collections, posters, prints, mail order
Catalogs: Occasional catalog

Fred Wilson Books

80 E. 11th St., Suite 334 (bet. University Pl. & Broadway)
New York, NY 10003 • (212) 533-6381
Hours: Mon.-Sat. Noon to 7 P.M.
Form of payment: Checks
Type of store: New, used
Subject Specialties: Chess
Owner: Fred Wilson

Year Established: 1973
No. of Volumes: 3,000
Sidelines and Services: Appraise chess collections, foreign language periodicals, Wed.-evening chess seminars
Catalogs: 3/year

Wurlitzer-Bruck

60 Riverside Dr. New York, NY 10024

(212) 787-6431 Fax: (212) 496-6525

Hours: By appointment only

Type of store: Antiquarian

Subject Specialties: Music • Autographs/Manuscripts • Opera
• Prints/Drawings • Illuminated Manuscripts

Owners: Marianne Wurlitzer, Gene Bruck

Year Established: 1975

Sidelines and Services: Prints and paintings of musical subjects,
musical autographs, musical ephemera

Collegiate Bookstore
at Yeshiva University

2539 Amsterdam Ave. (at 186th St.) New York, NY 10033

(212) 923-5782 Fax: (212) 927-5257

Hours: Mon.-Thu. 10 A.M. to 3:15 P.M.

Form of payment: Visa, MC; No checks

Type of store: New, used

Subject Specialties: Judaica

Year Established: 1987

Yeshiva University Museum Gift Shop

2520 Amsterdam Ave. (at 185th St.) New York, NY 10033

(212) 960-5390

Hours: Tue.-Thu. 10:30 A.M. to 5 P.M.; Sun. Noon to 6 P.M.

Form of payment: Checks

Type of store: New
Subject Specialties: Judaica
Manager: Eleanor Chiger
Year Established: 1977

Yu Lee Book Store

81 Bayard St. (bet. Mott & Mulberry Sts.)
New York, NY 10013 • (212) 349-0451
Hours: Mon.-Sun. 10:30 A.M. to 8 P.M.
Type of store: New
Subject Specialties: China (including Chinese Language
and Literature)

Zakka

510 Broome St. (bet. West Broadway and Thompson St.)
New York, NY 10013 • (212) 431-3961 Fax: (212) 431-5549
Hours: Mon., Wed.-Sun. Noon to 8 P.M. Closed Tue.
Form of payment: Visa, MC, AMEX
Type of store: New
Subject Specialties: Japan (including Japanese Language and
Literature) • Graphic Arts • Design • Art - Asian • Asian Studies
• New Age • Animation Art • Toys
Owners: Toshiki Okazaki, Miyuki Okazaki
Year Established: 1994

Irving Zucker Art Books

303 Fifth Ave., Suite 1407 (at 31st St.) New York, NY 10016

(212) 679-6332 Fax: (914) 692-7675

Hours: By appointment only

Form of payment: Checks

Type of store: Antiquarian

Subject Specialties: Illustrated Books • Art - General • Fine Arts • Prints/Drawings

Owners: Irving Zucker, Janis Zucker

Year Established: 1940

No. of Volumes: 600

Comments: Also stocks French modern illustrated books.

Neighborhood Index

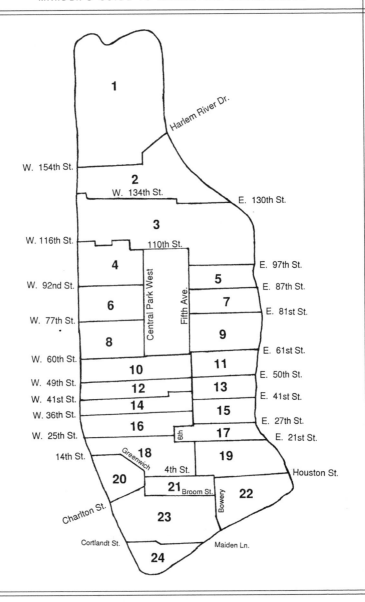

Cathedral Shop of Saint John
the Divine
Christian Science Reading Room
(1st Church)
Christian Science Reading
Room (7th Church)
Demes Books
First Things First
Funny Business Comics
Ideal Book Store
L. Kaplan Magazine and
Book Search
David Malamud Books
Isaac H. Mann
Jeryl Metz
Murder Ink
Naturalist's Bookshelf
Paperback Discounter—Video 83
Papyrus Booksellers
Pomander Books
Posman Books at Barnard College

AREA 5
Upper East Side: 87th to 96th Sts.
Zip code 10128
Jutta Buck, Antiquarian Book
and Print Sellers
Cooper-Hewitt Museum Shop
Book Department
Corner Bookstore
DG Antiquarian Books
William Doyle Galleries
V. F. Germack Professional
Photography Collectors
Solomon R. Guggenheim
Museum Bookstore

International Center of
Photography
Jewish Museum Book Shop
Kitchen Arts and Letters
The Military Bookman
National Academy of Design
Bookshop
Leona Rostenberg and Madeleine
B. Stern Rare Books
Charlotte F. Safir Books
Synod Bookstore
Weitz, Weitz & Coleman

AREA 6
Upper West Side: 77th to 91st Sts.
Zip code 10024
American Educational Systems
Bookstore
American Museum of Natural
History Museum Shop
Bart Auerbach
Barnes & Noble Bookstore
(Store No. 1979)
Book Ark
William G. Boyer
Jo Ann and Richard Casten Ltd.
Children's Museum of Manhattan
Chip's Bookshop
Corporate Book Express
Cultured Oyster Books
East-West Books
Roger Gross Ltd.
Gryphon Bookshop
Hauswedell & Nolte
(New York office)
Hayden Planetarium Bookstore
Kendra Krienke

AREA 9
Upper East Side: 61st to 80th Sts.
Zip code 10021
Appelfeld Gallery
W. Graham Arader III
Archivia: The Art Book Shop
The Asia Society Bookstore
Bookberries
Books & Co.
Bryn Mawr Bookshop
Susi Buchanan
Choices—The Recovery Bookshop
Christian Science Reading Room
    (3rd Church)
Christian Science Reading Room
    (8th Church)
Cornell University Medical
    College Bookstore
James Cummins Bookseller
Ex Libris
Leonard Fox Ltd.
Frick Collection
Bill George International
Good Earth Foods
Elliot Gordon Books
Charles Hamilton Autographs
Donald A. Heald Rare Books
    and Fine Art
Hudson News Bookstore
Hunter College Bookstore
Imperial Fine Books
Harmer Johnson Books
Kauffman International Ltd.
Kubies
Janet Lehr
Lenox Hill Bookstore
Madison Avenue Bookshop

Metropolitan Opera Gift Shop
Murder Ink
Paraclete Book Center
Phillips Auctioneers
Pryor & Johnson Booksellers
Bruce J. Ramer, Experimenta
    Old and Rare Books
Richard C. Ramer Old
    and Rare Books
Reinhold-Brown Gallery
Kenneth W. Rendell Gallery
Paulette Rose, Fine
    and Rare Books
Howard Schickler
David Schulson Autographs
Shakespeare & Co.
Sotheby's Book and Manuscripts
    Department
Stress Less Step
Stubbs Books and Prints
Ursus Books and Prints
Whitney Museum of American
    Art Bookstore
Whitney Museum of American
    Art Store Next Door

AREA 10
Midtown West: 49th to 59th Sts.
Zip codes 10019, 10020, 10103,
    10111, 10101, 10112
American Craft Museum
American Folk Art Books
American Management
    Association Bookstore
Barnes & Noble Bookstore
    (Store No. 1003)

Quest Bookshop
Rand McNally, The Map
    and Travel Store
Justin G. Schiller Ltd.
F.A.O. Schwarz Book Department
Urban Center Books

AREA 12
**Midtown West: 41st to 48th Sts.,
including the Theater District
Zip code 10036**
Animation Art Guild Ltd.
Christian Publications Book
    and Supply Center
Dianetics Center
The East Africa Safari Co.
Gemological Institute
    of America Bookstore
Gotham Book Mart and Gallery
HSA Bookstore
Hagstrom Map and Travel Center
International Center
    of Photography
JHM Video
Dan Redmon
Virgin Megastore Book Department

AREA 13
**Midtown East: 41st to 49th Sts.
Zip codes 10017, 10173, 10175,
    10176**
Asahiya Bookstores New York, Inc.
Barnes & Noble Bookstore
    (Store No. 1020)
Barnes & Noble Bookstore
    (Store No. 1051)
British Travel Bookshop

Christian Science Reading Room
    (5th Church)
Creative Living Bookstore (First
    Church of Religious Science)
E & D Books
Episcopal Book Resource Center
Glenn Horowitz Bookseller
Hudson News Bookstore
JBC Bookstore
H. P. Kraus Rare Books
    and Manuscripts
Scientific & Medical Publications
    of France
UNICEF House Gift Shop
United Nations Bookshop

AREA 14
**Midtown West: 36th to 40th/41st
Sts., including Garment District
(north)
Zip code 10018**
Adventist Book Center
E. W. Brill Antiquarian Books
Bus Terminal Books and Periodicals
Ginesta Eudaldo
Fashion Books and Magazines
E & B Goldbergs' Discount Marine
Hudson News Bookstore
Hudson News Bookstore
Manhattan Gaming Co.
New York Public Library Bookstore
OAN / Oceanie Afrique Noire
    Art Books

Barnes & Noble Bookstore
(Store No. 2538)
Baruch College Bookstore
Central Yiddish Culture
Organization
Christian Science Reading Room
(9th Church)
Samuel French Bookshop
K & M Camera
Victor Kamkin
Judith and Peter Klemperer
Magazine Center
Millers
Reference Book Center
School of Visual Arts Bookstore
Swann Galleries
Target Books and Music
United Synagogue Book Service

AREA 18
**Chelsea (south) and Greenwich
Village (northwest)**
Zip code 10011
Academy Book Store
America's Hobby Center
C. Virginia Barnes
Barnes & Noble Bookstore—
Annex (Store No. 1002)
C. Richard Becker
Book Scientific
Book Smart
Books and Binding
Books of Wonder
Chelsea Books and Records
Christian Science Reading Room
(10th Church)
Howard C. Daitz Photographica

B. Dalton Bookseller
(Store No. 1167)
A Different Light Bookstore
East-West Books
A. I. Friedman
Great Judaica Books
Integral Yoga Bookshop
Landy Fine Judaica
Lectorum Publications
Librairie Francaise
Macondo Books
Manhattan Comics and Cards
Metropolitan Book Auction
Metropolitan Book Center
Fred and Elizabeth Pajerski
Partners & Crime Mystery
Booksellers
Revolution Books
Roig Spanish Books
Skyline Books & Records
Rudolf Steiner Bookstore
Peter Tumarkin Fine Books
Unity Book Center
S. F. Vanni

AREA 19
**Houston to E 21st Sts., including
East Village, Stuyvesant, Gramercy,
New York University**
Zip codes 10003, 10009
Abraham's Magazine Service
Agueybana Bookstore
Angelica's Herbs
Arka Gift Shop
Asian American Bookshop
The Baha'i Bookstore

AREA 21
**Broome to 4th Sts., betw. 6th Av.
& Bowery; including Greenwich
Village, Soho (north), Little Italy,
& Bowery**
Zip code 10012
The Bilingual Publications Co.
CFM Gallery
Center for Book Arts
Chess Forum
Chess Shop
Children of Paradise
D.A.P. Bookstore at Exit Art
Dean and Deluca
Down East Enterprises
Eastern Mountain Sports
    (Store No. 35)
El Cascajero—the old Spanish
    book mine
Gallery 292
Granary Books
Solomon R. Guggenheim Museum
    Soho Bookstore
Hebrew Union College Bookstore
Housing Works Used Book Cafe
Illustration House
The Irish Bookshop
Lafayette Books
Mercer Street Books and Records
The New Museum of Contemporary
    Art Bookshop
New York Open Center Bookstore
New York University Book Center—
    Professional Bookstore
Nudel Books
Pageant Book and Print Shop
Perimeter

A Photographers Place
Printed Matter
Rizzoli Bookstore and Art Boutique
The Science Fiction Shop
6 Rays of Gold
Spring Street Books
Talas
Traveler's Choice Bookstore
Untitled / Fine Art in Print
Ursus Art Books in Soho
Village Comics

AREA 22
Lower East Side, Bowery
Zip code 10002
Elite Hong Kong
Jaffa Gate Bookshop
Stavsky Hebrew Bookstore

AREA 23
**Chinatown, Soho, Tribeca, City
Hall, Financial District (north)**
**Zip codes 10007, 10013, 10038,
    10278, 10281**
Alba House Cornerstone Book
    and Gift Shop
America East Book Co.
Ann St. Adult Entertainment Center
Art Market
Association of Independent Video
    and Film Makers
Biblio's Cafe and Bookstore
Borough of Manhattan Community
    College Bookstore
City Books Stores
Civil Service Book Shop
The Civilized Traveler

College of Insurance Bookstore
Computer Book Works
Dieu Donne Papermill—
   The Mill Store
Dokya Bookstore
Good Field Trading Co.
Virginia L. Green Rare Books
Heller Audiobooks
J. N. Herlin
Jung Ku Books and Stationery
Mona Levine
Living Word Books
New York Law School Bookstore
New York Nautical Instrument
   and Service Corp.
Oriental Culture Enterprises
Pace University Bookstore
Rizzoli Bookstore
Ruby's Book Sale
Science Fiction Mysteries & More!
Soho Books
South Street Seaport
   Museum Bookstore
Spoken Word
Strand Bookstore
Sufi Books
TwoSixtyOne Arts
United States Government Printing
   Office Bookstore
Philip Williams Posters
Yu Lee Book Store
Zakka

AREA 24
Financial District, Wall Street, World
Trade Center, Battery Park City
Zip codes 10004, 10005, 10006,
   10041, 10047, 10048, 10280,
   10281, 10282
Benjamin Books
Borders Books and Music
Castle Clinton Monument Bookstore
Christian Science Reading Room
   (Tri-State Reading Room)
The Civilized Traveler
Federal Hall National
   Memorial Bookstore
Fraunces Tavern Museum Store
Hudson News Bookstore
National Museum of the
   American Indian (Smithsonian
   Institution) Bookshop
Rizzoli Bookstore
Shakespeare & Co.
R. M. Smythe and Co.
Trinity Bookstore
Waldenbooks

Subject Index

Integral Yoga Bookshop
Koryo Books
Liberation Bookstore, Inc.
New York Open Center Bookstore
Quest Bookshop

Americana
American Folk Art Books
Appelfeld Gallery
W. Graham Arader III
Argosy Book Store
J. N. Bartfield
Bauman Rare Books
James F. Carr
Donald A. Heald Rare
    Books and Fine Art
H. P. Kraus Rare Books
    and Manuscripts
Martayan Lan
Metropolitan Book Center
The Military Bookman
The Old Print Shop
Pageant Book and Print Shop
Richard C. Ramer Old
    and Rare Books
Sotheby's Book and Manuscripts
    Department
Strand Bookstore
Strand Bookstore Rare
    Book Department
Swann Galleries
Weitz, Weitz & Coleman

Anarchism
Blackout Books

Angels
Everything Angels

Animals
Dog Lovers Bookshop
Tootsie's Children's Books

Animation
Supersnipe Comic Book Euphorium

Animation Art
Animation Art Guild Ltd.
Zakka

Anthropology
Continental Book Search
C. G. Jung Foundation Book Service
Liberation Bookstore, Inc.
OAN / Oceanie Afrique Noire
    Art Books

Anti-Authoritarianism
Blackout Books

Antiques/Collectibles
Acanthus Books
C. Richard Becker
Ralph D. Gardner
Gem Antiques
Hayden & Fandetta
Metropolitan Book Center
Theodore Roosevelt Birthplace
        National Historic Site Bookstore

Applied Arts
Hacker Art Books
Hayden & Fandetta

Architecture - Southeast Asian
OAN / Oceanie Afrique Noire
    Art Books

Arctic/Polar
Huckleberry Designs
South Street Seaport Museum
    Bookstore

Armenian Language
Fil Caravan Inc.

Arms and Armor
Huckleberry Designs
Metropolitan Museum of Art
    Bookshop
The Military Bookman

Art - African
Demes Books
Harmer Johnson Books
Liberation Bookstore, Inc.
OAN / Oceanie Afrique Noire
    Art Books
Studio Museum in Harlem Store

Art - American
American Folk Art Books
Fraunces Tavern Museum Store
Kennedy Galleries Book
    Department
Kolwyck-Jones Books on Art
Mona Levine
Madison Avenue Bookshop
Museum of American Folk Art
    Museum Shop
Studio Museum in Harlem Store

Whitney Museum of American
    Art Bookstore
Whitney Museum of American
    Art Store Next Door

Art - Ancient/Classical
Harmer Johnson Books
Mona Levine

Art - Art Deco/Art Nouveau
Leonard Fox Ltd.
Barbara Leibowits Graphics Ltd.

Art - Artists' Monographs
Ursus Art Books in Soho

Art - Asian
Asian Rare Books
Zakka

Art - Australia/Oceania
Harmer Johnson Books
OAN / Oceanie Afrique Noire
    Art Books

Art - Austrian
Galerie St. Etienne

Art - Avant-Garde
Howard Schickler

Art - Bauhaus School
Ex Libris

Art - Caribbean
OAN / Oceanie Afrique Noire
    Art Books

Metropolitan Museum of Art
   Bookshop at Rockefeller Center
Music Inn
New York Public Library Bookstore
Pageant Book and Print Shop
The Photographic Arts Center
Posman Books
Posman Books Annex
Printed Matter
Pryor & Johnson Booksellers
Reinhold-Brown Gallery
Rizzoli Bookstore
Rizzoli Bookstore and Art Boutique
Ruby's Book Sale
David Schulson Autographs
Myrna Shinbaum Books
   & Book Themes
Skyline Books & Records
Strand Bookstore
Strand Bookstore Rare
   Book Department
Three Lives and Co.
Tower Books
Union Square Art Books
Untitled / Fine Art in Print
Ursus Art Books in Soho
Ursus Books and Prints
Viewpoint Gallery
Virgin Megastore Book Department
Andrew D. Washton Books
   on the Fine Arts
Weitz, Weitz & Coleman
Philip Williams Posters
Irving Zucker Art Books

Art - German
Galerie St. Etienne

Art - German Avant-Garde
MJS Books and Graphics

Art - Judaica
Landy Fine Judaica

Art - Master Drawings
Pierpont Morgan Library Book Shop

Art - Medieval/Renaissance
Mona Levine
Metropolitan Museum of Art
   Bookshop, Cloisters Branch
Pierpont Morgan Library Book Shop
Andrew D. Washton Books
   on the Fine Arts

Art - Middle Eastern
Aurora Fine Books
Camel Book Co.
Fil Caravan Inc.
Sufi Books

Art - Modern
Arcade Books
Aurora Fine Books
CFM Gallery
Ex Libris
Leonard Fox Ltd.
Galerie St. Etienne
Solomon R. Guggenheim
   Museum Bookstore
Solomon R. Guggenheim Museum
   Soho Bookstore
J. N. Herlin
Kolwyck-Jones Books on Art
Barbara Leibowits Graphics Ltd.

Art Instruction
Ruby's Book Sale

Art Restoration
Talas

Asian Studies
The Asia Society Bookstore
Asian Rare Books
Asian American Bookshop
Janet Lehr
Richard C. Ramer Old
    and Rare Books
Zakka

Astrology
C. G. Jung Foundation Book Service
LifeVisions
New York Astrology Center
Quest Bookshop
6 Rays of Gold

Astromony
Hayden Planetarium Bookstore
Bruce J. Ramer, Experimenta Old
    and Rare Books

Atlases
See: Maps/Atalases/Cartography

Auction House
Christie's Book and Manuscript
    Department
William Doyle Galleries
Hauswedell & Nolte
    (New York Office)
Metropolitan Book Auction

Phillips Auctioneers
R. M. Smythe and Co.
Sotheby's Book and Manuscripts
    Department
Swann Galleries

Audio Books
Heller Audiobooks
Spoken Word

Australia
See History - Australia/Oceania

Autographs/Manuscripts
Appelfeld Gallery
Argosy Book Store
Bart Auerbach
J. N. Bartfield
Bauman Rare Books
Ronald Belanske Rare Books
    and Manuscripts
Black Sun Books
Cambridge-Essex Stamp Co.
Gary Combs Autographs
Eastside Books and Paper
Ex Libris
Fil Caravan Inc.
Ralph D. Gardner
Gotta Have It! Collectibles
Roger Gross Ltd.
Charles Hamilton Autographs
Lion Heart Autographs, Inc.
James Lowe Autographs, Ltd.
Les Perline & Co.
Phillips Auctioneers
Pierpont Morgan Library Book Shop
Pryor & Johnson Booksellers

Christian Science Reading Room
(10th Church)
Christian Science Reading Room
(12th Church)
Christian Science Reading Room
(14th Church)
Christian Science Reading Room
(Tri-State Reading Room)
Episcopal Book Resource Center
Kyobo Bookstore
J. Levine Books and Judaica
Living Word Books
Logos Bookstore
New York Bible Society
Saint Francis Bookstore
Trinity Bookstore
Union Theological Seminary
Bookstore

Bibles (foreign language)
American Bible Society Bookstore

Bibliography
See: Books About Books

Bicycling
Hagstrom Map and Travel Center

Biography/Autobiography
Aids Thrift Shop/Out of the Closet
Biography Bookshop
Bookleaves
Brazen Head Books
Nicholas Davies & Co.
Jonah's Whale
Lenox Hill Bookstore
Liberation Bookstore, Inc.

Joseph Patelson Music House, Ltd.
Pauline Books & Media
Theodore Roosevelt Birthplace
National Historic Site Bookstore
Charlotte F. Safir Books

Birds
Naturalist's Bookshelf

Black Comics
Amen Ra and Isis

Board Games
Chess Shop

Boating
E & B Goldbergs' Discount Marine
Hagstrom Map and Travel Center
New York Nautical Instrument
and Service Corp.
South Street Seaport Museum
Bookstore

Book Arts
Center for Book Arts
Dieu Donne Papermill—The Mill Store
Barbara Leibowits Graphics Ltd.
Talas

Book Collecting
Irving Oaklander Books

Book Plates
Irving Oaklander Books

Bookbinding
Talas

Canada
J. N. Bartfield

Canoeing
Down East Enterprises

Cartography
See: Maps/Atlases/Cartography

Catholicism
Alba House Cornerstone Book
    and Gift Shop
Saint Francis Bookstore

Cats
See: Pets

Ceramics
Gem Antiques
Hayden & Fandetta

Chemistry
Book Scientific
Computer Book Works

Chess
Chess Forum
Chess Shop
The Compleat Strategist
    (all locations)
Posman Books at Barnard College
Fred Wilson Books

Child Development
Brunner-Mazel

Children's/Juvenile
Aids Thrift Shop/Out of the Closet
Amen Ra and Isis
American Museum of Natural
    History Museum Shop
Appelfeld Gallery
The Asia Society Bookstore
Asian American Bookshop
Bank Street College Bookstore
Barnes & Noble Junior Bookstore
    (Store No. 1941)
Bauman Rare Books
Black Books Plus
Book Ark
Book Smart
Bookberries
Books of Wonder
William G. Boyer
Susi Buchanan
Chelsea Books and Records
Children of Paradise
Children's Museum of Manhattan
Civil Service Book Shop
Cooper-Hewitt Museum Shop
    Book Department
Corner Bookstore
Dean and Deluca
Demes Books
Dinosaur Hill Books
Doubleday Book Shops
    (Store No. 1601)
East Village Books and Records
Episcopal Book Resource Center
Ralph D. Gardner
Golden Books Showcase
Gozlan's Sefer Israel Inc.
Gryphon Bookshop

Christianity
See: Religion - Christianity

Christmas
James F. Carr
Pauline Books & Media
Tootsie's Children's Books

Christmas Keepsake Books
James F. Carr

Churchill, Winston
Chartwell Booksellers

Cinema/Films
Aids Thrift Shop/Out of the Closet
Animation Art Guild Ltd.
Applause Theater Books Inc.
Association of Independent Video
    and Film Makers
Book Ark
Bookleaves
Brazen Head Books
Drama Book Shop
Drougas Books
East Village Books and Records
Forbidden Planet
Ralph D. Gardner
Gotham Book Mart and Gallery
The Gulack Collection Theater
    and Cinema
Jay Bee Magazine Stores
Jonah's Whale
Mercer Street Books and Records
Metropolis Comics and Collectibles
Museum of Modern Art Book Store

New York University Book Center—
    Main Branch (Washington
    Square Bookstore)
Old Paper Archive
Saint Mark's Comics
Richard Stoddard Performing
    Arts Books

Circus
Richard Stoddard Performing
    Arts Books

Civil Service Study
Civil Service Book Shop

Classical Studies
Aurora Fine Books
Gotham Book Mart and Gallery
Ideal Book Store
Last Word Used Books and Records
Metropolitan Museum
    of Art Bookshop
Posman Books at Barnard College
E. K. Schreiber Rare Books

Collectibles
William G. Boyer
Jaffa Gate Bookshop

Colonial America
See: History - America - Colonial/
    Revolution

Colorplate Books
William Alatriste
J. N. Bartfield
The Book Chest

Liberation Bookstore, Inc.
Rhyme & Reason
Ruby's Book Sale
Charlotte F. Safir Books
Myrna Shinbaum Books
    & Book Themes
Stubbs Books and Prints
UNICEF House Gift Shop

Counseling
Choices—The Recovery Bookshop

Crafts
American Craft Museum
Civil Service Book Shop
National Museum of the American
    Indian (Smithsonian Institution)
    Bookshop
Ruby's Book Sale
South Street Seaport Museum
    Bookstore

Criminology
John Jay College of Criminal
    Justice Bookstore
Partners & Crime Mystery
    Booksellers

Cruising Guides (boating)
New York Nautical Instrument
    and Service Corp.

Cultural Studies
Posman Books
Saint Mark's Bookshop
Shakespeare & Co.

Current Events
Great Judaica Books

Dance
Drama Book Shop
Roger Gross Ltd.
Juilliard School Bookstore
Metropolitan Opera Gift Shop
Metropolitan Opera Gift Shop
Richard Stoddard Performing
    Arts Books

Decorative Arts
Academy Book Store
Acanthus Books
Arcade Books
Archivia: The Art Book Shop
C. Richard Becker
The Bohemian Bookworm
Cooper-Hewitt Museum Shop
    Book Department
DG Antiquarian Books
Fraunces Tavern Museum Store
Virginia L. Green Rare Books
Gryphon Bookshop
Hayden & Fandetta
Museum of the City of New York
    Museum Shop
Stubbs Books and Prints

Dentistry
New York University Book Store
    Health Sciences Bookstore

Design
Acanthus Books
Arcade Books

Pierpont Morgan Library Book Shop
Bruce J. Ramer, Experimenta Old
    and Rare Books
Leona Rostenberg and Madeleine
    B. Stern Rare Books
E. K. Schreiber Rare Books
Sotheby's Book and Manuscripts
    Department
Swann Galleries

Earth Sciences
El Cascajero—the old Spanish
    book mine

Eating Disorders
Choices—The Recovery Bookshop

Economics
Bauman Rare Books
Bookfinders General
Liberation Bookstore, Inc.
Revolution Books
United Nations Bookshop

Eddy, Mary Baker
Christian Science Reading Room
    (3rd Church)

Education
Bank Street College Bookstore
Continental Book Search
German Book Center N.A., Inc.
Teachers College Bookstore
    (Columbia University Graduate
    School of Education)

Electronics
New York University Book Store—
    Computer Store

Ellis Island
Castle Clinton Monument
    Bookstore

Engineering
Arcade Books
Barnes & Noble Bookstore—
    Main Store
Book Scientific
Columbia University Bookstore
Computer Book Works
Corporate Book Express
McGraw-Hill Bookstore

England
See: United Kingdom

Environment/Conservation/Ecology
Aperture Book Center
Arcade Books
Episcopal Book Resource Center
Good Earth Foods
Good Earth Foods
Kubies
Science Fiction Mysteries & More!
United Nations Bookshop
United States Government Printing
    Office Bookstore

Ephemera
James F. Carr
Eastside Books and Paper
Gallagher Paper Collectibles

Richard C. Ramer Old
and Rare Books
South Street Seaport Museum
Bookstore

Facsimile Editions
Abraham's Magazine Service
W. Graham Arader III

Family Dynamics
Choices—The Recovery Bookshop

Fashion/Costume/Clothing
The Bohemian Bookworm
Nicholas Davies & Co.
Fashion Books and Magazines
Fashion Design Books
Fashion Institute of Technology
Bookstore
Hayden & Fandetta
Idea Graphics Bookstore
Janet Lehr
Metropolitan Museum
of Art Bookshop
Museum of the City of New York
Museum Shop
Rizzoli Bookstore
Rizzoli Bookstore and Art Boutique
Stubbs Books and Prints

Feminism
See: Women's Studies

Fiction - Crime/Mystery/Suspense
Ronald Belanske Rare Books
and Manuscripts
Black Orchid Bookshop

G. Curwen Books
Heller Audiobooks
Liberation Bookstore, Inc.
Isaac Mendoza Book Company
Murder Ink
The Mysterious Bookshop
Paperback Discounter—Video 83
Partners & Crime Mystery
Booksellers
Rhyme & Reason
Science Fiction Mysteries & More!
Shakespeare & Co.
Skyline Books & Records
H. Valentine Books

Fiction - Fantasy/Horror
The Compleat Strategist
Forbidden Planet
Gryphon Bookshop
Jim Hanley's Universe
Heller Audiobooks
Saint Mark's Comics
Science Fiction Mysteries & More!
The Science Fiction Shop
Supersnipe Comic Book Euphorium
Jonathan White

Fiction - Gay/Lesbian
A Different Light Bookstore

Fiction - Historical
Glenn Horowitz Bookseller

Fiction - Religious
Church of St. Paul the Apostle
Book and Gift Shop

Book Ark
Brazen Head Books
Chartwell Booksellers
Chip's Bookshop
James Cummins Bookseller
G. Curwen Books
Demes Books
Ralph D. Gardner
Gotham Book Mart and Gallery
Gryphon Bookshop
Donald A. Heald Rare Books
    and Fine Art
Imperial Fine Books
James Lowe Autographs, Ltd.
Madison Avenue Bookshop
David Malamud Books
Murder Ink
Nudel Books
Partners & Crime Mystery
    Booksellers
Pryor & Johnson Booksellers
Dan Redmon
The Science Fiction Shop
Skyline Books & Records
Sotheby's Book and Manuscripts
    Department
Strand Bookstore
H. Valentine Books

Fishing
Chartwell Booksellers
James Cummins Bookseller
Hagstrom Map and Travel Center
SportsWords Ltd.

Folk Art
American Folk Art Books

Museum of American Folk Art
    Museum Shop

Folklore/Mythology
Books of Wonder
C. G. Jung Foundation Book Service
Tootsie's Children's Books

Food
See: Cooking

Fore-edge Paintings
J. N. Bartfield
Imperial Fine Books
Foreign Language Instruction
Baruch College Bookstore
French and European Publications
Heller Audiobooks
Lectorum Publications
Rand McNally, The Map
    and Travel Store
Traveller's Bookstore
United Nations Bookshop

Foxes
Dog Lovers Bookshop

France (including French Language
    and Literature)
Book Ark
French and European Publications
Librairie Francaise
Pathfinder Books
Paulette Rose, Fine and Rare Books
Scientific & Medical Publications
    of France

The Book Resource
Bookberries
Borders Books and Music
Bradlees
Bus Terminal Books and Periodicals
Coliseum Books
B. Dalton Bookseller
    (Store No. 1167)
B. Dalton Bookseller
    (Store No. 300)
Doubleday Book Shops
    (Store No. 1601)
Fordham University Bookstore
Green Arc Bookstore
Hudson News Bookstore
Jonah's Whale
Logos Bookstore
Macy's Department Store
    Book Department
Madison Avenue Bookshop
Penn Books
Penn Station Book Store
Reborn—14th St. Bookstore
Rhyme & Reason
Spring Street Books
Target Books and Music
Tower Books

Geography
The East Africa Safari Co.
Hagstrom Map and Travel Center

Geology
Gemological Institute of America
    Bookstore

Germany (including German
    Language and Literature)
Aurora Fine Books
Book Ark
German Book Center N.A., Inc.
Carla Hanauer
Skyline Books & Records
Peter Tumarkin Fine Books

Glass
Hayden & Fandetta

Golf
Larry Lawrence Rare Sports
SportsWords Ltd.

Government Publications
City Books Stores
United States Government Printing
    Office Bookstore

Grant, Ulysses
General Ulysses Grant National
    Memorial Bookstore

Graphic Arts
Comic Art Gallery
James Cummins Bookseller
Fashion Books and Magazines
A. I. Friedman
Irving Oaklander Books
Reinhold-Brown Gallery
Rizzoli Bookstore
Rizzoli Bookstore and Art Boutique
Justin G. Schiller Ltd.
Village Comics
Zakka

History - America - Colonial/Revolution
Castle Clinton Monument
   Bookstore
Federal Hall National Memorial
   Bookstore
Fraunces Tavern Museum Store
James Lowe Autographs, Ltd.

History - America 19th c.
Appelfeld Gallery
James Lowe Autographs, Ltd.
New-York Historical Society
   Museum Shop
Theodore Roosevelt Birthplace
   National Historic Site Bookstore
South Street Seaport Museum
   Bookstore

History - America 20th c.
Peter Hlinka Historical Americana
Theodore Roosevelt Birthplace
   National Historic Site Bookstore

History - Ancient
Metropolitan Museum of Art
   Bookshop
William H. Schab Gallery

History - Asia
Potala

History - Australia/Oceania
Harmer Johnson Books

History - Britain
Appelfeld Gallery
James Cummins Bookseller

History - Europe
German Book Center N.A., Inc.
Leona Rostenberg and Madeleine
   B. Stern Rare Books

History - General
Academy Book Store
Aids Thrift Shop/Out of the Closet
Alba House Cornerstone Book
   and Gift Shop
Barnes & Noble Bookstore
   (Store No. 2618)
Bauman Rare Books
Bookfinders General
William G. Boyer
Brazen Head Books
Cambridge-Essex Stamp Co.
Chelsea Books and Records
College of Insurance Bookstore
Cooper-Hewitt Museum Shop
   Book Department
Corner Bookstore
Crawford Doyle Booksellers
El Cascajero—the old Spanish
   book mine
Glenn Horowitz Bookseller
Ideal Book Store
Imperial Fine Books
Jonah's Whale
Last Word Used Books and Records
Lion Heart Autographs, Inc.
Madison Avenue Bookshop

How-To Books
The Bilingual Publications Co.

Human Rights
United Nations Bookshop

Humanism
E. K. Schreiber Rare Books

Humanities
William H. Schab Gallery
Strand Bookstore
Three Lives and Co.

Humor
The Book Chest
Comic Art Gallery
Huckleberry Designs
Rhyme & Reason
Village Comics

Hungary (including Hungarian
   Language and Literature)
Puski-Corvin Hungarian Books

Illuminated Manuscripts
H. P. Kraus Rare Books and
   Manuscripts
Pierpont Morgan Library Book Shop
Kenneth W. Rendell Gallery
Sotheby's Book and Manuscripts
   Department
Wurlitzer-Bruck

Illustrated Books
Appelfeld Gallery
W. Graham Arader III

Richard B. Arkway
J. N. Bartfield
Black Sun Books
The Bohemian Bookworm
Book Ark
William G. Boyer
Martin Breslauer
Jutta Buck, Antiquarian Book
   and Print Sellers
James Cummins Bookseller
Demes Books
Virginia L. Green Rare Books
Jim Hanley's Universe
Donald A. Heald Rare Books
   and Fine Art
Illustration House
Kendra Krienke
Barbara Leibowits Graphics Ltd.
MJS Books and Graphics
Jeryl Metz
Naturalist's Bookshelf
Nudel Books
Elizabeth Phillips
Pryor & Johnson Booksellers
Dan Redmon
William H. Schab Gallery
Justin G. Schiller Ltd.
Sotheby's Book and Manuscripts
   Department
Peter Tumarkin Fine Books
Ursus Art Books in Soho
Ursus Books and Prints
Irving Zucker Art Books

Illustration - Modern
TwoSixtyOne Arts

Central Yiddish Culture
    Organization
Gozlan's Sefer Israel Inc.
Great Judaica Books
Hebrew Union College Bookstore
Ideal Book Store
Jaffa Gate Bookshop
Jewish Book Center of the
    Workmen's Circle
Jewish Museum Book Shop
Judaica Experience
Landy Fine Judaica
J. Levine Books and Judaica
Isaac H. Mann
Metropolitan Museum of Art
    Bookshop at Rockefeller Center
Evelyn Pearl
Charlotte F. Safir Books
Myrna Shinbaum Books
    & Book Themes
Spring Street Books
Stavsky Hebrew Bookstore
Peter Tumarkin Fine Books
United Synagogue Book Service
West Side Judaica
Collegiate Bookstore
    at Yeshiva University
Yeshiva University Museum
    Gift Shop

Juvenile Development
Bank Street College Bookstore

Kent, Rockwell
Cambridge-Essex Stamp Co.

Knitting
Idea Graphics Bookstore

Koran
Fil Caravan Inc.
Touba Khassyitt Books & Tapes

Korea
Koryo Books
Kyobo Bookstore

Labor
Unity Book Center

Landscape Architecture
Acanthus Books
Urban Center Books

Latin America
El Cascajero—the old Spanish
    book mine
Ginesta Eudaldo
Liberation Bookstore, Inc.
Pathfinder Books
Richard C. Ramer Old
    and Rare Books

Law
Barnes & Noble Bookstore—
    Main Store
Bauman Rare Books
Benjamin Cardozo School
    of Law Bookstore
Columbia University Bookstore
New York Law School Bookstore

Literature - European to 1900
William Alatriste

Literature - General
Academy Book Store
Aids Thrift Shop/Out of the Closet
Barnes & Noble
Bauman Rare Books
The Bohemian Bookworm
Book Ark
The Book Chest
Bookberries
Bookfinders General
Bookleaves
Books & Co.
Bryn Mawr Bookshop
Chelsea Books and Records
Chip's Bookshop
Coliseum Books
Continental Book Search
Corner Bookstore
Drougas Books
East Village Books and Records
Jim Hanley's Universe
Heller Audiobooks
Glenn Horowitz Bookseller
Imperial Fine Books
Jonah's Whale
Last Word Used Books and Records
Lenox Hill Bookstore
Lion Heart Autographs, Inc.
Madison Avenue Bookshop
Mercer Street Books and Records
New York Public Library Bookstore
New York University Book Center—
    Main Branch
Pace University Bookstore

Pageant Book and Print Shop
Papyrus Booksellers
Pierpont Morgan Library Book Shop
Posman Books
Posman Books Annex
Charlotte F. Safir Books
Saint Mark's Bookshop
David Schulson Autographs
Shakespeare & Co.
Spring Street Books
Strand Bookstore
Three Lives and Co.
Tompkins Square Books
Tower Books
Ursus Books and Prints
Viewpoint Gallery

Literature - Latin American/Caribbean
Agueybana Bookstore
The Bilingual Publications Co.
Hispanic Society Bookshop

Literature - Medieval/Renaissance
Leona Rostenberg and Madeleine
    B. Stern Rare Books
E. K. Schreiber Rare Books

Literature - Modern
Ampersand Books
Ronald Belanske Rare Books
    and Manuscripts
Biblio's Cafe and Bookstore
Brazen Head Books
Chip's Bookshop
Cultured Oyster Books
Firsts and Company

Marbling
Talas

Maritime
See: Nautical/Maritime

Marketing
Baruch College Bookstore

Martial Arts
Kinokuniya Bookstore

Marxism
Pathfinder Books
Revolution Books

Massage
Come Again

Mathematics
Bleecker Street Books
Book Scientific
Chelsea Books and Records
Computer Book Works
New York University Book Store—
    Computer Store
Bruce J. Ramer, Experimenta Old
    and Rare Books

Medicine
Argosy Book Store
Richard B. Arkway
Barnes & Noble Bookstore—
    Main Store
Bookfinders General
Columbia-Presbyterian Medical
    Center Bookstore

Cornell University Medical
    College Bookstore
Corporate Book Express
Jonathan A. Hill Bookseller
J. P. Medical Books
Martayan Lan
Mount Sinai Medical Bookstore
New York University Book Store—
    Health Sciences Bookstore
Bruce J. Ramer, Experimenta Old
    and Rare Books
Scientific & Medical Publications
    of France

Men's Studies
C. G. Jung Foundation Book Service
Paths Untrodden Book Service

Metaphysics
Creative Living Bookstore (First
    Church of Religious Science)
New York Open Center Bookstore
Pauline Books & Media
Quest Bookshop
6 Rays of Gold
Rudolf Steiner Bookstore
Unity Center of Practical
    Christianity Bookstore

Metiodism
C. Virginia Barnes

**Middle Eastern Languages
and Literature**
Asian Rare Books
Camel Book Co.
Fil Caravan Inc.

National Parks
Castle Clinton Monument
    Bookstore

Native Americans
Drougas Books
Harmer Johnson Books
Liberation Bookstore, Inc.
National Museum of the
    American Indian (Smithsonian
    Institution) Bookshop
New York Open Center Bookstore
Natural Healing
East-West Books

Natural History
American Museum of Natural
    History Museum Shop
J. N. Bartfield
Jutta Buck, Antiquarian Book
    and Print Sellers
Demes Books
Donald A. Heald Rare Books
    and Fine Art
Jonathan A. Hill Bookseller
Naturalist's Bookshelf
Bruce J. Ramer, Experimenta Old
    and Rare Books
Traveller's Bookstore
Ursus Books and Prints

Nature
Good Earth Foods
Kubies

Nautical/Maritime
Richard C. Faber Jr.

E & B Goldbergs' Discount Marine
Hagstrom Map and Travel Center
Peter Hlinka Historical Americana
Arnold B. Joseph
The Military Bookman
New York Nautical Instrument
    and Service Corp.
Richard C. Ramer Old
    and Rare Books
South Street Seaport Museum
    Bookstore
United States Government Printing
    Office Bookstore

Naval
See: Nautical/Maritime

Navigation
New York Nautical Instrument
    and Service Corp.

Netherlands
Carla Hanauer

New Age
Drougas Books
Everything Angels
C. G. Jung Foundation Book Service
New York Open Center Bookstore
Zakka

New York City
Arcade Books
Bookberries
Castle Clinton Monument
    Bookstore
Fraunces Tavern Museum Store

Ornithology
See: Birds

Painted Finishes
Archivia: The Art Book Shop

Paper Conservation
Dieu Donne Papermill—
   The Mill Store

Papermaking
Dieu Donne Papermill—
   The Mill Store

Paperweights
Gem Antiques

Paralegalism
Interboro Institute Bookstore

Parapsychology
Lectorum Publications

Parenting
Corner Bookstore

Pastoral Care
Episcopal Book Resource Center

Performing Arts
Aids Thrift Shop/Out of the Closet
Applause Theater Books Inc.
Book Ark
Bookleaves
William G. Boyer
Chip's Bookshop
G. Curwen Books

Dramatis Personae Booksellers
Roger Gross Ltd.
Gryphon Bookshop
Mercer Street Books and Records
Joseph Patelson Music House, Ltd.
Richard Stoddard Performing
   Arts Books
Strand Bookstore

Personal Growth
LifeVisions

Pets
Dog Lovers Bookshop

Philately
Cambridge-Essex Stamp Co.
Phillips Auctioneers

Philosophy
Academy Book Store
Biblio's Cafe and Bookstore
Book Ark
Bookberries
Books & Co.
Chelsea Books and Records
Continental Book Search
Dahesh Heritage Fine Books
East Village Books and Records
German Book Center N.A., Inc.
Gotham Book Mart and Gallery
Great Judaica Books
Ideal Book Store
Integral Yoga Bookshop
Last Word Used Books and Records
Mercer Street Books and Records
Posman Books

Poetry

Asian American Bookshop
Biblio's Cafe and Bookstore
Corner Bookstore
Cultured Oyster Books
Dahesh Heritage Fine Books
A Different Light Bookstore
East Village Books and Records
Gotham Book Mart and Gallery
Glenn Horowitz Bookseller
Housing Works Used Book Cafe
Huckleberry Designs
Imperial Fine Books
Jonah's Whale
Mercer Street Books and Records
New York Public Library Bookstore
New York University Book Center—
    Main Branch (Washington
    Square Bookstore)
Pomander Books
Posman Books
Posman Books Annex
Posman Books at Barnard College
Revolution Books
Saint Mark's Bookshop
Shakespeare & Co.
Unity Book Center

Poland

Kosciuszko Foundation

Politics/Political Science

Biblio's Cafe and Bookstore
David Malamud Books
Pathfinder Books
Posman Books at Barnard College
Revolution Books

Leona Rostenberg and Madeleine
    B. Stern Rare Books
Saint Mark's Bookshop
Science Fiction Mysteries & More!
United Nations Bookshop
Unity Book Center

Popular Culture

Applause Theater Books Inc.
Biblio's Cafe and Bookstore
G. Curwen Books
Drougas Books
Everything Angels
Forbidden Planet
Jim Hanley's Universe
Tower Books
Virgin Megastore Book Department

Porcelain

Hayden & Fandetta

Portuguese

Hispanic Society Bookshop
Richard C. Ramer Old
    and Rare Books

Portuguese Exploration

El Cascajero—the old Spanish book
    mine

Poster Art

Reinhold-Brown Gallery

Poster Books

Irving Oaklander Books

Creative Living Bookstore (First
Church of Religious Science)
East-West Books
Integral Yoga Bookshop
C. G. Jung Foundation Book Service
Last Word Used Books and Records
New York Open Center Bookstore
The Book Store of the New York
Psychoanalytic Institute
Papyrus Booksellers
Posman Books
Posman Books Annex
Shakespeare & Co.

Public Service
New York University Book Center—
Professional Bookstore

Publishing
Dahesh Heritage Fine Books
Irving Oaklander Books

Quilts
Idea Graphics Bookstore

Radical Issues
Blackout Books
Revolution Books

Radio/Television
Applause Theater Books Inc.
Drama Book Shop
Forbidden Planet
Jay Bee Magazine Stores
Museum of Television and
Radio Gift Shop
Pauline Books & Media

Ray, Man
Virginia L. Green Rare Books

Railroads
See: Trains/Railways

Recipes
Dean and Deluca

Recovery
Choices—The Recovery Bookshop
LifeVisions

Reference
Aids Thrift Shop/Out of the Closet
American Management Association
Bookstore
W. Graham Arader III
Barnes & Noble Bookstore—
Main Store
Civil Service Book Shop
Corporate Book Express
Drama Book Shop
French and European Publications
New York Public Library Bookstore
Pace University Bookstore
Reference Book Center
Ruby's Book Sale
United States Government Printing
Office Bookstore

Religion - Christianity
Adventist Book Center
Alba House Cornerstone Book
and Gift Shop
American Bible Society Bookstore
Calvary Christian Book Store

New York Open Center Bookstore
Potala

Riding
Kauffman International Ltd.

Roosevelt, Theodore
Theodore Roosevelt Birthplace
    National Historic Site Bookstore

Royalty
James Lowe Autographs, Ltd.

Russia (including Russian
    Language and Literature)
Arka Gift Shop
Fil Caravan Inc.
Victor Kamkin
Russian House
Russica Book and Art Shop

Samovars, Russian
Fil Caravan Inc.

Sandoz, Mari
James F. Carr

Scandinavia
Swedish Book Nook

Scholarly Publications
Books and Binding
Metropolitan Museum of Art
    Bookshop at Rockefeller Center

Science
Richard B. Arkway

Bauman Rare Books
Biblio's Cafe and Bookstore
Bleecker Street Books
Book Scientific
Children's Museum of Manhattan
Corporate Book Express
Jonathan A. Hill Bookseller
H. P. Kraus Rare Books
    and Manuscripts
Lion Heart Autographs, Inc.
Martayan Lan
McGraw-Hill Bookstore
Bruce J. Ramer, Experimenta Old
    and Rare Books
David Schulson Autographs
Technical Career Institute
    Bookstore
Tootsie's Children's Books

Science Fiction
See: Fiction - Science Fiction

Scientology
Dianetics Center

Scripture Study
Alba House Cornerstone Book
    and Gift Shop

Sculpture
Museum of Modern Art Book Store

Secretarial Studies
Interboro Institute Bookstore
Technical Career Institute
    Bookstore

El Cascajero—the old Spanish
    book mine
Mercer Street Books and Records

Sociology
Last Word Used Books and Records

Sociology - Afrocentric
Liberation Bookstore, Inc.

Space Exploration
Hayden Planetarium Bookstore

Spanish Language and Literature
The Bilingual Publications Co.
Book Ark
Da Dochi Bookstore
El Cascajero—the old Spanish
    book mine
Ginesta Eudaldo
French and European Publications
Hispanic Society Bookshop
La Bohemia Bookstore
Lectorum Publications
Macondo Books
Moria Libreria
Pathfinder Books
Pauline Books & Media
Richard C. Ramer Old
    and Rare Books
Roig Spanish Books
Tootsie's Children's Books

Spiritual Healing
First Things First

Spiritual Teaching
East-West Books

Spirituality
Alba House Cornerstone Book
    and Gift Shop
Cathedral Shop of Saint John
    the Divine
Choices—The Recovery Bookshop
East-West Books
Episcopal Book Resource Center
Eve's Garden International
Everything Angels
HSA Bookstore
Logos Bookstore
Matchless Gifts
Pauline Books & Media
Potala
Saint Francis Bookstore
Sufi Books
Trinity Bookstore

Sporting Books
Donald A. Heald Rare Books
    and Fine Art

Sports
J. N. Bartfield
James Cummins Bookseller
Eastern Mountain Sports
Jonah's Whale
Larry Lawrence Rare Sports
Ruby's Book Sale
SportsWords Ltd.
Traveller's Bookstore

The Gulack Collection—
    Theater and Cinema
Housing Works Used Book Cafe
Jonah's Whale
Juilliard School Bookstore
Metropolitan Opera Gift Shop
    (both locations)
Museum of the City of New York
    Museum Shop
Old Paper Archive
Posman Books
Posman Books Annex
Shakespeare & Co.
Richard Stoddard Performing
    Arts Books

Theology
Alba House Cornerstone Book
    and Gift Shop
Cathedral Shop of Saint John
    the Divine
Episcopal Book Resource Center
Everything Angels
Last Word Used Books and Records
Logos Bookstore
New York Theological Seminary
    Bookstore
Paraclete Book Center
Pauline Books & Media
Saint Francis Bookstore
Trinity Bookstore
Union Theological Seminary
    Bookstore

Theosophy
Quest Bookshop

Torah
Fil Caravan Inc.

Toys
Comic Art Gallery
Tootsie's Children's Books
Village Comics
Zakka

Trade Catalogs
Eastside Books and Paper

Trademarks
Idea Graphics Bookstore

Traditional Healing
Sufi Books

Trains/Railways
Eastside Books and Paper
Arnold B. Joseph
Penn Books
Tootsie's Children's Books

Transportation
America's Hobby Center
Jonah's Whale

Transvestitism
Paths Untrodden Book Service

Travel
Aids Thrift Shop/Out of the Closet
Appelfeld Gallery
W. Graham Arader III
Richard B. Arkway

Urban Planning
Arcade Books
Urban Center Books

Vedic Scriptures
Matchless Gifts

Video Production
Applause Theater Books Inc.
Association of Independent Video
    and Film Makers

Visual Arts
School of Visual Arts Bookstore

Walpole, Horace
DG Antiquarian Books

Walt Disney
Animation Art Guild Ltd.

War
See: Military/War

War ames
The Compleat Strategist

Watercolors
Leonard Fox Ltd.
Donald A. Heald Rare Books
    and Fine Art

Western Americana
J. N. Bartfield
Janet Lehr

Wine
Dean and Deluca
Kitchen Arts and Letters

Wizard of Oz
See: Baumiana

Wolves
Dog Lovers Bookshop

Women's Studies
Choices—The Recovery Bookshop
Drougas Books
East-West Books
Episcopal Book Resource Center
Eve's Garden International
Jewish Museum Book Shop
C. G. Jung Foundation Book Service
New York Open Center Bookstore
New York University Book Center—
    Main Branch (Washington
    Square Bookstore)
Pathfinder Books
Posman Books at Barnard College
Revolution Books
Paulette Rose, Fine and Rare Books
Saint Mark's Bookshop
Union Theological Seminary
    Bookstore
United Nations Bookshop
Woodcuts
Old Paper Archive

Writer's Guides
Murder Ink

About the Author

WILLIAM MARDEN has long been involved with libraries and the book trade. With a master's degree in library science from Columbia University, Marden has worked for some of the country's leading rare book dealers, collectors, and research libraries. His first edition of <u>Marden's Guide to Manhattan Booksellers</u> was recognized by the New York Public Library in 1994 as "one of the outstanding reference works of the year." He currently resides in New York City with his wife and daughter.

OTHER TITLES AVAILABLE FROM CITY & COMPANY

Title	Retail
How To Find an Apartment in New York	$12.95
New York Book of Beauty (cloth)	$16.00
New York Cat Owner's Guide	$9.95
New York Book of Coffee & Cake (cloth)	$16.00
Cool Parents Guide to All of New York	$12.95
New York Book of Dance	$14.00
New York Dog Owner's Guide	$9.95
Good & Cheap Ethnic Eats	$9.95
Good & Cheap Vegetarian Dining	$9.95
Jones Guide to Fitness & Health	$9.95
Ken Druse's New York City Gardener	$15.00
How To Make New York a Better Place to Live	$9.95
Marden's Manhattan Booksellers	$16.00
How To Meet A Mensch in New York 2nd Edition	$12.95
New York Book of Music	$15.00
New York Book of Tea (cloth)	$15.00
New York Chocolate Lover's Guide (cloth)	$16.00
New York's 50 Best Nightspots	$9.95
New York's 50 Best Places to Find Peace & Quiet	$9.95
New York's 50 Best Secret Architectural Treasures	$9.95
Psychic New York	$13.00
Shop NY: Downtownstyle	$15.95
Shop NY: Jewelry	$15.95
A Year In New York (cloth)	$20.00

You can find all these books at your local bookstore, or write to:
City & Company 22 W. 23rd St NY, NY 10010, 212-366-1988

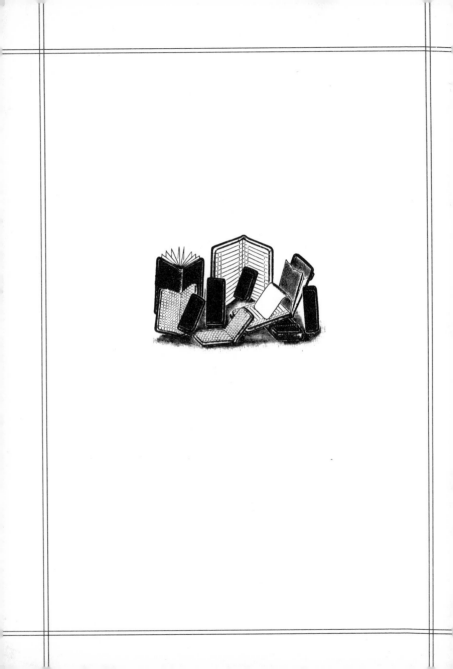